D0214568

# LIBERATORS
### of the
## FEMALE
## MIND

Contributions in Women's Studies

THE CHAINS OF PROTECTION: The Judicial Response to Women's Labor
Legislation
*Judith A. Baer*

WOMEN'S STUDIES: An Interdisciplinary Collection
*Kathleen O'Connor Blumhagen and Walter D. Johnson, editors*

LATIN AMERICAN WOMEN: Historical Perspectives
*Asunción Lavrin*

BEYOND HER SPHERE: Women and the Professions in American History
*Barbara J. Harris*

LITERARY AMERICA, 1903-1934: The Mary Austin Letters
*T. M. Pearce, editor*

THE AMERICAN WOMAN IN TRANSITION: The Urban Influence,
1870-1920
*Margaret Gibbons Wilson*

Edward W. Ellsworth

# LIBERATORS
## of the
# FEMALE
# MIND

The
Shirreff Sisters,
Educational Reform,
and the Women's Movement

*Contributions in Women's Studies, Number 7*

GREENWOOD PRESS
WESTPORT, CONNECTICUT • LONDON, ENGLAND

**Library of Congress Cataloging in Publication Data**

Ellsworth, Edward W
  Liberators of the female mind.

  (Contributions in women's studies ; no. 7 ISSN 0147-104X)
  Bibliography: p.
  Includes index.
    1. Social reformers—Great Britain—Biography
  2. Education of women—Great Britain—History.
  3. Feminism—Great Britain—History. 4. Shirreff,
  Emily Anne Eliza, 1814-1897. 5. Grey, Maria Georgina Shirreff.
  I. Title. II. Series.
  HQ1595.A3E44        301.41'2'0922   [B]   78-67910
  ISBN 0-313-20644-9

Copyright © 1979 by Edward W. Ellsworth

All rights reserved. No portion of this book may be
reproduced, by any process or technique, without the
express written consent of the publisher.

Library of Congress Catalog Card Number: 78-67910
ISBN: 0-313-20644-9
ISSN: 0147-104X

First published in 1979

Greenwood Press, Inc.
51 Riverside Avenue, Westport, Connecticut 06880

Printed in the United States of America

10  9  8  7  6  5  4  3  2  1

*In loving memory of my parents*
Marguerite Drummey Ellsworth
*and*
Edward William Ellsworth

*"What is a woman's right, and fitting sphere?"*
*How best she may, with free and willing mind,*
*Develop every special genius,*
*Retaining and perfecting every charm*
*And sweetness sung of old, so, evenpaced,*
*Walk in a joint obedience with man,*
*And equal freedom of the law of God,*
*Up to the height of an immortal hope.*
*Vainly would any poet, tho' he own'd*
*The "double-nature" of the poet breed,*
*Paint the completed circle of her powers,*
*Whose germs await the future, undisclosed.*
*What she will be, she can alone define,*
*Nor knows she yet, but dimly feeling strives*
*To gain the fair ideal; what she will do*
*Is folded in her nature, as the flower*
*Is folded in the bud, or masterpiece*
*Of statuary in marble. She is not*
*Like some dead animal whose nerves and veins,*
*Bones, muscles, functions, powers and highest use*
*Can be defined by an anatomist*
*Brooding above her with a sharpen'd knife.*

"Summer Sketches, Lillian's Second Letter, July, 1853," Bessie Rayner Parkes [Belloc], *Poems*, 2nd ed. (London: John Chapman, 1855), pp. 165-66.

# Contents

# Acknowledgments

I have deep gratitude and much appreciation for assistance given by many people at various stages in the preparation of this book.

I found a warm welcome and cooperation from the staffs at the depositories which contain Shirreff manuscript material, the Cambridge University Library; Girls' Public Day School Trust Archives, 26 Queen Anne's Gate, London; the North London Collegiate School Archives, Canons, Edgeware, Middlesex, England; and in particular the gracious hospitality of Miss Marion E. Shilito, Assistant Archivist, the Maria Grey Training College Archives, Twickenham Road, Hounslow, London; the George Baily Library, University of Vermont; and the British Library of Political and Economic Science, London School of Economics, University of London.

I also found invaluable to my research and writing published material and the services of the staffs at the British Library, the Institute of Historical Research, University of London; Widener Library, Harvard University; the Boston Public Library; and the Wheelock College Library and in particular Miss Marie Cotter, librarian and director. I wish to give a special accolade to Mr. Rodney Armstrong, director, and the staff of the Boston Athenaeum, who provided the milieu as well as easy access to its superb collection which made research and writing a joy.

The perceptive suggestions made by the editorial staff of the Greenwood Press added immeasurably to the final product.

Miss Patricia Barone typed much of the first draft of the manuscript efficiently and with good cheer. President Gordon Marshall and the Board of Trustees of Wheelock College kindly gave assistance for the final preparation of the manuscript.

Lastly I owe special and profound thanks to members of my family, my late aunt Anna M. Drummey, who had much interest in all my work and in particular in this project; my sister and brother-in-law Mary Ann and Alfred MacIntyre; and my aunt Clara Drummey, who provided encouragement and the personal support which is invaluable in day-to-day research and writing.

*Edward W. Ellsworth*

# LIBERATORS
## of the
# FEMALE
# MIND

# 1

## Lives of Quiet Endeavor

The personal lives of the Shirreff sisters, Emily Anne (1814-1897) and Maria Georgina (1816-1906) unfolded in a quiet and regular pattern. Wealth, pleasant associations with intellectuals from several countries, and personal moral rectitude stimulated a life of service marked by sobriety, moderation, and lack of social strife and personal conflicts. The dynamism and creative energy of the sisters appeared in their public lives which they undertook as a duty and joy. They joined the band of Englishwomen and men drawn from the comfortable parlors of the middle class, the drawing rooms of the aristocracy, and the squalid habitations of the working class who throughout the nineteenth century had a single-minded dedication to a glorious venture to make the lives of fellow citizens more satisfying and meaningful as well as create new patterns—or reshape existing ones—for human progress. Doubtless the times encouraged such activity; a fairly flexible social structure, an expanding economy, political liberalism, and a partial merging of spiritual values with humanitarianism provided an impetus that caused public-spirited citizens to feel that movement and change were possible and ideals could be implemented in a substantive fashion.

Emily Shirreff and Maria Shirreff Grey grew into young womanhood in an era of major change in British political, economic, and social affairs. At an impressionable age, when they engaged in serious study and intellectual exploration, the reform program of the 1830s brought the upper middle class to which they belonged into new positions of power and influence. They also saw as an omen of progress liberalism in France which triumphed by the Revolution of 1830. When they finally put their thoughts on paper at mid-century, Chartism had been defeated, but keen observers of the political scene saw that political life was still in flux and more change was in the offing.

The message and work of the Shirreff sisters had great impact on British society of the last third of the nineteenth and early twentieth centuries. They sought to widen in nondramatic ways the vision and personal satisfaction of females whose lives on the surface were replicas of their own, that is, upper-middle-class women restricted by convention and education, who suffered thereby cultural deprivation and ennui. By virtue of deeds they stood in the forefront of the corps of Englishwomen who, in the latter half of Victoria's reign, brought women of social refinement, ambition, and intellect into active participation in what may be called a middle-class activist culture which had been by and large both male-oriented and male-dominated. As a necessary component of that mission they explored varied facets of women's lives and in the process reassessed the female world which led to selective confrontations about existing patterns of life. But of equal moment, on a vast array of matters which concerned basic values of the era, they simply presented a female viewpoint and gave a vital dimension to the Victorian *zeitgeist*.

The Shirreffs set forth in their writings the basic educational goals that had been agreed upon by many of the most influential women educators and women's rightists of the last third of the century. Their educational goals were predicated on a change of attitude toward women by society and an alteration of some concepts and prejudices held by women. But primarily the Shirreffs created structures and organizations which brought into operation the ideals and suggestions to which they and their allies subscribed; they laid the foundation of a national educational system for girls at the secondary level, a valid teacher-training pattern for that level of education, a revamped, in fact a new, national system of early childhood education and the teacher training structure to sustain it. Above all they gave to female preparation for life a stamp which endured, an educational system based on Victorian views of life and its purposes.

The Shirreff sisters' crusade for female education was expansive and idealistic and also rooted in an essentially middle-class view of women's needs, potential, and role in society. It is clear from their writings that they consciously focused on middle-class womanhood. When the sisters wrote their major polemical works, *Thoughts on Self Culture Addressed to Women* (1850) and Emily's *Intellectual Education and Its Influence on the Character and Happiness of Women* (1858) as well as novels, the middle-class male society had carved out a comfortable place within the British Establishment. The sisters desired to bring women into an effective position in that coalition which guided societal developments and thereby make it more responsive to the needs of the nation.

Their adult years fell into two phases. Until early middle age Emily and Maria Shirreff Grey spent their lives out of the public eye. In that period by family ties and personal conviction they were drawn to Whig political principles. Maria married the nephew of the second Earl Grey, prime minister (1830-1834). When they undertook educational work in the last third of the century, they found allies in the reform-oriented Liberal Party, Henry Bruce, Lord Aberdare, Anthony Mundella, and Lord Frederick Cavendish.[1] Their close female supporter, Lady Stanley of Alderley, was a leader of the Liberal Unionist Association. British liberals as well as many Whigs in the first half of the century were fascinated with the concept of freedom and therefore explored its meaning and varied dimensions. Moderation and reason were pillars of liberal ideology. Liberal thought focused on issues which had relevance to women who examined their place in family life and society and contributions to be made, for example, the relationship of freedom to necessary forms of collective planning and responsibility, the reconciliation of a well-organized society and its needs with full expression for the individual, achievement of security without regimentation, and viable ways to release the energies of all people. John Stuart Mill infused liberal thought with concern for the suffering of individual members of society and stressed that abridgment of freedom of one individual inflicted evil on all. These attitudes of Mill, dramatically shaped by Harriet Taylor, were compatible with the political and social liberation of women, and of course Mill became a champion of women's rights.[2]

Emily Shirreff's work for early childhood education came in the wake of the Forster Act sponsored by a Liberal government. It established a national system of elementary education, the condition a priori for the kindergarten pattern that Emily sought.

A biographer of Harriet Martineau, popular Victorian writer and critic of her times, described her particular brand of liberalism; it was much in accord with that of the Shirreffs, her contemporaries. It was liberal in the sense of one concerned with freedom, both positive and negative, as a goad to do right as well as an injunction to remove restraints.

The referents and ordinances of the free society were supplied by natural laws, not yet entirely disclosed, which operated as inescapably as the laws of mechanics or the laws of political economy....What evils remained as the attainment of a truly free society drew near were curable by education and the benevolence commanded by necessarian morality, and until they were cured, they were tolerable because the adjustments were sure and progress and perfection certain.[3]

Emily Shirreff and Maria Shirreff Grey in the middle of the century responded to the pull between the realities of life as they saw them and their idealistic goals. The women's movement meant for them an effective response to women's need and right to knowledge of all sorts in order to fulfill their humanity. Further, it meant their liberation from the petty cares of the household and asinine round of duties of the fashionable world, so that they could pursue constructive social work and professional activity which, in the Shirreffs' ideology, was a natural outgrowth of intellectual maturity. On the other hand, the Shirreffs believed that women had to fulfill their spiritual role as legitimate custodians of the moral code and undertake the duties of male helpmate as well as motherhood. The reconciliation of the two foci came about for the Shirreffs in their detailed plans for education for young females and children; education was the agency to achieve an equilibrium between personal and societal demands on the one hand and familial life on the other.

In the second phase of their adult years, in the 1870s and 1880s, the sisters engaged in dedicated organizational activity and the adaptation of their ideas to the needs and expanding hopes of British society. In the process their attitudes toward politics underwent change.

The sisters reacted to the triumph of democracy in different ways. Maria said about her sister, "She held till quite late in life to the liberal principles with which we had started in 1830, till her fear of democracy overcame her love of liberty, and for the first time in our long lives we stood in opposite camps and our hitherto perfect union on every serious question was broken to the deep but vain regret of both."[4] The divergence of opinion which developed between Maria and Emily was reasonable, given the tensions within liberal ideology; it elevated interests and intelligence to a supreme position. Walter Bagehot rejected the British Reform Act of 1867 which invested the workingman with the vote, and John Stuart Mill accepted it; both came to their decision on the basis of the liberal ideology of intelligence. For her part Maria in the eighties linked the women's movement to the aspirations of the working class and was receptive to socialism and the cooperative movement.[5]

Emily Anne Shirreff, born on November 3, 1814, and her sister Maria Georgina, born sixteen months later on March 7, 1816, belonged to a family and social class which in a number of ways exemplified the spirit of nineteenth-century Britain. Well-born, materially comfortable, oriented to public service, and dedicated to familial responsibility, they were members of that upper-middle-class, purposeful community which emerged as a dynamic factor in the country. Their father, a career naval officer, eventually reached the rank of rear admiral. He had a French Huguenot connection, specifically Chevalier Bayard of New York whose family had migrated to America at the revocation of the Edict of Nantes (1685). His sister, and later Maria his daughter, married into the prestigious Grey family, facilitating valuable social and intellectual contacts for the Shirreff family. Their mother Elizabeth Murray Shirreff, daughter of the Honorable David Murray, was a grandniece of the sixth Baron Elibank, who married the daughter of David Montelieu, baron of St. Hypolite.

At the ages of five and six respectively the two girls had a French-Swiss governess, Mademoiselle Adele Piquet who spoke no English. Their immersion in French culture took on a new character half a dozen years later, when in 1826 the family took up residence at St. Germain en Laye about twelve miles from Paris where they remained until 1829. In that year Mademoiselle Piquet had to leave the household due to illness in her family. Three subsequent governesses did not prove satisfactory. Captain Shirreff decided to send his eldest daughter Caroline (born in 1812), Emily, and Maria to a boarding school. Upon the suggestion of Lady Frances Webster Wedderburne, he chose a school in Paris. Lucy Wedderburne, daughter of Lady Wedderburne, was the only other English student enrolled in the establishment. The Shirreff girls remained at the school less than a year; they disliked the primitive living conditions and the poor food there. Indeed Emily's health broke down after two months, and she had to withdraw.

Emily at the age of seven had suffered a devastating infantile fever. Until then she had been a precocious child who had been able to write compositions in prose and verse. The sickness left her memory a blank, and she even had to relearn the alphabet. Moreover, it left her in fragile health. Maria wrote of her condition.

Her life from that time was a ceaseless struggle with pain and its consequent depression of spirits, —a struggle carried on, however, with such indomitable courage and perseverance, that outside her own family and most intimate friends none knew at what a cost she gained knowledge for herself and gave help in every form to others, nor that the brightness and charm of her society were not the outflow of a naturally bright temperament, but the result of self-mastery over a naturally depressed and disponding one![6]

After the girls' disastrous experience at school, Mademoiselle Piquet returned to the Shirreff household and took charge of them.

In 1829 Captain Shirreff took command of the Warspite, and in order to live frugally, the family moved to Avranche in Lower Normandy, where the girls at an impressionable age came into contact with exemplars of the French intelligentsia. They formed a friendship with Monsieur Angot, country gentleman and member of the Chamber of Deputies, his son Alphonse, and a friend of the family, Monsieur de Beaumont. Monsieur Angot was a political liberal who opposed the restrictive ordinances issued by Charles X. He branded them unconstitutional and joined two hundred deputies in a formal protest. Emily and Maria acquired an interest in politics and liberal thought in quiet discussions with Monsieur Angot and his friends. Maria recalled the thrilling experience of hearing the news of the Revolution of 1830 and being present in the central square of Avranche when the French tricolor was raised. "We gained our first experience of intimate intercourse with men of large and fine cultivation, whose conversation was a liberal education in itself, an experience to be repeated so often in our lives, and to which we owed more than I could put into words."[7]

In the following year Shirreff became captain of the port of Gibraltar, and the family shortly thereafter moved to the British post. There followed a series of experiences for the Shirreff girls which broadened their cultural contacts in new directions. Emily, however, suffered greatly from seasickness on the three-week voyage to Gibraltar. Indeed, fever endangered her life. Two sons of the family died, adding much sorrow to the girls' lives. William, a semi-invalid in mind and body, died in 1829 and Henry, a young midshipman whom Emily adored, in 1833. The removal of the male members of the family increased the interest of the Shirreff parents in their daughters Emily, Maria, Caroline, and Katherine, the youngest (born in 1818).

The family explored areas of southern Spain and North Africa rich in history and cosmopolitan cultural influences. Parents and children visited centers like Seville but also spent time in out-of-the-way spots like Chiclana where no one spoke English. The Shirreffs remained in Gibraltar until 1834, so that the girls became very familiar with the area, in particular the Tangiers region. The sisters' lengthy residence there stimulated their first literary work, *Letters from Spain and Barbary*, published in Britain in 1835. Observation of customs, scenery, and life of the people of an exotic area was one of the literary exercises which the age accepted as appropriate for women. And so the Shirreff sisters, the joint authors, tested their skills and gained confidence in a traditional pattern.

The education of the Shirreff girls in their late teen years continued to be in large measure in their own hands. Maria gave a clear statement on the topic in reference to Emily. "She was almost, I might say after thirteen, entirely self-taught, yet few women have attained more large and varied culture. She had no home facilities or helps for study, owing to circumstances neither she or her family could control, but she made the opportunities she did not find and her works remain to show to what purpose she attained."[8]

Their father had a limited formal education. When he was a young boy, he ran away from Westminister School to go to sea as a middy under Sir Home Popham. In maturity he had great respect for learning, collected a reputable library in science, and eagerly sought association with intellectuals. Self-study in astronomy gave him a store of knowledge and thus access to scientific circles in Britain. At Gibraltar he established a private astronomical observatory and guided his daughters in science studies.

Elizabeth Murray Shirreff, their mother, was a kind and gentle person who had no inclination to pursue learning of any sort and indeed discouraged it for females because she considered it inappropriate for them. But in reflections about her youth, Maria showed no resentment of her mother's attitude. Maria noted that although Mrs. Shirreff did not encourage frivolity in her daughters, she had a deep interest in them and a constant concern for their welfare. During their early childhood years she read to them from material considered appropriate for girls and taught them needlework. Maria felt that she effectively communicated her own appealing qualities of sweetness and serenity of temper, "a guileness of heart and mind which made her incapable of suspecting evil in others as of harbouring it in herself."[9] Maria said that she created an atmosphere of priceless moral healthfulness so valuable to young girls growing into womanhood. Parental attitudes in the Shirreff home were warm and supportive of their children; the girls had opportunity to develop their minds and personalities.

The years at Gibraltar were crucial to the self-development program of the Shirreff sisters. They had initiated a regular study of languages and the humanities which became a source of personal pleasure, a resort when beset by ill health and family cares, and the basis for their later ideology of female cultural fulfillment. Maria expressed the value of study to her cousin.

Every exertion you make to cultivate your mind, to strengthen your powers of reasoning, to increase your knowledge will repay you a thousand fold. To an existence so destitute of all external enjoyment—these inward resources are doubly precious. I doubt whether you yourself are aware of the powers of your own mind.... I feel sure that you are capable of every effort necessary to obtain that great object of life, a well-balanced, well-regulated, well-trained mind."[10]

During her stay at Gibraltar, Emily Shirreff renewed her commitment to Christianity which remained throughout her adult years. She noted in a letter that Dr. Barrow, a young clergyman, had convinced her that the very font of life was a cheerfulness that came from a just view of oneself and one's relationship to God and fellow beings. She observed that in the wake of her religious renewal, the fits of depression about her health which she had periodically experienced had disappeared. "I for one have reason indeed to feel thankful for the change improved religious feeling has worked in me." The religious sentiment of the sisters seems to have been solidified through contact in 1835 with Lady Tarleton of Cheltenham. Maria wrote, "She was a deeply religious woman, and her influence awakened in both Emily and me a deeper religious feeling and a faith in the great truths of religion, which through all the changes and moral and mental developments of later years, the doubts and misgivings which must come to all thoughtful minds...we never lost again."[11]

Emily generally devoted eight hours a day to study. Since she arose at six o'clock and did not retire until midnight, she could have a varied social and family life in addition to the hours she set aside during the day and evening for gaining knowledge.

Emily and Maria returned to England in 1834 due to an outbreak of cholera at Gibraltar. They remained in their homeland except for several months in late 1837 and early 1838 when they returned for a stay at Gibraltar. On their return to England the Shirreffs formed close ties with the Grey family, in particular the Honorable Mrs. Grey, a sister of William Shirreff and wife of a brother of the second Earl Grey, the prime minister. William Grey, son of the family and future husband of Maria, encouraged the two sisters to undertake serious study of philosophy in which he was interested.

He directed their attention to the writings of Francis Bacon, John Locke, and Dugald Stewart. William had financial investments in a wine firm, but his primary interest was scholarly research. Maria and Emily also had a valuable mentor to their intellectual growth and reading program in Lord Gage, a cousin of their father. They spent several months in 1836 at his estate of Firle in Sussex. Maria noted that he had an extensive library which they used, and he graciously guided their explorations.

During the last five years of Admiral Shirreff's life he held posts in Britain, in 1841 at Chatham, the Deptford Dockyard, and Victualling Yard. In the final year of his life he had command of the Portsmouth Dockyard. At her father's death in 1847 Emily wrote an epitaph which recounted his somewhat unknown years and unsung naval services which she described as not known to "storied page" but "not unfruitful to his country's fame."

> His was the daring soul, the steadfast will,
> The generous ardour death alone could still;
> And his heart that knew no throb of fear,
> Yet still could melt when pity claimed a tear.
> When love held sway, or weakness to him sued,
> Gentle as a woman in her gentlest mood;
> Nor cold the heart, nor still the pulse where flowed,
> Not all in vain, the Bayard's stainless blood,
> Shafts which the base still aim at noblest worth
> At him full oft were hurled while yet on earth,
> And faults attendant on high natures still
> Oft pointed out with Envy's murderous skill;
> But cease they now; fallen the true and brave.
> E'en foes are dumb before the silent grave.[12]

In their homeland Emily and Maria, who were attractive and in comfortable material circumstances, received invitations from prestigious social circles. A group oil portrait of the four Shirreff girls in late adolescence and one of Emily depict attractive young women of the era in fashionable party gowns with simple but modish hair styles and sweet countenances. Both maternal and paternal sides of the family were connected by marriage to several aristocratic families which opened to them a whole series of drawing-room doors. Also of prime import, Emily became the protégée of Mr. and Mrs. Richard Napier whom she met at Deptford in 1840. Indeed she devoted herself to their care when they became infirm and was rewarded for her devotion at their death with a sizable life income. The Napiers were gifted people. Richard, afflicted with ill health and poor sight, did not engage in public affairs as his elder brother Sir Charles, who conquered Scinde, did. Nor did he have the stature of his brother William who wrote a history of the Peninsular War. Maria Shirreff, who also had a close relationship with the childless couple, described Richard Napier as humane and intelligent. "What it was to live with those two I cannot describe; the wit, the wisdom, the humor, the tenderness which made their conversation unlike I have heard before or since; their almost ideal standard of rectitude, of duty . . . made their friendship as bracing as it was genial."[13]

The Napiers brought the Shirreffs into contact with many people of intellect and sagacity; one of the most important, Henry Bruce, married a niece of Napier. Bruce served as undersecretary for state in the Home Department in the Palmerston government (1862-1864). His interest and work in education had special value to the Shirreffs. In April 1864 he became vice-president of the Committee of Council on Education, then secretary in the Gladstone ministry and lord president of the council in 1873, and then was elevated to the peerage as Lord Aberdare.

The Shirreffs engaged in a life-style which, to many women of their social class, produced intellectual vacuity. They, however, artfully combined lengthy visits to lavish country homes, parties, and heavy family responsibilities due to illness with a regimen of study and a coherent life of the mind which led to vigorous activities within associations and agencies to further an ideology of female intellectual development which they slowly evolved.

The regular social contacts which the sisters established with leading scientists of the era shaped their intellectual outlook and educational development. They had a close and warm friendship with Sir William Grove, lawyer, judge, and scientist, who had won public recognition in 1839 with his invention of the Grove battery. In mid-century he received various marks of honor, the chair of experimental philosophy at the London Institution, vice-presidency of the Royal Institution, and presidency of the British Association.[14] The Shirreffs had a long and rewarding friendship with Mary Somerville, Britain's foremost woman scientist of the Victorian era, who gained an array of honors from her science peers and learned societies, the Royal Astronomical and the Royal Geographical societies. Like the Shirreffs she spent much of each year in her later life in Italy due to the ill health of her husband, Dr. Somerville.[15] Sir Charles Lyell and his family became close friends of the Shirreffs, particularly Maria. His eminence in geological studies led to the headship of several science organizations, a knighthood, and in 1864 a baronetcy.[16] Lord Wrottesley, lawyer, astronomer, president of the Royal Society and British Association, also was one of the science fraternity which the Shirreffs saw often. Sir George Biddell Airy, astronomer royal, became a confidant of the Shirreff sisters when their father was at Deptford, close to the Greenwich Observatory. The sisters also had pleasant social contacts with Sir John Herschel and Professor Whewell.[17]

In the drawing rooms of their wide circle of friends they had opportunities for social contact with other intellectual leaders like Maurice, Herbert Spencer, Thomas Huxley, John Tyndall, Benjamin Jowett, and George and Harriet Lewin Grote, who gave vivacity to the cultural life of the era. Maria said of their circle, "Society reached its perfection; full of interest, full of wit, full of fun even, but absolutely empty of gossip and incapable of ill-breeding. Such a society may, and I suppose does, still exist somewhere, but I have never met with its equal since."[18]

Each of the Shirreff sisters had a dominant male influence in her life in addition to their father. Maria, in January 1841 at the age of twenty-five, married her first cousin, William Thomas Grey, nephew of the second Earl Grey, who was the first love of her life. The marriage necessitated a number of readjustments. Emily, who had been very close to her sister, was disturbed by the turn of events. Their cousin wrote about the courtship and Emily's reaction to it.

It was quite amusing to see Willie turned into a lover, he did not disguise his preference, everything she did he admired, even to her screaming the scales; poor Emily was quite left in the background, and had no other resource but to talk to me, and talk we did by the hour about the flirtation that was going on before our eyes. I must say Emily did not at all encourage the attachment but on the contrary interrupted the tête-à-têtes whenever she could, she is a dear good girl, and I like her very much and value her friendship, she appreciates Willie thoroughly and willingly she says gives up her Darling Minnie to him.[19]

Maria admitted that the marriage was "a crushing blow to Emily."

In the wake of the marriage Emily's health, which had been a continuing problem, deteriorated; from childhood she suffered bouts of neuralgia. The warm relationship between the sisters, however, was reestablished, since William showed affection for Emily and encouraged their close rapport. The newly married couple took a cottage at Wargrave, and Emily lived with her parents.

Upon marriage Maria also faced the short-lived opposition, or perhaps more accurately the resentment, of her sister-in-law who had not been aware of the love match which blossomed quickly and seemed peeved that she had not learned of the turn of events. Maria, the new bride, wrote to her sister-in-law Maria.

I have refrained hitherto from writing to you, as I would not but be conscious that you must at first have felt toward me as towards a thief who in your absence had crept into your house and robbed you of your treasure. I cannot help hoping that this feeling has passed away, and that you are assured that you have lost nothing but on the contrary gained a sister.... At least I will try to be deserving of your love by making Willie as happy as I can, and I think even now if you could see his bright looks you would forgive me all my misdemeanors. Dearest Maria, will you not look forward cheerfully with me to the many busy mornings and merry chatting evenings we shall spend together.[20]

Maria revealed that William had gone to church with her on Christmas and received the sacraments.

In 1847 the Greys moved into Maria's mother's home in Lowndes Square where Emily resided. Admiral Shirreff had purchased the house just prior to his death. The new living arrangements provided the opportunity for Maria and Emily to write *Thoughts on Self Culture Addressed to Women*, completed in December 1849. William Grey financed the publication; it sold well enough to cover expenses and make a profit. It came out in a second edition in 1854. In 1851 Mrs. Shirreff went to Switzerland to nurse her youngest daughter Katherine who was recuperating from a serious illness. Emily accompanied her mother and sister. Richard Napier and his wife joined the Shirreffs in Switzerland, and the group proceeded to Italy where they met Maria and her husband. Katherine Shirreff met her future husband Clarence Hilton on the tour, and she and her mother returned to London to prepare for her wedding in August 1852. Emily remained in Italy with Richard Napier, his wife, and Lord and Lady Napier. She returned to London just in time for Katherine's marriage. In 1854 a second edition of Emily's and Maria's novel *Passion and Principle* appeared as a part of the popular Railway Series published by Routledge.

Thomas Henry Buckle, who met Emily Shirreff in the spring of 1853, became her close friend and guide and she became his confidant with whom he discussed his hopes and the vast historical study which he envisaged as the major opus of his life. Buckle sent reading lists to both Emily and Maria, as he also developed a close friendship with Maria and William Grey. When the Shirreff sisters met Buckle through mutual friends, he was an unknown man of thirty-three who had spent his life in quiet but rigorous study. Possessed of a modest fortune, he did not have to seek employment and his widowed mother shielded him from the bothersome routines of life. She was the crucial person in his life who encouraged him in his intellectual pursuits. The Buckles, mother and son, and the Shirreffs, in particular Emily, found much pleasure in regular social contact. Maria assessed the friendship. "The intimacy became so close, and occupied so large a place in our lives while it lasted that it seems strange in looking back to realize how short a time actually witnessed its beginnings and close."[21]

After his death Helen Taylor, an editor of his works, affirmed the assessment of Maria Shirreff Grey. In reference to Emily Shirreff she wrote, "You saw him, as I understand, in circumstances in which he was seen by no one else now living except Mrs. Allat [his sister]."[22] With Buckle and his mother conversation turned often to penetrating intellectual, especially literary and philosophical, subjects, which gave the Shirreffs insights into many areas of knowledge and a torrent of ideas.

In his diary Buckle passed favorable judgment on the Shirreffs' *Thoughts on Self Culture*, published prior to his contact with the sisters. He willingly offered to help Emily with her writing on education. "I take great interest in what she is doing, or about to do, on female education." And to Emily he wrote in 1855, "There is no particular reason why I should hurry in my own works, and there is reason why I should assist you, if I can; the reason being simply the selfish one of doing myself a pleasure."[23] He assisted her in the publication of *Intellectual Education*. "What! Faint at the eleventh hour. Impossible. Surely you do not mean that you despair about your book because it can not be all that you wish. . . . Pray go on: then let me see it; and trust the rest to me, to Mr. Parker [the publisher], and to the public! Me first! and the public last!"[24] He was delighted with the finished product. Maria said his influence on Emily "was that of a strong and fruitful stimulus to independent exertion rather than in changing the direction of her efforts or her views of life."[25]

He encouraged Emily to study Dutch, and she was able to read Grotius. With the assistance of Richard Napier, Emily learned Latin and a little Greek. Both sisters were fluent in French, Spanish, and Italian. Later in life Emily learned to read German. Emily read Buckle's work and made suggestions. Indeed his journal revealed that the only major advice that he took was from Emily. On April 1, 1857, he observed that he had sent part of chapter twelve to Miss Shirreff to read, and a week later he said he had made alterations in chapter fourteen which she had suggested. In 1858 he wrote, "I have adopted at least five out of six of every emendations you proposed." Buckle's first public lecture, "Influence of Women on the Progress of Knowledge," was delivered at the Royal Institution in March 1858 after the publication of the first volume of his *History of Civilization*.[26] In the opinion of Buckle's latest biographer, Emily convinced him that mankind was severely harmed by neglect of women's education. At that juncture Buckle had emerged from obscurity and was the lion of the London season.

The death of Mrs. Buckle in March 1859 plunged her son into utter despair, and his health deteriorated. He saw less of the Shirreffs. He wrote to Maria, "If we were now to meet, it would distress your warm heart." Work, his great joy, became difficult. Two years later, on the eve of his trip to the Near East he emphasized that fact. "Everywhere I go I soon feel restless, and after the first novelty I want to go elsewhere."[27] He sailed from Southampton in October 1861, and seven months later died of typhoid fever at Damascus. Helen Taylor, stepdaughter of John Stuart Mill and a liberated woman of the era, agreed to edit Buckle's Common Place Books, and Emily Shirreff promised to add a biographical memoir to it. However, in August 1869 Emily withdrew from the project. Material that she had discovered caused her to feel that Buckle had deceived her. Letters revealed that he had a liaison with Elizabeth C. Faunch, a widow of humble circumstances; probably he financially aided her and wanted her to come to the Near East. Apparently his relationship with Emily Shirreff was purely platonic, but in later life she revealed at least to one person that he had asked her to marry him, and Buckle's biographer feels that had he lived, marriage might have occurred.[28] After the first sting of the Faunch affair Emily relented and added a short biography of Buckle to Helen Taylor's work.

Emily's sketch was full of praise, but the flaws she had discovered in him doubtless gave her a needed perspective. With her interest in education and self-development, she naturally featured those areas in her analysis of Buckle.

Having won everything by his own exertions, and never tried his strength against others, he sometimes appeared to underrate, sometimes to overrate, the common average of ability and of attainments. Accordingly, in his work we occasionally find points elaborately dwelt upon and enforced by repeated quotations which few would have been inclined to dispute; and occasionally, on the other hand, a belief in the ready acceptance of some principles which the majority of men are still far from acknowledging. A man who had gone through the normal routine of education and of life would not, even with half his ability, have fallen into these mistakes.

On another point he judged others too much by his own standard. To himself, recognising a truth and accepting it as a principle to be acted upon, were one and the same thing; and I believe it was his ignorance of the world that made it hard for him to admit how feebly in general men are stirred by an appeal to their understanding. The very common inconsistency between opinions and practice which perhaps saves as much evil in one direction as it causes in another, was so foreign to his own mind that he often failed to allow for it. The profession, for instance, of intolerant views in religion or politics made him look upon the persons who professed them, as if they were prepared to carry them into practice, as perhaps they might have done in times when the symbols of their religious or political allegiance had a living power among men.[29]

In assessing the Shirreff family's friendship with Henry Buckle and his mother, Emily revealed facets of the sisters' own habits and pleasures. Quiet discussion with friends in pleasant surroundings was one of their chief joys in life. "The interest and charm of conversation are like the fleeting lights and shadows on a landscape, and what they add to the beauty can never be rendered, however faithful the sketch."

In the early fifties the Shirreffs were in an optimistic mood about the development of western civilization, in accordance with the outlook of large numbers of educated men and women in Britain. With Buckle they visited the Crystal Palace in 1854. Emily recalled the attitude of their party on that occasion.

We were not altogether disabused at that time of the illusions of a new era of peaceful progress which the first Exhibition of 1851 had seemed to inaugurate. It is true that we were even then in the first stage of the Crimean War; but many still believed that the struggle would quickly end; the glorious days, the dark months of suffering yet to come were little anticipated. Still less did any prophetic vision disclose to us the dire future that was to bring the Indian Mutiny, the American war, the battlefields of Italy and Denmark, of Germany, and of France; or tell us that twenty years after nations had met in amity, and seemed pledged to run a new course of friendly emulation, we should be plunging deeper and deeper into the barbarism which turns the highest efforts of man's skill and inventive power towards producing instruments of destruction.[30]

In the spring of 1859 William Grey became a sleeping partner in his firm of Block, Grey and Block so that he could spend his time in scholarly work in the fields of mathematics and Greek literature and philosophy. But almost immediately he showed signs of illness which led in five years to a paralytic stroke and death. The Greys, after William's retirement, went abroad with their eighteen-year-old nephew, William Duberly, the son of William's sister, Caroline. The three were joined by Maria's younger sister Katherine, her husband Clarence Hilton, and their seven-year-old daughter Emily. Clarence had developed the first signs of a creeping palsy which slowly incapacitated him. He did not die, however, until 1884 but for several years before that lost control of his body. The only consolation to his family was the clarity of his mind during his years of physical debility.

Emily remained in London in 1859 to nurse her mother and the Napiers. The Greys returned to England in the summer of 1860. The following winter Emily helped nurse her brother-in-law, George Bowyear, at Halstead. Caroline Shirreff had married Bowyear in 1849. Her nursing duties concluded, Emily went to Saville House to supervise the care of the Napiers. In 1862 she suffered a severe infection from a carbuncle on her neck so near a major artery that it was extremely difficult to treat. In the summer and fall of that year she endeavored to restore her health by visiting the British countryside and Switzerland. In January 1863 she again undertook nursing chores. For three months she cared for Mrs. Hay, her devoted friend since the time when the Shirreff family lived in North Africa. Mrs. Hay's daughter Louisa Norderling was in Sweden, the homeland of her deceased husband who had been a member of the Swedish Dragoon Guards. Sickness came again to the Napier family, and Emily responded and cared for Richard. Then she traveled to the Bowyear home at Ramsgate to help nurse her mother who lingered between life and death for several weeks but recovered and lived until 1873.

Despite the varied calls on her strength and energy, Emily found time for intellectual activity. She wrote "Our Modern Youth" for *Fraser's Magazine* and a pamphlet, *The Chivalry of the South*.[31] The latter was a stirring defense of the Union position in the American Civil War. She recorded her regret at not being able to do more intellectually satisfying work but also a determination to persevere.

The more time is cut up the more I require to keep command of what is left, and not to let my mind be frittered with my time. Some steady occupation in small measure I will keep up unless all strength of purpose and intellectual worth are gone from me. God grant if I live to read this next December, it may not be with the bitter scheme of failure.[32]

In March 1864 William Grey died. In sorrow Maria visited, for short periods, her sister-in-law Mrs. Duberly, widowed a few days before Maria, and then the Bowyears and Hiltons. She then stayed with her mother at Richmond, so that she could be close to Mrs. Hay, her daughter Louisa, and the Napiers. Maria proposed that her mother and Emily stay permanently at her home at Cadogan Place. The acceptance of the offer allowed Emily to divide her time between Maria's home and Saville House, the seat of the Napiers, whose health made them increasingly dependent on her.

At that juncture Emily was fifty and Maria forty-eight. The sisters' letters written in the previous decades of their youth and early middle age shed almost no light on Maria's feelings about her marital life or on Emily's feelings about the prospect of marriage. Emily, perhaps due to ill health, was her father's favorite, and in turn she was devoted to him. He declined a post in South America because he was afraid of the impact a long and rough sea voyage would have on her delicate health. Possibly her poor health made her apprehensive about marriage and its responsibilities. At her father's death, when she was in her early thirties and still of marriageable age, she sought emotional attachment to older people; the Napiers, as has been pointed out, provided an important intellectual lift to her daily life and became, in effect, surrogate parents with all that that relationship demanded from middle-class females in Victorian Britain. Emily's friendship with Buckle developed within the framework of a close rapport with his mother, and when Mrs. Buckle died, the close contact between Henry and Emily waned.

Maria appears to have had a compatible marriage with William. Indeed, she observed that a happy marriage was fulfillment for a woman. In the pattern of the younger generation in middle-class Victorian families, Maria and William developed their daily routines, social activities and holidays with attention to the interests of their extended families—the Greys and the Shirreffs. During the last five years of his life, William was an invalid whose mind was affected by his illness. In Maria's novel *Love's Sacrifice*, the heroine, Maria, spent years in devoted care of her husband, Archie, who was in poor health and mentally irresponsible. In that novel

Maria Grey gave a stirring affirmation of a life devoted to the care of loved ones.

She had pursued with undeviating steadfastness the course she had laid down for herself, and had found in the benevolence which had become a passion with her, a substitute for the affections which fate had denied. To soothe suffering, to give pleasure, to aid by all means which her vast wealth and large cultivated intelligence supplied, every cause which promised to relieve the ills and promote the welfare and improvement of suffering humanity, seemed to give her all the happiness she was capable of feeling.[33]

At William's death, Maria's age, limited income, and stolid appearance made remarriage unlikely; in contrast, her heroine made an idyllic second marriage.

The 1860s were absorbed almost entirely with family cares. Maria said they were too full of sickness and sorrow to leave time or strength for any work beyond "that which each day's needs enforced on body, heart, and mind." But the sisters did have some enjoyable respites. In 1866 Maria and Emily attended the annual meeting of the British Association for the Advancement of Science at Nottingham. They served as hostesses for the president that year, Sir William Grove. But hardly had they finished that pleasant task and attended the weddings of Sir William Grove's daughter and Maria Duberly when they learned that their dear aunt, Eliza Shirreff, had suffered a paralytic stroke. She was moved from Lord Gage's residence to her home in London. Maria daily attended her aunt until she died a year later. During this nursing stint Maria wrote her novel *Love's Sacrifice*. She found literary and intellectual activity as rewarding as did Emily at that time.

While Maria looked after her aunt, Emily took care of Mrs. Richard Napier in her last illness and then remained with Richard after the death of his wife. He was desperate with grief, and Emily's attempts to buoy his spirits put great pressure on her nervous system. In late 1867 Maria contracted smallpox, and Emily left Napier to care for her mother who also had come down with the disease. During her family's illness Richard Napier died. His death left Emily disconsolate and crushed because she had not been present when he wanted and needed her most.

In order to raise Emily's spirits, Maria took her on a European tour while the Bowyears cared for Mrs. Shirreff. Maria and Emily visited Count and Countess Villers de Boursier at the Château de Giracourt in Lorraine. They then proceeded to Switzerland. Maria renewed her vigor on the trip, but Emily continued in a sorrowful mood and in a weakened physical condition. After several months the sisters returned home.

In January 1869 Emily, still in poor health, went abroad again in the care of Margaret Threw, the former housekeeper of the Napiers, and remained out of the country nine months. On two occasions she was near death. At Nice she mistook belladonna lineament for a nerve medicine and fell unconscious for nine hours. Shortly thereafter at Rome she suffered a severe attack of dysentery which greatly weakened her physically. After recovering, she returned to London because her mother was ill again.

The Shirreff sisters entered upon the last generation of the century with determination to fulfill their familial obligations but also to find personal intellectual satisfaction and make a contribution to society. They embarked upon their public life. Maria joined the Charity Organisation Society and stood for the election to the Chelsea School Board. Emily for a short time served as headmistress of Girton.

Personal sorrow continued to surround them. Their sister Caroline died, and after a few months at Girton College Emily resigned her post and went to care temporarily for her newly widowed brother-in-law at Harbledown. In order to gain a needed perspective, she went abroad in the spring of 1871 with Maria's niece by marriage, Emily Duberly, and the latter's friend May Stirling, the future Lady Lyell. In June 1873 Mrs. Shirreff died, and Maria wrote lovingly of her. "In the home of our middle age she was the sweetest, gentlest presence, almost childlike in the simplicity of her character, her enjoyment of every little pleasure still possible to her, almost saintlike in the silent patience with which she bore her terrible load of pain."[34] After her funeral Emily and Maria went to Switzerland to commune with nature that so often refreshed them in times of sorrow.

In the autumn of 1873 they returned to their educational labors in England. After vigorous work through the winter Maria traveled with Madeline Norderling to Gibraltar to visit Sir John Drummond Hay; minister to Tangiers, for the marriage of his daughter. She visited places associated with her pleasant youth and was entertained by another close friend, Admiral Sir Augustus Phillemore, at Gibraltar. In the meantime Emily in late 1873 went to Cambridge to nurse her nephew Henry Bowyear, a student at Caius College, who had caught typhoid fever.

After successfully bringing Henry back to health, Emily met Maria at Genoa in order to visit the Novello family whose members were devoted friends in the sisters' later years of life when they resided in Italy for lengthy periods. Vincent Novello, a musician and music publisher of London, had been part of the effervescent social circle in the British capital before his move to Italy. His partner in the publishing business, Cowden Clarke, married Novello's daughter, May Victoria. They became prominent literary figures in London and were especially interested in Shakespearean lore. In 1856 they moved to Nice and remained there until 1861 when they established their home in Genoa.

Another close confidant of the Shirreffs was Clara, Countess Gigliucci, of Rome, who prior to her marriage in 1848 was Clara Novello, concert and operatic singer of continental renown. Clara Novello Gigliucci had a deep affection for the Shirreff sisters.

In 1873 I had the happiness of knowing Mrs. W. Grey and her sister Miss E. Shirreff, of educational and literary celebrity, and they both became from the first, dearest of friends. For them, in delicate health and rarely able to attend concerts or theatres, I took to singing again, and Mrs. Grey's birthday, 7th of March, was always kept musically; sometimes Sgambati joined us.... Some rare times I sang also in my own house, for a few friends at their request.[35]

Countess Gigliucci was interested in the work of the Shirreffs and social issues of the day and explored varied topics in her regular *conversazione*. Her most recent biographer noted that liberals in Italy in the unification era were hopeful of social regeneration through education, and the Froebel advocates were welcomed as vital heralds of that process.[36]

During the seventies and eighties the Shirreffs spent much time in Italy and became members of a vivacious Anglo-American circle in Rome. The sisters enjoyed a long and rewarding relationship with United States minister to Italy George Perkins Marsh and his wife. He belonged to the New England intellectual aristocracy. He had been a brilliant student at Dartmouth College, served in the United States Congress, and had been minister to Turkey prior to assuming the diplomatic post in Italy in 1861. He remained there twenty-one years. Marsh became an authority on English philology and etymology and was one of the founders of the modern conservation movement. He wrote *Man and Nature; or Physical Geography as Modified by Human Action* (1862). Both Marsh and his wife Caroline were avowed feminists. They formed close friendships with women who pioneered in medicine, education, and the arts. He took a position on the ability of women vis-à-vis men compatible with that of the Shirreffs. "We know next to nothing at all about the relative powers and capacities of the two sexes," he wrote. And, he added, nothing would be known until "we make woman legally and socially the peer of man; afford her equal, if not identical means of education, and give free scope to the natural laws."[37] The Marshes founded an orphan asylum in Florence to raise leaders for the schools who would promote the type of education which Marsh said he hoped would teach Italian women to respect themselves by compelling men to respect them. Maria observed, "We met every visitor to Rome worth knowing at the Marshes'."[38]

William Story, American sculptor of note who resided in Italy during his creative years, was another of the American community in Rome whose company the Shirreffs enjoyed. They established lasting friendships with Americans who visited the Eternal City for shorter periods; probably the most attractive to them was Mrs. Elliot Cabot of Boston, member of one of the first families of Massachusetts who contributed much to the cultural life of that region. During their years in Rome the sisters maintained Sunday afternoon soirees which attracted a vivacious, cosmopolitan clientele of English people, Americans, and Italians. Joshua Fitch, a devoted co-worker for the cause of women's education in Britain, visited them in Italy and was pleased with their drawing room." At their Sunday afternoon gatherings we met Mr. Adolphus Trollope and many other interesting English and Italian residents."[39]

Emily continued to be plagued with ill health in the mid-seventies. In the spring of 1875 Maria Grey and her niece, Emily Hilton, took Emily Shirreff to Italy. They visited the Italian cities of Rome, Naples, and Sorrento, but Emily's health did not improve, and they went north to Switzerland which had a bracing effect on her. Emily remained in Switzerland, and Maria and her niece returned to London. The following year Emily remained in Italy through the winter. Accompanied by her brother-in-law Thomas Bowyear, Maria joined her there in the spring.

Despite long lives—Emily lived until eighty-two and Maria to ninety—the sisters had more than a normal share of personal and family illness. Yet their difficulties at times appeared to be stimulants to intellectual and organizational exertions which they pursued doggedly. Maria noted on one occasion that the Shirreffs had a great propensity to rally after every difficulty. Despite illness, they carried on a quiet but vigorous social life. They enjoyed small dinners with compatible friends.

The Shirreff sisters were deeply devoted to each other but were still independent spirits. Emily and Maria had differing views about politics in their late middle age. Each had an educational focus that led to major accomplishment, varied organizational work, and publication of their ideas, all of which supported their self-esteem and sense of usefulness. Emily had a sharp tongue in youth and was prone to employ sarcasm. In maturity, when engaged in varied public activities, she had a gracious manner and resorted to the sharp retort only when provoked. Both sisters found platform oratory an ordeal, but it was a particular chore for Emily. Much of the success of the sisters resulted from their ability to achieve a rapport with the middle-class and aristocratic circles in which they moved so comfortably, although keenly aware of their intellectual and social shortcomings.

At the end of 1877 Emily's health stabilized for a while, but Maria had a riding accident with Lord Aberdare at Duffryn from which she never fully recovered. "I got patched up and broke down again more than once but, at last, I had to take to my bed at the end of December, and though I recovered from the serious illness which kept me there for three weeks, I never recovered from the nervous prostration which preceded it and followed it."[40] Then in 1882

Emily's eyesight became seriously impaired, and she sought medical advice in both Italy and Switzerland. Although she improved greatly, the condition brought back the cycle of illness and consequent depression.

The increasing intensity of illness which afflicted Maria Grey at the end of the seventies required lengthy visits abroad. In 1879 Maria wrote, "It is a sad wrench, but London life is altogether too much for me—my only chance for recovering strength is being out-of-doors which this climate makes difficult even in summer and impossible in winter. Emily also suffers an aggravation of all her great miseries."[41] Apparently she was afflicted with severe migraine headaches. Enforced inactivity brought in its wake depression that had earlier engulfed Emily. Maria had to give up her activities on behalf of the Maria Grey Training College, which had just been founded and needed her guidance, as well as the several other educational ventures that had given her a real sense of accomplishment. Emily, who was with Maria in Rome in 1879, wrote to Frances Mary Buss,

We have had of course much passing enjoyment in the beautiful scenery we have dwelt amongst, but there is a dark shadow over all. It is not perhaps reasonable, when sixty is long past, to mourn that an active career is cut short, but you know better than anyone how in dealing with education, one must still feel that no one worker can be spared—do we not know all the best are overworked.

A few months later Maria Grey gave personal testimony of her sadness. "All my idleness and care of my useless self has not brought me nearer than I can see or feel towards ever joining it [work for education] again." Emily also yearned to engage in work. "I have wished for a task, and yet for the only task I had—one of writing for the Fröbel Society—I was quite unfit."[42]

The lengthy sojourn in Rome lifted the sisters' spirits and seemed to improve their health. In November 1880 Maria wrote, "We are enjoying Rome, and the weather is exquisite. We have not yet thought of a fire and live with open windows from morning till night—the beauty of the damsels, St. Peter's standing out against the greying sky—which I see evening after evening from my sofa is indescribable, and market life quite a different thing from what it would be in London."[43] At Christmastime she observed that they experienced cloudless skies and floods of sunshine, but the air had become cold as ice, and "I feel stiffened by it and not so wonderfully active as I was during the exquisite month of November." They had left their hotel and taken sunny rooms "at the foot of the great stairs."[44]

The Shirreff sisters became much absorbed with their adopted country. Emily studied Roman and Italian history, literature, and art. Maria, directed by the Italian artist and personal friend Gabriel Cavelli, went into the countryside to sketch. They took part in discussions about reform of the Roman Catholic Church on the lines of Dr. Dollinger's Old Catholic Church. They lived in Italy in the wake of the declaration of papal infallibility and moved in circles that disliked the tightening of control of the church by the papal curia. Maria and Emily also assisted the missionary work of Luigi Capellini among Italian soldiers.

The sisters always enjoyed the beauties of nature. Marie described the special appeal of the area surrounding Rome. "It is indeed the Eternal City...in the vast grassy sea of Compagna, losing itself on one side in the blue of the real sea, and on the other bound by the semicircle of exquisitely shaped and coloured mountains, and everywhere the life of the past; the shepherd and his sheep resting in the shade of the imperial arches of eighteen centuries ago."[45]

Happily the sisters revived sufficiently to carry forward their educational work in the mid-eighties. In February 1885 Emily wrote to Caroline Marsh that London life seized a person and dragged her into a vortex of perpetual motion till she had no strength of brains left. Emily noted that she had completed a paper for the Froebel Society and planned other writing, but much work was left undone. Maria had joined a new society for the training of governesses. "She has spoken several times and as well as before her illness, but I dread the fatigue."[46]

Emily Shirreff examined in 1880 the essential qualities of friendship as she had conceived it during many decades of her life. "Those to whom mental sympathy has always been the strong, if not the strongest link of friendship, have in this case a great advantage over others, because while we outlive other and lighter needs of our nature, the need for mental companionship never is lost, and this enjoyment can never cease to give, after close affection, the truest zest to life."

Both Maria and she were emotionally attached to nieces and nephews, but Emily made a brief reference to the bittersweet nature of attachment to young people not of one's own flesh. "How strongly we childless women cling to those young creatures, who seem almost our own, till we are cruelly reminded that our claim is but a shadow...that may any day be set against us."[47] Emily in old age liked to have young people around her. The Shirreff home was always open to young distant relatives and other young people who were in London for varying periods of time for educational or cultural activities.

Emily Shirreff and Maria Grey in the eighth decade of the century, when they were in the forefront of the feminine educational crusade, presented the image of gracious gentility. One contemporary described Maria as "sweet Mrs. Grey with the touch of old world stateliness." Emily was said by Emily Davies "to have a stoical way of talking which attracts me." She added that Emily was ladylike and gentle, and she was a good student. A former pupil at Girton College remembered her in a similar way, as beautiful and beautifully dressed, the fine ladylike type. Augustus Hare in 1877 characterized Maria Grey as a little lady with glistening silver hair, simple, with a bright, active mind.[48] Two photographs of the sisters taken when they were past middle life show them as small, plump, white-haired women garbed in the traditional manner of prosperous elderly ladies of the era—dark dresses of rich cloth, shawls, several pieces of jewelry, and white lace caps.[49] In fact they resembled Queen Victoria, in clothing and size, at the same time.

Throughout their adult years the sisters lived in comfortable homes in the West End of London, in Lowndes Square, Cadogan Place, and finally at 41 Stanhope Gate, Queen's Gate, Kensington. Maria gave a personal account of the rising cost of living in the West End in the later half of the nineteenth century. When Maria's husband bought the lease to the property in Cadogan Square, the rent was 102 pounds per year, the house was assessed for 50 pounds, and government rates (taxes) amounted to 80 pounds. In 1884 the rent was 300 pounds, the assessment for the parish 150, and the government rates 250.[50] The sisters then moved to Emily's house in Kensington.

In 1888 Maria became a total invalid; in that year she made her last trip from the bedroom downstairs to the dining room of the Kensington house. From the time they were in Rome the previous year the growing weakness of the sisters had been apparent. Emily commented to Frances Mary Buss, "I am quite well in health but ten years older as regards infirmities and feebleness than I was last winter. My poor sister gets no respite from great neuralgia which cuts her off from work and play. At present she cannot bear the motion of a carriage for above half an hour at most, and how we are ever to get back to England, I do not see."[51] The sisters had to make the decision whether to remain permanently in Italy or Britain, and they decided upon their homeland.

Emily in spite of her age kept fairly active for the next few years. In 1890 she made a series of summer visits; the Shirreffs had since youth been entertained at gracious homes during the summer months. This particular year she went to Castle Howard, Thirlstane, the estate of Lord Napier, Douglas Castle, Sir Leonard Lyell's home at Kinnordy, and to the duchess of Northumberland's at Alnwick.

In 1892 Maria wrote to Frances Mary Buss rejecting her suggestion that she should write an account of the women's movement in Great Britain. She did so on two grounds: first, her own declining strength, and second, that someone of stature, preferably a man in the public eye should do it so that many people would read it.

No dear friend—that cannot be so far as I can see. All that is left to my sister for writing or thinking power is pledged to her Fröbel propaganda— I—even if I were not so completely disaffected as I am—have been too unsuccessful as a writer ever to try the public again. Even my *Last Words* which I thought had a chance of popularity in the special public I addressed have only in three years reached 2-1000. But I do wish someone who has the public ear would write a history of the women's movement in England, educational, political, and social since the Queen's accession. If we could get a man to do it like John Morley or Lord Rosebery, people would learn what a wonderful and important event it has been—and far reaching in its consequences. It is a new world since my youth. I cannot write more. I am weaker than usual just now.[52]

In 1894 Emily fell in Sir William Napier's garden at Oaklands, broke her arm, and injured her right side which led to complications of her nervous system.

In the early nineties the sisters at an advanced age lost dear friends of decades, Louisa Norderling, née Drummond-Hay, their intimate friend of fifty-nine years, and her brother Sir John Drummond Hay who had served at the Morrocan Legation for forty years and retired in 1885. Others whose passing left a void were Lady Stanley of Alderley, Lord Aberdare, and their brother-in-law the Reverend Thomas Bowyear.

In their personal lives and work the Shirreff sisters exemplified a development of the nineteenth century described by Clara Collet at the end of Victoria's reign.

During the last twenty years a very striking change has made itself apparent. In some branches the extension of the working period of a woman's life has been so great that it has even brought back to useful, hopeful enterprise women who had settled down to the colourless, dreary, monotonous round prescribed for the unattached elderly.... Indeed, what I wish to lay stress on as a fact for which to be thankful is that the period of youthful interestedness has been very greatly extended.

Women had been considered aged at fifty at the opening of the century. Maria Grey was in her mid-fifties when she stood for election to the Chelsea School Board and both sisters close to sixty when they began their energetic work in the fields of secondary education for girls and early childhood education.[53]

During 1896 Emily slipped into a state of twilight mental and physical existence which lasted until her death in March 1897. She was buried in Brompton Cemetery after services in St. Peter's Church, Cranley Gardens. Maria lived almost a decade longer in her bedroom at 41 Stanhope Gate which was the extent of her physical world. However, she received visits, wrote letters, and remained interested in the Maria Grey Training College, Brondesbury. She died September 19, 1906.

The two sisters had shown an indomitable spirit in the continual search for self-fulfillment and service and equal devotion to self-realization for members of their sex of all ages. The epitaph on Emily's gravestone accurately stated their mission. "She did with all her might the work God gave to her to do for the better education of women, girls, and little children; and for this work generations yet unborn shall rise up and call her blessed." The epitaph was especially appropriate. The Shirreff sisters applied to their own lives the essentially Victorian ethic that they urged upon English-women in their various speeches and writings: women should seek self-fulfillment by developing their intellectual and spiritual natures in conjunction with family obligations. They insisted that despite cares and burdens of all sorts, women, if properly motivated, could have a life of the mind and make a contribution to the betterment of fellow creatures. They claimed that satisfaction and contentment came by such a commitment. Maria Grey passed an encomium upon her dear friend Caroline Crane Marsh that also applied to her sister and herself. "Rejoice evermore, God gives you thoughts . . . to rejoice . . . whatever He lays upon you whether of doing or, harder still, learning you have done."[54]

# 2

## The Difficulty of the Search for Equality

The Shirreff sisters and others who shaped female education and the women's rights cause in the Victorian era faced formidable opposition. Nevertheless, Britain had a heritage of a female intelligentsia and exploration by women of ways in which they could achieve personal fulfillment. The women's movement, however, prior to the nineteenth century lacked a coherent framework. Women who sought to expand their knowledge and enjoy a fruitful intellectual life usually worked without much encouragement from other women of like mind. They did not have a network of supporting organizations or indeed any clarity of goals. They also lacked a cadre of the opposite sex to advance their cause and give social approval and dimension to their point of view. Nonetheless, Britain in the early modern age, the hundred years between 1660 and 1760, had produced a reputable and cosmopolitan female intelligentsia.

A group of brilliant women, including the duchess of Newcastle, Mrs. Katherine Philips, Mary North, Dorothy Osborne, Margaret Blagge, Lady Pakington, the countess of Warwick, Lady Fanshawe, and Lucy Hutchinson, was active in the Restoration era. Their intellectual vivacity had been stimulated by the breaking of some of the traditional constraints on life during the Puritan-Parliamentary upheaval, stimulating new feelings of involvement in a society undergoing marked political, economic, and religious change. But an orderly scheme for female development did not emerge from the mercurial, uncoordinated, and isolated work of that league of learned women.

Yet women late in the seventeenth and in the first half of the eighteenth centuries employed their literary and intellectual talents in a diversified manner; religion and theology, practical beneficence, drama, and general learning came within their purview. Others engaged in painting and appeared on the stage, the latter of course not an acceptable activity for women of position and wealth. Boarding schools for girls existed in the late seventeenth and early eighteenth centuries, but their character in regard to curriculum, faculties, and general milieu established for their students remains obscure. Charity schools were primarily training centers for girls who entered domestic service.

The heritage which the Shirreff sisters carried on was not merely that of the learned woman; they also followed in the path of the female who drew plans for new patterns of education appropriate for her sex. Mary Astell in the late seventeenth century set forth the need for a new college with a diversified curriculum for women as well as increased freedom of person and occupational opportunities for them.[1] Even though she tolerated male supremacy in family relationships, she challenged contemporary educational thought and social conventions that dealt with women as inferior beings and brought on herself the scorn of Jonathan Swift and the rebuke of Sir Richard Steele. Daniel Defoe, on the other hand, supported the concept of a new education for females.

A century later Mrs. Elizabeth Montagu, a leading blue stocking, suggested establishment of a women's college to an unsympathetic Mrs. Barbauld, and Catherine Macaulay in *Letters on Education* (1790) urged a level of education for females equal to that available to males.[2] But without doubt Mary Wollstonecraft was the most progressive and innovative female education philosophe of the late eighteenth century. In major educational assumptions and goals the Shirreffs were in accord with her. Mary Wollstonecraft believed that the perfectability of males and females had to proceed apace, that females were entitled to an education equal to that of males, and that if encouraged to develop their minds, females would manifest talents and abilities equal to males. She insisted that women were human beings before they were sexual beings and had been kept in submission throughout history. Education meant to her not simply acquiring knowledge but also development of judgment and cultivation of intellectual independence. She sponsored coeducation, easy conversational methodology, and physical exercise as a part of an educational regimen.[3]

Mary Wollstonecraft's political radicalism, specifically her sympathy and rapport with the ideology of the French Revolution and its leaders and her sponsorship of social equality as well as her violation of the moral code decreed by society for her sex—an illegitimate daughter, attempted suicide, and flouting of the marriage code—were used by opponents of women's rights in the nineteenth century to depict women innovators as political radicals, at best indifferent to moral precepts or possibly even sexual libertines.[4] Actually for whatever reason, tactical or ideological, Mary Wollstonecraft in her publications expressed no sympathy for a free and active sexual life for women. In fact she held to the view of many Victorian female writers that sexuality was morally reprehensible, redeemed by parenthood and imposed on women by men. She saw motherhood as a primary duty of females and argued that education should be designed to fit women to fulfill that function adequately.[5]

But in the opening decades of the nineteenth century the Wollstonecraft ideology was relegated to a backwater. Maria Edgeworth and Hannah More preached for females passivity and acceptance of the status quo.[6] The middle-class male established for the woman of his segment of society the desirable roles: keeper of the household, bearer of his children, and shaper of their early years. The growing prosperity of the upper middle class in the early Victorian period fostered an indulgent attitude by males toward women in regard to decoration of their homes, adornment of their persons, and a life-style which emphasized social grace and superficial refinement. In *The Best Circles* (1973), which explores polite society from a combined historical and sociological stance, the provocative thesis is that the pattern of life of upper-middle-class and aristocratic women was a vital part of a control mechanism.

In nineteenth-century England upper- and middle-class women were used to maintain the fabric of society, as semiofficial leaders but also as arbiters of social acceptance or rejection. By effectively preventing upper- and middle-class women from playing any part in public life whatsoever, the Victorians believed that one section of the population would be able to provide a haven of stability, of exact social classification in the threatening anonymity of the surrounding economic and political upheaval.[7]

Just at the time that an adverse evaluation of female education by the Taunton Commission was presented to the general public, *Punch* published an encomium of the education of the old order which prepared a young woman of social status for success in polite society.

I know that it is the fashion to run down the present system of female education, but has not my daughter learned to dance, to sing, to speak a little French, to dress her hair becomingly, to play croquet, to discuss with knowingness every topic of the day, to amuse herself from morning until night? And is not this the acceptable curriculum of female education in this great country?[8]

Stirring affirmations of the subordinate position of the female based on God-given or nature-ordered laws were made from pulpit and platform and in great detail in tracts and periodicals. In 1841 in the *Edinburgh Review* Thomas Henry Lister (1800-1842) made the simplistic declaration of female inferiority to which large numbers of men of education and accomplishment subscribed. He attended Westminster School and Trinity College, Cambridge. In 1834 he was a commissioner for inquiring into the state of religious and other instruction in Ireland and performed a similar task in Scotland the following year. In 1836 he became registrar-general of England. His contemporary fame rested on his career as a novelist, *Granby* (1836), *Herbert Lacy*, half a dozen other novels, and a successful play *Epicharis* (1829). Lister contrasted male and female qualities: females had less active courage than men, "more excitability of nerve," and more enthusiasm and sympathy but were inferior in close and logical reasoning. Women, he charged, were less dispassionate and less able to place feelings in subjection to judgment than men, possessed less power of concentration and generalization, were less capable of steady and concentrated attention, and although their patience equaled that of men, their spirit of perseverance did not.[9] Lister denied women direct access to political and public life. Even though he recognized that women were treated unfairly by the law in matters of property and family rights, he admitted only indirect political action as tolerable to rectify the injustice.

Finally Lister claimed that it could not be argued with any plausibility that man owed his superiority to education rather than nature. He said it was clear that even in art and poetry, which somewhat depended on qualities that were seemingly most developed in female natures, men had reigned supreme.[10]

But during the first generation of Victoria's reign a distinguished group of public-spirited and educated women challenged the obscurantist views of the anti-feminists and set before society legitimate aspirations for women which ran the gamut from adequate education to new employment opportunities and full civil and legal rights, including the vote and freedom to be involved in solutions of social issues of the age. By and large they were middle-class women, often of dissenting religious background, moderate in program and supportive of the evolving Victorian ethic of moral rectitude. Marion Kirkland Reid, daughter of a merchant of Glasgow, was married to Hugo Reid, chemist, writer of educational material, and president of the Hunterian Society. Mrs. Reid in *A Plea for Women* (1843) stated forcefully the case for equality of male and female in matters of education and legal rights.

Lady Sydney Owenson Morgan married Thomas Morgan, physician to her patron, the marquis of Abercorn. Lady Morgan, a successful novelist and leader of a sparkling social circle, received a 300-pound per annum pension from Lord Melbourne, the first of her sex so honored. In 1840 Lady Morgan presented *Woman and Her Master*, a polemic against the unconscionable oppression of women throughout the ages in all continents and cultures. She examined the degraded status of females in primitive societies, the aborigines in Australia, Indians of America, the tribes of Africa, but also peoples in the Far East, in China and India, in biblical Hebrew communities, and in classical Greece and Rome. She saw a relief from the dismal grip of male subjugation by opening to women the storehouse and resources of knowledge.

But where lies the oversight? Can it be one, astounding in its obviousness, and all important in its mischief? While codes have been reformed, institutes nationalized, and the interests of orders and classes have been minutely attended to, has one half of the human species been left, even to the present moment where the first rude arrangements of a barbarous society and its barbarous laws had placed it. Is woman still a thing of suffrance and not of rights?[11]

Lady Morgan's study of vast sweep brought upon her the scorn of a number of male critics who charged that she had a superficial approach and misread facts. Despite some validity to the charges, she gathered an impressive array of material.

Anna Brownell Murphy Jameson (1812-1860), daughter of an Irish artist, governess, wife of a barrister from whom she separated, achieved modest fame as an art commentator and miscellany writer.[12] She traveled extensively and formed a warm appreciation of intellectual life in Germany. Her confidant there, Ottilie von Goethe, gave her access to the Weimar intelligentsia, August Wilhelm von Schegel, Ludwig Tieck, and Moritz Retzsch. Madame Mohl provided her a similar entré to cultural circles of Paris. In England she had close contact with such major female writers and intellectuals of the era as Barbara Leigh Smith Bodichon, Elizabeth Browning, Harriet Martineau, Maria Edgeworth, Harriet Lewin Grote, Mary Mitford, Elizabeth Gaskell, Joanna Baillie, and Sarah Austin. The latter wrote to Anne Jameson, "Have you read Miss Shirreff's last book? There are excellent things in that, in quite a different direction, but no less wholesome or true."[13]

In two works *Communion of Labour: A Second Lecture on Social Employment of Women* and *Sister of Charity* she set forth the social service duties in which enlightened women could profitably engage. She called for both education and legislation. "The woman cries out for the occasion and the means to do well her appointed and permitted work, to perform worthily her share in the national communion of labour." Moreover, Anna Jameson maintained firmly that all programs for public good for which men and women did not work in common had in them seeds of discord and decay.

In the midst of our apparent material prosperity, let some curious or courageous hand lift up but a corner of that embroidered pall which the superficial refinement of our privileged and prosperous classes has thrown over society and how we recoil from the revelation of what lies seething and festering beneath! How we are startled by glimpses of hidden pain, and covert vice, and horrible wrongs done and suffered. Then come the strange trials before our tribunals, polluting the public mind. There are great blue books piled up before Parliament, filled with reports of inspectors and committees. Then eloquent newspaper articles are let off like rockets into an abyss, just to show the darkness—and expire. Then we have fitful clamorous bursts of popular indignation and remorse; hasty partial remedies for antiquated mischiefs; clumsy tinkering of barbarous and inadequate laws;—then the vain attempt to solder together undeniable truths, admitted falsehoods into some brittle, plausible compromise;—then at last the slowly awakening sense of a great want aching deep down at the heart of society.... Yes I have the deepest conviction, founded not merely on my own experience and observation but on the testimony of some of the wisest and best men among us, that to enlarge the working sphere of woman to the measure of her faculties, to give a more practical and authorized share in all social arrangements which have for their object the amelioration of evil and suffering, is to elevate her in the social scale; and that whatever renders womanhood respected and respectable in the estimation of the people tends to humanize and refine the people.[14]

In 1859 in fulfillment of that goal she attended the annual Social Science Congress at Bradford in order to take part in the proceedings concerning women's employment and education.[15] A few months later she died at the age of forty-eight.

Barbara Leigh Smith Bodichon, daughter of a distinguished humanitarian and radical politician, in addition to art work turned her attention to the discrimination women suffered before the law, in *A Brief Summary...of the Most Important Laws Concerning Women* (1854). She set forth the horrendous consequences of the legal discrimination against women in economic, family, and public life. She also focused on women's employment needs in *Women and Work* (1857). Her sizable financial contribution helped launch Girton College. Prior to her marriage Mrs. Bodichon was a member of the so-called Langham Place circle, a group of educated, middle-class women who carried on various feminist activities at 19 Langham Place, London. This dynamic and dedicated band, including Bessie Rayner Parkes, Emily Davies (founder of Girton College), Elizabeth Garrett Anderson (medical pioneer), Jessie Boucherett (writer and promoter of employment opportunities for females), and Adelaide Proctor (popular poetess and daughter of Byron Proctor) expanded the intellectual horizons and opportunities for employment for women. They focused initially on education and employment needs of middle-class women but broadened their sphere of interest to embrace the needs of working-class women.[16]

*The Englishwoman's Journal*, made possible by the financial investment of Barbara Bodichon, drew upon the editorial talents of Bessie Rayner Parkes. Later its successor in terms of focus and interests, *The Englishwoman's Review*, came under the supervision of Jessie Boucherett and kept alive the missionary zeal. *The Englishwoman's Journal* presented the views of leaders of the era on subjects of major concern to women. It gave a considerable amount of attention to the issue of women's suffrage. Mrs. Bodichon wrote on the subject, and Miss Boucherett together with Emily Davies and Elizabeth Garrett Anderson formed a committee to circulate the first petition for female enfranchisement, which John Stuart Mill brought to Parliament. The *Journal* contained reviews of books of interest to women, information on female organizations, female educational, legal, and legislative goals, and developments in the area of women's rights in foreign countries. Jessie Boucherett, when she became editor of *The Englishwoman's Review*, called for greater analysis of the needs of working-class women and their problems.

The *Victoria Magazine* (1863-1880) for women, edited by Emily Faithfull, had a transitional character in that it combined the entertainment focus of earlier women's periodicals—fiction, drama, music, travelogues—with material on work opportunities for women, their varied problems, and suggested reforms. Miss Faithfull employed female compositors in her printing establishment.

Emilia Jessie Boucherett, daughter of Ayscoghe Boucherett, high sheriff of Lincolnshire, engaged in philanthropy in her home region of Market Rosen where she supported a dispensary and cottage hospitals. She had a fine sense of humor, studied nature by regular treks in the countryside, and rode to the hounds with great ardor. In 1863 she interpreted Samuel Smiles' ideology for women in *Hints on Self Help: A Book for Young Women*. She set forth as a primary goal for them a satisfying livelihood. She discussed the value of knowledge and the practical uses to which it could be applied. She made a catalogue of the qualities which had to be developed—the power to reason clearly, self-reliance founded on self-knowledge, confidence, common sense, and perseverance. Realistically she observed that choice of occupations depended upon social position, education, and opportunities. Above all Jessie Boucherett urged women to become independent. She advised them that teaching and needlework were overcrowded occupations. She offered other possibilities, such as nursing, copying law papers, and working as clerks and bookkeepers, and wanted women to consider entering their father's businesses and becoming grocers, bakers, booksellers, and managers of various types of shops, even though women had not usually been considered for such positions. Miss Boucherett told women not to be dazzled by the innocuous term genteel and to be willing to enter occupations not covered by that meaningless description.[17]

In 1859 in the *Edinburgh Review* Harriet Martineau lent her support to the efforts of women to gain access to diversified employment. She drew upon varied source material to support her case: Madame Bodichon's *Woman and Work* (1857), treatises by Mrs. Austin and Dr. Elizabeth Blackwell, and official material in the Census of 1851, the *Report of the Assistant Poor-law Commissioner on Employment of Women and Children in Agriculture* (1843), and *Minutes of the Committee of Council of Education* (1855-1856). Miss Martineau believed that male jealousy had barred women from industrial occupations of all sorts, had been in evidence with every step made by civilization, and had pauperized women. She pointed out that from whatever sources information came, it had become clear that old obstructions had to be removed from the free development and full use of the powers of every member of the community. "In other words, we must improve and extend education to the utmost; and then open a fair field to the powers and energies we have educed. This will secure our welfare, nationally and in our homes, to which few elements can contribute more vitally and more richly than the independent industry of our countrywomen."[18]

Bessie Rayner Parkes dedicated her work *Essays on Woman's Work* (1865) to Anna Jameson. She described six different desires that had emerged to reshape women's place in British society. "Let women be thoroughly developed. Let women be thoroughly rational. Let women be pious and charitable. Let women be properly protected by law. Let women have fair chance of a livelihood. Let women have ample access to all stores of learning."[19] And she asked women who did not need to work to associate freely, and on terms of equality, with those who had to labor so as to bring about a new social milieu. "It will become a respectable and desirable thing for a woman to become a good poet, novelist, or artist. In time it will no longer be half a disgrace for a lady to become an 'independent factor' in any other post but that of a governess." Bessie Parkes pointed out that 43 percent of women above the age of twenty were either single or widowed, and the necessity to earn a living was therefore a paramount issue to them and society. She made a special plea for women to consider the trades and not limit their sights to teaching. In order to facilitate women's entrance to small businesses of all sorts, she suggested that women establish small cooperatives. "If twenty ladies would club together five pounds a piece they might open a stationery shop.... The same principle might be applied to grocery, drapery, and to other articles of common consumption."[20]

Frances Power Cobbe, Anglo-Irish writer and philanthropist who dealt with problems of servant girls, called for opening university degrees to women at the Social Science Congress of 1862. In that same year she noted in an article in a popular monthly that 30 percent of females in England would not marry. She pleaded not to make marriage for Englishwomen a Hobson's choice.[21] "It is only on the standing ground of a happy celibacy that a woman can make a free choice in marriage."[22] Miss Cobbe claimed that if women had options to pursue varied careers, a sharp reduction in unhappy marriages would take place. She wanted them to enter the fields of medicine, journalism and literature, science, and fine arts as well as teaching and nursing. She scorned those in her country who depreciated the old maid and at the same time poked fun in scathing terms at husband hunting. She rejected William Rathbone Greg's emigration scheme. "No false charity to criminals. Transportation or starvation to all old maids."[23] And about a generation later Sarah Sharp Hamer under the pseudonym of Phillis Brown in *What*

*Girls Can Do* documented the widened occupational opportunities which had come to women during the previous half century.[24]

In 1881 Miss Cobbe believed that the educational work of Mrs. Grey, Miss Shirreff, Miss Buss, Miss Beale, and the founders of Girton, Newnham, and the other women's foundations at the universities had prepared the way, "the only safe and sound way for all future achievement of our sex in the fields of literature and public work."[25] She denied that public life would lead women to neglect family duties.[26] She was at one with the Shirreffs in the claim that men and women rose or fell together, and humanity could only advance in a common pattern. Miss Cobbe repudiated bohemian manners which she saw as a threat to the women's movement. She demanded of women chastity, temperance, truthfulness, and courage and found substantiation for her position in Kant's *Metaphysic of Ethics*.

Mary Taylor, close friend of Charlotte Brontë and the model for her character Rose Yorke in *Shirley* (1849), wrote "The First Duty of Women," which appeared in fourteen installments in the *Victoria Magazine* between 1865 and 1870 and subsequently as a book. Charlotte Brontë made her strongest references to the wretched restrictions on single women of genteel background in *Shirley*. "Then seek for them an interest and an occupation which shall raise them above the flirt, the manoeuverer, the mischief-making tale bearer. Keep your girls minds narrow and fettered,—that will still be a plague and a care, sometimes a disgrace to you. Cultivate them—give them scope and work." Mary Taylor spoke for the inherent right of every woman to learn to earn in order to avoid a loveless marriage, penury in widowhood, and wretched despondency as an unwanted guest in some household. She condemned submissiveness and empty lives without purpose.[27]

Helen Dendy Bosanquet was the daughter of the Reverend John Dendy, a Unitarian minister. In 1894, the year before her marriage, she analyzed in the *National Review* the Report of the Royal Commission on Labour. She focused on the material it gathered about female industrial employment. She contended that pay scales for women, which were markedly lower than those for men, had to be remedied by action of trade unions, but the myriad of health hazards that resulted from poor hygienic working conditions and lack of safety precautions demanded government action in better inspection and enforcement.[28] But Helen Dendy felt that the crucial factor in the industrial inferiority of women was the character of their employment; many of them who worked had no independent economic position but were mere adjuncts to men. "Want of skill, irregularity, inferiority of work, all the minor causes to which low wages are often attributed, may be reduced to this one cause: that in the majority of cases the men are earning the living, and the women are working either for pocket money or for an escape from the monotony of home life."[29] Unfortunately, Helen Dendy said, the women who worked by choice set both the wages and standard of work for their sisters who worked by necessity, but she felt that situation could be remedied as it had been in regard to Lancashire weavers. But despite a basic optimism about the future for women in industry, she made a scathing assessment of conditions in her own day. "We can forgive the most inveterate abusers of employers; we can look leniently upon the wildest schemes of Socialism; we can almost find it in our hearts to seek excuses for Anarchists themselves when we reflect upon the cold-blooded indifference to suffering, the hardhearted brutality of employers which is depicted in the sober evidence of the pages before us."[30]

Helen Dendy married Bernard Bosanquet and continued to write forcefully about the necessity to meet economic needs of British women of all classes by adequate education and enlarged employment opportunities. Bernard Bosanquet, philosopher of T. H. Green's school of idealism, gave up an academic career and became involved in the activities of the Charity Organisation Society. Indeed the Bosanquet family were zealots for that cause. Helen was the district secretary of Shoreditch when she married. She later served on its council with her husband and also edited the *Charity Organisation Review*. Bernard's brother Charles B. P. Bosanquet served as its first secretary, and a close friend at Balliol succeeded his brother in that post. Helen Bosanquet observed that a good education for girls was a good investment for society. "Let the hundreds of women testify who are earning an independent living by thorough and honest work instead of being inefficient and underpaid nursery governesses."[31] She was most interested in opening up skilled trades and industrial employment at a sophisticated and supervisory level to women. "Women must be educated above the level where they need fear rivalry with machinery, they must be taught to use their intellect as well as muscles."[32] She pointed out that "economy, industry, method, and self-control," which were imparted by specialized education for technical employment, were also desirable qualities in the domestic circle.[33]

But sentinels stood at occupational gates and approved of only limited access for women. William Rathbone Greg, son of a mill owner of Manchester and a member of the dissenting intelligentsia, became comptroller of the stationery office but gained public recognition as an essayist. He offered suggestions to solve what he called the problem of "redundant women," single females whose number he fixed at 1,500,000. Greg sponsored the emigration of 500,000 women to British dependencies where they were needed for the marriage market.[34] In addition he favored admittance of women to lower levels of industry and business to become compositors, tailors, telegraph workers, and factory hands together with expansion of traditional work areas of teaching and nursing. Greg, however, barred women from the higher echelons of the labor force, in particular the professions and politics. "The cerebral organization of the female is far more delicate than that of man: the continuity and severity of application needed to acquire real mastery in any profession or over any science are denied to women, and can never with impunity be attempted by them; mind and health would almost invariably break down under the task."[35]

Clara Collet in a report in 1894 endeavored to show that increased employment of women did not lead to the loss of men's jobs but was usually supplemental to male employment. "No fact comes out more clearly than that the occupations in which women and girls have been employed on work hitherto done by men and boys are those in which the employment of the latter has increased at an abnormal rate."[36] At the opening of the twentieth century Clara Collet voiced a realism about women and work in Britain.

Our pioneers were full of enthusiasm in their journey to the promised land where sex barriers should be removed and sex prejudices die away. Those of us who passed through the gates which they opened for us were often unpopular among those we left behind and were delighted with the novelty of the country before us. The next generation are coming into the field under new conditions. To begin with, it is realised that work is work; next, that economic liberty is only obtained by the sacrifices of personal freedom; that there is nothing very glorious in doing work that any average man can do as well, now that we are no longer told we cannot do it. The glamour of economic independence has faded, although the necessity for it is greater than ever. Further, although it used to be true that a smaller proportion of the girls who distinguished themselves most at school and at college married than was the case among the girls in the lower forms, this no longer holds good.... And this after all means progress for the race.[37]

When she wrote this assessment, Miss Collet was more than forty years old but had decades of vigorous work ahead of her. She did not die until 1948. She graduated from the North London Collegiate School and University College, London, taught in a secondary school, worked for Charles Booth from 1888 to 1892, and served as assistant commissioner for the Royal Labour Commission of 1892. She became labor correspondent and then senior investigator for the Board of Trade (1893-1917), and finally a member of the Trade Boards (1921-1932).[38] She was accurate in her observation about the unpopularity of the female pioneers. Throughout the nineteenth century the moderate female reformers faced hostility from members of their own sex.

In the late Georgian and early Victorian eras a plethora of women wrote guidebooks of various sorts for their sisters. The majority of female commentators urged British females of all ages to accept their status in society and find satisfaction in humble submission to the fate that God had ordained for them. Charlotte Yonge, whose first work appeared in 1844 and last in 1901, decreed for her countrywomen self-effacement, domestic labor in the family circle, and intellectual subordination to men. In *Womankind* she gave in polemical terms the attitudinal guidelines which appeared in a less direct fashion in her fiction. She told women to accept their inferior status. Charlotte was a heroine to the Girls Friendly Society and edited one of its periodicals, *The Monthly Packet*, for several decades.[39] The Anglican girls' organization by 1911 had 1,707 branches, its Mothers Union 6,969, and a membership of almost 195,000.[40] The Girls Friendly Society called upon girls to be pious, be modest, be submissive to all recognized authority, and not pursue female rights which were seen as divisive to familial and social cohesion.[41] Sara Stickney Ellis in a series of guidebooks, *The Women of England, The Wives of England, The Daughters of England,* and *Mothers of Great Men,* set forth patterns of thought and action to sustain the male-dominated society.[42] She suggested ways for women to find humble satisfaction in their status of subordination.

Some women, among them Mrs. A. J. Penny and Mrs. John Sandford, advised their sisters on proper outlets for their energies. They told women to accept the male world as constituted, and spend themselves in tasks unwanted by others and in religious devotion. Elizabeth Poole Sandford in *Woman, in Her Social and Domestic Character* (1831) presented the ideal female qualities, delicacy, amicability, and piety. She felt that a woman's mind was doubtless incapable of the originality and strength requisite for "the sublime." She advised women to be encouragers and imitators of genius and decried their prevalent vices such as fickleness, want of judgment, and gossiping.[43] The social constraints against even private study for girls in many families were described by Sara Stephen in *Passages From the Life of a Daughter at Home* as well as by the Shirreffs in their numerous writings.[44]

Lynn Linton, novelist, and one-time newspaper correspondent in Paris in 1868, in a series of articles in the *Saturday Review* attacked the artificiality and lack of fulfillment of Englishwomen of the upper and middle classes, but she did not advocate that they seek new activities. She told them to revitalize traditional areas of interest and accept feminine inferiority and the duty to serve men as helpmates.

In all countries, then, the ideal woman changes chameleon-like, to suit the taste of man; and the great doctrine that her happiness does somewhat depend on his liking is part of the very foundation of her existence. According to his will she is bond or free, educated or ignorant, lax or strict, housekeeping or roving; and though we advocate neither the bondage nor the ignorance, yet we do hold to the principle that by the laws which regulate all human communities everywhere, she is bound to study the wishes of man, and to mould her life in harmony with his liking.[45]

In 1883 in the preface to her works she affirmed the opinion of fifteen years earlier,

I neither soften nor retract a line of what I have said. . . . And I think now, as I thought when I wrote these papers, that a public and professional life for women is incompatible with the discharge of their highest duties or the cultivation of their noblest qualities. I think now as I thought then, that the sphere of human action is determined by the fact of sex, and that there does exist both natural limitation and natural direction.[46]

The prestigious *Saturday Review* in which Miss Linton's articles appeared was one of the chief anti-feminist journals. It developed the theme that for their own good and that of society women should remain in the home. Their subordinate status was justified on the basis of female intellectual inferiority and the need for women to impart to society a needed grace.[47]

Dina Maria Craik (1826-1887), children's writer and novelist who married a partner in Macmillan and Company and established a social and literary circle at Hampstead, wrote forcefully against equality of the sexes; she called such an assertion blasphemous. She rejected political enfranchisement of women and their entrance into higher education and the professions. She insisted that men and women had entirely different vocations: one was abroad, the other at home, one external, the other internal, and one active, the other passive. No woman living entirely in and for the world she believed, could be truly happy. "I repeat our natural and happiest life is when we lose ourselves in the exquisite absroption of house, the delicious retirement of dependent love." She urged women to engage energetically in the traditional role of wife and mother, and in those spheres of activity she demanded work and diligence. "Let the superstructure be enjoyment, but let its foundation be in solid work—daily, regular conscientious work; in its essence and results as distinct as any 'business' of men. What they expend for wealth and ambition, shall not we offer for duty and love."[48]

Margaret Lonsdale in the *Nineteenth Century* deplored the appearance of women on the public platform. Miss Lonsdale had drawn a profile of the type of woman she admired, Dora Pattison, sister of Mark Pattison, in *Sister Dora*. Miss Pattison taught school but abandoned the profession to enter the Sisterhood of the Good Samaritan. She spent herself tirelessly in nursing work in the hospital at Walpole and died of cancer at forty-five.[49] Miss Lonsdale, who saw no deleterious impact on health in arduous nursing chores, denounced platform speaking by women because it undermined their health. She believed that women who engaged in public oratory stepped down from the pedestal of gentleness, softness, and quiet dignity because public speaking demanded self-assertiveness which ran counter to the aforementioned feminine virtues. She branded the female platform speaker as "dreadful" with a hardened countenance and manner. "No repose, outward or mentally, is to be found in her society; she produces a strong impression of unnaturalness and living in antagonism with the world around her."[50] Yet Miss Lonsdale admitted that women orators gained attention; she observed that the names of such women and the principles they espoused were bandied about in half the drawing rooms of London.

Anna Maria Fielding Hall, prolific writer and editor of *The Saint James's Magazine* and *Sharpe's London Magazine*, in her various novels, particularly *The Worn Thimble: A Study of Woman's Duty and Woman's Influence* (1853), set down the quiet pattern of domestic subordination required of females. She wrote in her most popular novel *Marian* (1840) that the affectation of philosophy in a woman was dangerous and flew in the face of nature. Her most stark presentation appeared in her husband's *Book of Memories of the Great Men and Women of the Age* (1871). "I am quite sure the leading, guiding, and controlling impulse of women is to render themselves agreeable and helpful to men. . . . It is so, and it ever will be so, in spite of the 'stray minded' who consider and describe as humiliation that which is woman's glory, and should be her boast."[51]

Elizabeth Missing Sewell, who began her career as a fiction writer with *Amy Herbert* (1844), wrote more than three dozen works for women and also conducted a girls' school. In *Principles of Education Drawn from Nature and Revelation and Applied to Female Education in the Upper Classes* (1865) she set forth the acceptable conservative educational pattern for the genteel young lady. The chief aim of such intellectual development was inculcation of clearly defined attitudes and responsibilities toward God, family, and society, specifically self-discipline, devotion to religious principles, sexual purity, humility, and simplicity. Male intellectual standards of measurement she insisted could not be used with females. By adolescence Miss Sewell claimed that boys had outdistanced girls in mental prowess. She felt that not one girl in a hundred would be able to master the subject matter required for an Indian Civil Service Examination. Miss Sewell considered that a woman needed a general cultivation in order to be her husband's companion and to entertain his guests. "A woman who declaims or instructs has forgotten her vocation and is utterly out of place; but when she makes use of her own sense and information to make others talk well, her influence is of inestimable use."[52]

By the seventies when the Shirreffs were deeply involved in their organizational work for female education, a cadre of influential critics of male-female intellectual equality sought substantiation for their position in science, particularly in Darwinian thought. The simple assertions of the type made by Henry Lister, although expressed time and time again throughout the Victorian age, became less relevant in the late years of the century due to the work of pioneer female educators and entrance of women into new occupations and professions. At the same time many critics of women's quest for full intellectual equality were less strident and caustic in the tone and content of their refutations.

One group of commentators wished to redefine the male-female partnership and upgrade women's role and scope of action with the provision, however, that they remain under male tutelage in crucial areas of public and private life. A second group explored in some detail and from various stances the reasons why women could not and should not try to achieve full equality with men. Of course commentators often subscribed to both positions. Opponents of intellectual equality challenged the type and emphasis of education for young women propounded by the reform-minded female educators: the use of education by women to enter higher levels of the economic market place and its impact on traditional family life.

Clerical opposition to women's search for an equitable place in British society covered a wide spectrum of viewpoints. The Reverend John Bennett in *Strictures on Female Education*, published at the end of the eighteenth century, presented his cause as somewhat inherent in Revelation. It was an error and indeed an absurdity, he said, to compare men and women because God had formed them to supplement one another, and their abilities suited the sphere in which He wanted them to move. Women, he considered, had "a more brilliant fancy, a quicker apprehension, and more exquisite taste than men but restlessness of sensibility and inquietude of imagination debarred possibility of great attainments."[53] He added that if women were constituted to have male firmness and depth, it would have been at the expense of their most telling attractiveness. "They would cease to be women, and they would cease to charm."

William Landels, a Baptist minister, represented the more flexible clerical outlook manifest late years in the nineteenth century. He served from 1855 to 1883 at the Diorama Chapel, Park Square, Regents Park, London. Landels contended that a woman's physical constitution was unfit for the competition and jostling of public life, and similarly her mind was formed to play her primary role in the privacy of the home. He believed that any serious attempt to do man's work destroyed a woman's unique traits. The cleric however supported a female's access to the franchise when a householder, either a widow or mature single woman. He advised that female education should not be directed to preparation for careers in the professions. He endorsed the right of women to study science, art, and literature, not as the major focus of their lives but as an elegant and agreeable pastime. He wanted a woman's education directed to qualifying her to be man's companion and not his plaything. Landels admitted women's need to find livelihoods but assigned them modest tasks, "counting buttons, measuring tea and sugar in small quantities, making entries of the simplest sort, and performing light manufacturing jobs that entailed delicate manipulation rather than great strength or skill."[54]

With diverse considerations in mind, social commentators probed the impact of women's intellectual and economic liberation on two major foci of the Victorian age, marriage and the family. Alexandra Sutherland Orr had a cosmopolitan background. Born in Russia where her grandfather was court physician, she lived in India with her husband, a British officer, until his death in the mutiny. In London she moved in literary and artistic circles, became a confidant of Robert Browning after the death of his wife, and wrote his biography which was well received by the public. In the *Nineteenth Century* in 1879 she advanced the theory that liberation of women would have an adverse impact upon the female psyche and be debilitating to family life. She used Darwinian thought to support her contention. She observed that adaptation occurred constantly, and the female of a species brought up under a rule of life departing from its original form must itself depart more and more from its original type. "We must remember that an altered rule of life means also an altered ideal and that existing ideals are more or less distinctly present in every influence to which the growing mind, whether male or female, is subjected."[55]

Mrs. Orr subscribed to the view that certain qualities were an inherent part of maleness and femaleness; women were tender, men strong, women proficient in domestic life, and men in public life. She insisted that when boys and girls learned to think alike, engaged in similar patterns of learning, and competed for the same posts, a drastic change would occur in the innate feelings between the sexes. "The ideas, true or false, natural or conventional, which cluster round the feeling of women's distinctive existence, and in great measure sustain it, will pass away because circumstances will directly tend to change her but because she will lose in equal proportion the secondary consciousness of her former being as reflected in the minds of men."[56]

Alexandra Orr admitted that the impetus to liberation was rooted in the very real problem of how to provide a livelihood and financial independence to a large segment of single women. Nevertheless, she said, the movement led inevitably to a hostility to the basic ideal and conditions of conjugal and domestic life. Women, Mrs. Orr said, were intelligent but not creative, and their success had to come by contact with other minds. "That men possess the productiveness which is called genius, and women do not, is the one immutable distinction that is bound up with the intellectual idea of sex." She believed that if the female liberation process could be halted with the steps that had been taken in her era, all would be well, but that seemed impossible, and the most devastating evils would surface only in the succeeding generations because many of the traditional values and ideals still prevailed. Men and women of the future she saw as frightening creatures. She asked what would be the character of offspring of "men and women in whom remains in the correlative sense, in which alone the word has any meaning, sex neither of intellect or soul."[57] The *Journal of the Women's Education Union*, edited by Emily Shirreff, took Alexandra Orr to task for writing an article filled with false reasoning, incorrect statements, and hostility under the guise of sympathy to women's rights.[58]

Constance Naden (1858-1889), a young Englishwoman, died in the midst of a bright career. A poet and naturalist, she gained intellectual guidance at the Birmingham and Midland Institute, Mason College, and local intellectual societies. She traveled extensively on the European continent and in India. Upon her death Herbert Spencer passed a high judgment on her abilities. "I can think of no woman, save George Eliot, in whom there has been this union of high philosophical capacity with extensive acquisition. Unquestionably her subtle intelligence would have done much in furtherance of rational thought, and her death has entailed a serious loss." But Spencer used the occasion to note that "the mental powers so highly developed in a woman are in some measure abnormal and involve a physiological cost which the feminine organization will not bear without injury more or less profound."[59] In an addendum Spencer noted that women's intellects under special discipline yielded greater results than male intellects but at a terrible cost, the decrease of women's maternal functions. The physical impact of overworked mental capacities, Spencer implied, damaged a woman's reproductive system by causing derangement.

Spencer's opinion was not uncommon. Similar arguments against the intellectual equality of men and women surfaced in the last third of the century with considerable vigor, stemming from the interest of the era in biological research. Dr. Henry Maudsley presented the theory in the *Fortnightly Review* in 1874 that an intensive development of the intellect of females in adolescence and early maturity permanently damaged their health and caused a dysfunctioning of their bodily systems, in particular the reproductive and nervous. "Each sex must develop after its kind." Maudsley contended that females expended a great deal of energy during puberty, and education had to take that situation into account. He asserted that nature had marked out motherhood as women's primary function in their most productive years. Maudsley rejected the claim that certain qualities in the female were products of social conditioning and environment and maintained they were inherent in the fundamental character of her sex, in particular qualities of mind related to teaching children and assisting man as a helpmate.

For substantiation of his theory that any violation of the sexual laws of nature had serious consequences for females, Maudsley sought the opinions of several American physicians. Dr. Edward Hammond Clarke (1820-1877) received his undergraduate degree at Harvard College and his medical training at the University of Pennsylvania. Clarke served as professor of *materia medica* at Harvard College from 1855 to 1872. In *Sex in Education* he presented case histories of a number of women who had attended American colleges and had been incapacitated by excessive intellectual strain. Clarke commented that these women suffered "irregularity, imperfection, and arrest or excess function of bodily systems followed by pallor lassitude, debility, sleeplessness, headache, neuralgia, and worse ills."[60] When these women became mothers, Maudsley reported that their physicians recorded the appearance of a "variety of troublesome and serious diseases." Maudsley also examined the opinions of Dr. Nathan Allen, a prominent Massachusetts physician, a graduate of Amherst College and the University of Pennsylvania Medical School, who noted that women of the type described by Clarke were often unable to nurse their infants. "In consequence of the great neglect of physical exercise and the continuous application to study, together with various other influences, large numbers of our American women have altogether an undue prominence of the nervous temperament."

Maudsley also had recourse to the opinions of a third American physician, Dr. Weir Mitchell, a prominent Philadelphia neurologist. Mitchell wrote that the American pattern of female education was most destructive to health. "She [the American female] is not fairly up to what Nature asks from her as wife and mother. How will she sustain herself under the pressures of these yet more exacting duties which nowadays she is eager to share with man?"[61] Maudsley attacked John Stuart Mill's position that men owed their supremacy to the law of the strongest which they had used to keep women in brutal subjugation. Maudsley had recourse to social Darwinism and asked was it not proper for the strongest to make use of his strength so as to excel and move civilization forward rather than accommodate to the weakest? But also he asked for women the opportunity to fulfill their true capacity for mental culture and free development of their talents which were not of the same caliber or in the same areas as men's.[62]

Dr. Elizabeth Garrett Anderson, eminent physician, made a telling response to Maudsley in the same journal. She said the illnesses which Dr. Clarke identified as prevalent among American women were, according to independent medical observers, more in evidence among fashionable and idle women than those who engaged in vigorous education. She challenged the thesis that intellectual activity was detrimental to the health of normal girls who entered puberty; indeed, she felt that physical activity of an intensive sort could be far more damaging. She noted that Maudsley had presented no substantial evidence to support his contention.[63] Dr. Anderson observed that many of the health difficulties experienced by American young women which had been outlined by the several physicians quoted by Dr. Maudsley were due to poor diet, particularly an abundance of sweets, improper clothing, sedentary habits, and lack of exercise. The physician denied that the education developed for English girls was debilitating to their health; university education usually came after they had reached full maturity. Dr. Anderson also called attention to the fact that English education had established the same goals for young men and young women but allowed them to be reached by separate paths and so did not put men and women into direct confrontation with each other. Moreover, she insisted that physical education and recreational programs had an important place in British educational schemes for girls.[64] A few years later, in 1880, 1881, and 1884, Dr. Anderson in a series of letters to the London *Times* defended the British female educational system against the recurring charge that it placed inordinate demands on students.[65]

George John Romanes, graduate of Caius College, Cambridge University, studied at John Burden Sanderson's physiological laboratory at the University of London and formed a close friendship with Charles Darwin. Throughout his lifetime he conducted research in the fields of physiology and mental evolution, lectured at various educational centers, and moved in the highest intellectual circles of the capital.

Darwin had shown that what Hunter had designated as secondary sexual characteristics occurred throughout the whole animal kingdom. He referred to the secondary sexual differences as a bodily kind, plummage, horns, and so forth. Romanes however, claimed that the secondary sexual differences were also a mental sort, that is, the male differed physiologically from the female in the animal kingdom. He saw a major distinction in mankind: a female brain of a smaller size than the male which resulted in less creativity and productivity by women in higher areas of intellectual work. He judged that male superiority did not manifest itself until adolescence. In some areas he considered that women had conspicuous advantages, refinement of the senses or higher evolution of the sense organs, and rapidity of perception which led to rapidity of thought. He listed the preeminent female qualities as affection, sympathy, devotion, self-denial, modesty, patience, reverence, and veneration. Heroism in women he traced to unselfish emotions, and the aesthetic sense he judged to be stronger in women than in men. Romanes considered that women had a major impact on the value structure. He said that the positive qualities of the male led often to the negative values of insularity, self-assertiveness, and selfishness.

Human value is a very complex thing, and among the many ingredients which go to make the greatness of it, even intellectual power is but one and not by any means the chief. The truest grandeur of that nature is revealed by that nature as a whole, and here I think there can be no doubt that the feminine type is fully equal to the masculine, if indeed it be not superior.

Romanes championed women's educational programs of all sorts. "Therefore, learning as learning can never deteriorate those [feminine] qualities." He insisted that the inauguration of the women's rights movement would be considered by historians one of the great marks of progress of the nineteenth century. He had witnessed momentous changes and ferment. During his undergraduate days at Cambridge University, Girton and Newnham colleges had been established and evoked amusement and chagrin within the academic community there. But Romanes said times had changed, and the opening of university education to women had become a cause for gratification among the educated community. Nevertheless, Romanes designated the Girls' Public Day School Company of the Shirreffs as of equal importance to the university pattern for women.

It is of much more importance even than this that the immense reform in girls' education which has been so recently introduced by the Day School Company working in conjunction with the University Board and Local Examinations has already shaken to its base the whole system, and even the whole ideal of female education so that there is scarcely a private school in the country which has not been more or less affected by the change.

He said that the movement, however, had to be channeled. He raised a disturbing specter, that demanding curricula could damage women's health by "the protracted effort and acute excitement" which was a significant ingredient in the system of school and university examinations.[66]

Edith Simcox in the *Nineteenth Century* issued a rejoinder to Romanes' thesis of feminine intellectual inferiority. She maintained that men and women used their brains on the problems and goals which their society and racial group set before them. A large part of women's brain power, she said, had been directed to cajoling Samson. She noted that men moved from fighting to political and social functions which shaped the development of civilization, while women in primitive eras were confined to the tent and homestead and cut off from the educational influence of political power and free association with equals who shaped the destiny of nations. Once the gulf formed between the occupations and interests of men and women, Miss Simcox stated, it tended to widen and perpetuate itself. Moreover, she explained that women had not moved forward as rapidly as some people expected when they gained access to education because a flowering occurred mainly when an entire class of people was engaged in occupations which suggested and stimulated fresh thought. She contended that women had been barred from what she called the social life of the intellect. Miss Simcox asked that judgment be held in abeyance on women's brain power until they had achieved propitious circumstances which encouraged intellectual and artistic productivity. "If we are disposed to take a cheerful view of the moral future of the race—we must look forward, not to a continued difference between the functions and ideals of the sexes, but to the evolution of an ideal of human character and duty combining the best elements in the two detached and incomplete ideals."[67]

Significantly intellectual leaders of the era who favored wide-ranging educational patterns and public activities of all sorts for women nevertheless placed their upgraded status in a traditional setting as a helpmate of males and an enricher of domestic life. John Ruskin in *Sesame and Lilies* spoke for a revitalized educational system for women. He believed that a girl's education in its structure and content of study should be about the same as a boy's. And yet he considered that the major purpose of education for women was enrichment of the lives of husbands. "A woman ought to know the same language, or science, ably so far as may enable her to sympathise in her husband's pleasures and in those of his best friends."[68] Ruskin wanted women to master elementary knowledge but not simply gain a superficial grasp of material. He also advised women to explore studies which had become traditional for them, literature, art, and music, but beyond that he wished that their enlightenment be cast in a framework to strengthen their moral fiber. Ruskin considered that female education of a formal and informal kind had been conducted as if it aimed to create sideboard ornaments. He charged that girls' schools were more interested in imparting social usages than virtue, courage, and truth which were the pillars of humanity. He asked how sound education could be procured by girls when their teachers had the status of inferior beings. Ruskin accepted a role for women in public affairs, in "the ordering, in the comforting, and in the beautiful adornment of the state." The male function he saw as maintenance, advance, and defense of the state. The best strength of man was shown in his intellectual work and woman in her daily deeds and character.

*Sesame and Lilies*, based on two lectures by Ruskin in Manchester in 1864, appeared in print the following year. In a preface to a fifth edition of the work almost a generation later Ruskin observed that since the initial publication, novel methods of education and systems of morality had come into vogue. Indeed he mentioned specifically as not "without a measure of prospective good" college education for women and out-of-college education for men. Ruskin recognized that *Sesame and Lilies* was appropriate for young people of the upper and middle classes and wholly of the old outlook and so ignored without contention or regret the ferment of surrounding elements. "Thus the second lecture, in its very title, 'Of Queen's Gardens,' takes for granted the persistency of Queenship, and therefore of Uncourtliness or Rusticity. It assumes, with the ideas of higher and lower rank, those of serene authority and happy submission; of Riches and Poverty without dispute for their rights, and of Virtues and Vice without confusion of their natures."[69] In 1876 Ruskin in *Letters to Young Girls* defined women's work as fivefold: "to please people, to feed them in dainty ways, to clothe them, to keep them orderly, and to teach them."[70]

Alfred Lord Tennyson endorsed for females a thorough and penetrating development of their intellects and a pattern of education for them comparable to that for males. In *The Princess* (1847) Tennyson advocated a woman's college which he described in detail more than a generation before establishment of the women's colleges at Cambridge University. Indeed the founders of Queen's College (1848) discussed their project with Tennyson.[71] The Girls' Public Day School Company took its motto from Princess Ida. "Knowledge is now no more a fountain seal'd."

> We...
> Will clear away the parasitic forms
> That seem to keep her up but drag her down—
> Will leave her space to burgeon out of all
> Within her—let her make herself her own
> To give or keep, to live and learn and be
> All that not harms distinctive womanhood.

In truth *The Princess* was an educational treatise for women. Tennyson was reported by his friends to believe that higher education of women was one of the great social issues that had to be dealt with in his era.[72] On one hand he rejected the idea that women from an intellectual standpoint were simply undeveloped males. On the other, he disliked female pedantry and sought as a primary objective development of female imagination, inborn spirituality, and a sympathy with the noble and beautiful. He exalted motherhood. Tennyson, like Ruskin, emphasized woman's role as man's helpmate and reputable intellectual companion, but neither man gave serious attention to woman as a self-sustaining human being with ambition and aspiration independent of the male or family unit.

> My wife, my life, Oh we will walk this world,
> Yoked in all exercise of noble end,
> And so thro' those dark gates across the
>     wild
> That no man knows. Indeed I love thee; come,
> Yield thyself up: my hopes and thine are one:
> Accomplish thou my manhood and thyself
> Lay thy sweet hands in mine and trust to me.[73]

Indeed, even Victorian novelists who dealt in a sympathetic manner with female education and intellectual activity usually placed wifely aspirations in the premier place. Elizabeth Barrett Browning pleaded for reexamination of women's position in society in *Aurora Leigh*. Marian Erle and Aurora Leigh were central characters for her exploration of the female search for fulfillment. She spoke out against victimization of women by fate and "carniverous man." Aurora, intellectual, ardent, and generous, rebelled against her aunt's inculcation of submissiveness, deference to status, and wealth as well as "furtive and cloistered virtue."[74] Elizabeth Barrett Browning had recourse to the French revolutionary credo—liberty, equality, and fraternity—which she saw as a viable guideline for women to use to achieve their goals in the last half of the century. In like manner the Shirreff sisters, in particular Maria in her last polemical work, used the revolutionary slogan as a battle cry. Yet significantly at the conclusion of the Browning novel *Aurora Leigh* the chief character placed love before her devotion to art in sweet surrender to Romney.

> Art is much, but love is more.
> O Art, my Art, thou'rt much, but Love is more!

Art symbolises heaven, but Love is God
And makes heaven. I, Aurora fell from mine.
A simple woman who believes in love.
And, hearing she's beloved, is satisfied
With what contents God.[75]

Annie Edwards, prolific novelist of the last third of the century, wrote *A Girton Girl* (1885). She observed, "Girl wranglers may come, girl optimists may go. The heart of woman remains unchanged. The heart of woman tends towards marriage." In the closing pages of the novel, heroine Marjorie Bartrand, a young woman who had cherished the goal of attending Girton College, gave it up for love and marriage. Geoffrey Arbuthnot said, "Can you give up everything for me?...Your dream for years had been Girton. Do you desire still to become a Girton student, or—? I desire that you shall guide me, was the answer. Marjorie Bartrand had proven herself a very woman after all."[76]

# 3

## The Shirreff Sisters' Analysis of Women in Society

A number of considerations shaped the assessments and programs of the Shirreff sisters for the middle- and upper-class woman. They desired her full development which meant for them education of her mind, cultivation of her spiritual nature, and freedom to participate in public and economic life. Their philosophy of development drew upon the heritage of the eighteenth-century Enlightenment, especially a veneration of the human mind and its ability to give coherence and order to each life. They had confidence that an enlightened intellect was able to sustain an individual amidst personal tribulations, sorrow, oppression, and the irksome routines of life. Indeed, the superior status of man in history, they felt, had resulted not merely from his physical strength and stamina but also from command of his mind and the ability to use it for well-defined purposes. In the preface to *Thoughts on Self Culture Addressed to Women* (1850) they wrote that they sought to point out the principles "by which conscience may be enlightened, reason cultivated, the will brought into accordance with God's will, and the whole mind developed to the degree of perfection of which it is capable."[1]

The Shirreff sisters protested the patriarchy of the middle-class, one-family household. Ideologues of the middle class in their society often denounced personal dependence and hierarchy, but it was cherished in the family circle. Eric Hobsbawm has pointed out that "the crucial point is that the structure of the bourgeois family flatly contradicted that of bourgeois society. Within it freedom, opportunity, the cash nexus, and the pursuit of individual profit did not rule."[2]

In the mid-century decades Emily and Maria did not challenge the role of the male as breadwinner in the family. They desired first to gain for women latitude within the domestic circle so that they could be truly civilizers of society and educators of the young which was their legitimate role. The sisters felt that it was imperative for women to liberate themselves from ignorance; they then could examine with clarity what they owed to themselves, family, and society. Secondly, they wanted to free women from total absorption, in fact bondage, to narrow household duties and the absurd round of activities imposed by the world of fashion. Although a generation later the Shirreffs broadened their view of the possibilities open to women in realms beyond the domestic life and likewise at that point approved of women's aggressive pursuit of professional careers and social justice, they never withdrew their injunction to women to seek above all personal fulfillment within a domestic and familial setting.

The Shirreffs adhered to a traditionalist view of woman as composed of a higher nature and a lower one which struggled for supremacy, on one hand a proclivity to be a sexual temptress and pleasure seeker who gratified the senses and gave inordinate value to material goods and on the other hand custodian of humanity's highest aspirations.[3] Man and the society that he had constructed throughout the ages, the sisters charged, had nurtured in diverse ways the lower side of woman.

The Shirreff sisters saw enlightened intellect as a sure guide to achievement of the potentialities of human nature, but unlike the purely secularist thinkers of the eighteenth century, they subordinated this intellect to Christian humanism. They wanted man and woman to adhere to a clear-cut moral code that demanded sexual abstention prior to marriage, familial and social responsibility, and the primacy of the spiritual nature. However, they rejected absorption with dogma rather than daily practice of Christian virtues, clerical domination of the lives of women, and ecclesiastical intolerance. The Shirreffs sought by education the pursuit of truth, human conscience controlled by spiritual guidelines, and exploration of the means to apply veracity, justice, and tolerance in daily life.

The Shirreff sisters conceived of benevolence as a crucial principle of Christianity; it embodied for them sympathy, charity, and positive familial feelings that led to daily acts of kindness. The means to achieve a moral discipline, they said, were habitual self-examination, self-control that meant submission to preordained Christian concepts, and management of aggressiveness which led to cheerfulness.

"Be ye perfect as your Father which is in Heaven is perfect" were the words of Him whom we profess to follow; and such is the very standard set before us, evidently pointing to an infinite series of toils and endeavours never certainly to be accomplished on earth; and who shall tell through what forms of being hereafter to be carried on. Such, then, being the law under which we strive for improvement, it is evident that there can be no end to our labour and it follows that when we cease to gain ground, we actually begin to loose it, and the arrest of progress is but another word for deterioration.[4]

They ascribed to that spiritual injunction which moved the believer to song—"work, for the night is coming" when no man can work. Their writings contain a Broad Church spirit. In sum the Shirreff sisters wanted the principles of Christianity to shape the response of women to the secular problems of their lives. The core of their credo was applied altruism and Christian citizenship. The world, they recognized, moved toward a rational progressive and secular framework, and they tried to promote the concept that religion is morals. They were, therefore, in contact on that point with John Stuart Mill, Henry Sidgwick, and T. H. Green.

The Shirreffs defined happiness as that which satisfied the mind and heart. It meant involvement in the lives of others and provided fulfillment to the individual because it was rooted in spiritual aspirations, affections, social *solidarité*, and utilization of the intellect to expand and enrich ideals.[5]

In mid-century Emily and Maria studied the writings of a number of English philosophers. They gained ideas from Dugald Stewart who had supported the intellectual equality of men and women and other English worthies of previous years such as Lord Bacon,

Bishop Butler, David Hume, and Adam Smith. But the sisters also studied the writings of nineteenth-century intellectual leaders such as J. S. Mill, Archbishop Whately, Sir James Mackintosh, Sir John Herschel, Professor Sedgwick, Sir Charles Lyell, and Thomas Mayo, president of the Royal College of Physicians, in particular his *Pathology of the Human Mind* (1838).[6] In 1854 Henry Buckle sent material by Auguste Comte to Maria.[7] The Shirreffs read nineteenth-century historians Alphonse de Larmartine, Francois Guizot, Adolphe Thiers, and George Grote.

The Shirreff sisters in their first major presentation to women, *Thoughts on Self Culture Addressed to Women* (1850), asked for a general recognition that women held a subordinate position in society. From a moral stance, they said, that position was unconscionable because God had ordained an equality of sexes. But they also focused on the irksome life which women endured as a result of that servile status. Dependence and inactivity seemed to the sisters the main burdens of women to which all others were related. They urged women to search for a worthy partnership.

She will then neither seek to be his tyrant nor consent to be the puppet in his hands; she will neither hug an ignoble chain nor struggle by craft to shake off a natural bond: but, strong in her real independence of mind, she will stand, such as God created her, the meet companion for man, fitted to share with him the duties and joys, the hopes and responsibilities of existence.[8]

In that first polemical work and in subsequent essays the sisters endeavored to promote liberation of women without strident attacks on males. Their attitude can be traced to several motives. First, from a tactical point of view, they believed hostility was self-defeating. Emily Shirreff in *Intellectual Education* (1858) stated a principle which the sisters tried to promote in their subsequent careers—avoidance of controversy on a highly emotional issue which plagued the women's rights movement in the late nineteenth century, the quesion of equal intellectual capacity of men and women. Emily observed that the intellectual claims of women were advanced in an unselfish spirit by some of the ablest men in Britain whose aid was vital to the achievement of feminine goals, and it was both unwise and unjust to divide society into hostile camps on sex lines on a subject related to self-esteem that evoked in many cases irrational responses.

In the 1850s, on the question of women's right to participate equally with men in various occupations, the Shirreffs took a pragmatic position colored by what they considered a somewhat bittersweet gift from God—motherhood. It placed restrictions on and limited women as well as invested them with obvious power and satisfactions. They asked women to be aware of the male burdens which were an inseparable part of occupations of the nineteenth century—seemingly inordinate demands upon an individual's time and energy and the encouragement of highly competitive and indeed aggressive feelings. With such conditions so widespread Emily Shirreff asked women to recognize the amount of physical stamina needed to gain entrance to an occupation and compete in the economic world as constituted. She brought the issue to the fore because she wanted women to place their desires or economic need for an occupation in juxtaposition to the demands of family life. So the sisters made clear that they wanted women to make decisions about possible occupations from an individual and pragmatic stance—How did work relate to their personal needs and patterns of their family circle? After the sisters had become involved in public life in the 1870s, had experienced both its burdens and satisfactions, and had seen opportunities for women to pursue a number of occupations dramatically expand, they considered it feasible and most desirable for many married as well as single women to undertake a career.

Emily Shirreff feared that a wide assault by women on occupations preempted until then by men would have an adverse impact on male-female relationships and familial life. She wanted to proceed on the matter in a careful and paced manner.

What will be the moral effect on society, what the influence on women's happiness, when men have ceased to be protectors to become rivals, when the appeal to their generosity, to the loftier qualities of their nature is dropped, leaving only the eagerness and irritation of contest coupled with probable contempt for oft defeated competitors? What hold will then be left to women save through those feelings which might always give them power for a time?[9]

Emily Shirreff sought to preserve at all costs what she called innate feelings of men and women toward each other. Man's noblest affection, she said, blended in a positive way with protection and sheltering care, and women's love embraced trusting tenderness and the desire to invest the loved one with an ideal excellence.[10] She judged the crucial ingredient in the male-female relationship the character of the latter's dependence. But in fact she maintained that the relationship had to be variable and highly individualistic because of the range of abilities, personalities, and duties of men and women.

Almost a generation after the Shirreffs' initial approach to British women, Maria Grey at the start of her educational work at Belfast spoke forcefully for equality of women.

Is she a complete human being, the co-equal, and partner of man in all that constitutes true humanity as expressed in the words of Scripture:—"God created man in his own image. In the image of God created he him, male and female created he them"? or is woman only the spare rib of a man; an inferior and incomplete human creature, formed for his use and pleasure, a nought which has no value till another figure is placed before it? I need scarcely tell you that I hold the first to be the true view of women, and that the second has, consciously or unconsciously, with more or less clearness and definiteness, been held by men in general from the days of Eve till now, and is at the bottom of all their modes of dealing with women in the family, in society and in legislation. And sorely have too many women avenged the humiliation by using the power conceded to them—the power all their education has been directed to strengthen—their power over the senses and passions of men to degrade, to frivolise, to turn from noble ends and worthy efforts, the manhood which had so failed to recognise their womanhood. It is against this view we must strive to the utmost. We are always hearing in scorn or in approbation of women's rights. Let us contend for her right of humanity, her right to be considered a free and responsible agent, with a life of her own, a soul of her own, objects and interests of her own, which she may legitimately pursue, independently of the objects and interests of man. Let us also contend that the special function of motherhood which nature has assigned to her, gives us qualities which constitute the perfect mother as those qualities of the human mind and soul, requiring to develop them the highest training.[11]

On the issue that was most vexatious—intellectual equality of men and women—Maria bent the knee to the male in an article in the *Fortnightly Review* in 1879 as Emily had done in *Intellectual Education* twenty years earlier. Maria gave man a primacy of intellect or what she called the power of intellect.

There is, however, no evidence to show that the inferiority of the woman amounts to actual deficiency in any of the qualities belonging to man. It is rather like the difference between the right hand and the left. The left hand can be trained to do equally what is done by the right hand, and with naturally left-handed people does it better; but the right has, as a rule, just that slight superiority which prevents any hesitation as to which shall be used.

Maria, however, insisted that women had been handicapped in the race of life in the main by life-style, social conditioning, and education. Perhaps her major message was that the sexes were more similar than different.

The result of the comparison of the moral and intellectual powers of men and women seems to be that human nature is substantially the same in both, and the common expression—How like a man-How like a woman! should be translated into—How like what men and women generally have been made by conditions of life, education, and inherited aptitudes, from generation to generation, causing certain qualities to be more or less developed in each sex taken as a whole.[12]

She denied that women were specially endowed with the qualities traditionally assigned to them of modesty, tenderness, self-devotion, delicacy, quickness of perception, and idealism which reached its height in religion.

In like manner Maria asserted that men were not endowed to any greater degree than women with the virtues of courage, truthfulness, generosity, and magnanimity. The vices attributed to women—vanity, frivolity, meanness, artifice, jealousy, and spite—were, she insisted, produced by the conditions under which they lived and appeared equally in men when placed in the same circumstances. Clearly the Shirreffs did not challenge the division and social structure of domestic roles, but they rejected the stereotypes

of what constituted maleness and femaleness in the human character and spirit. That message was given by other contemporary feminists. Emily Faithfull, writer, lecturer, and editor of the *Victoria
Magazine*, five years later wrote, "The grandest human characters
include the selfsame qualities, the true man being much of the
noble woman and the noble woman having somewhat of the true
man. It is time to reject as heathenish the notion of separate codes
of virtues and to look for modesty in men and courage in
women."[13]

As the century drew to a close, Mrs. Grey commented that the
country was in a transition era—the old age of faith and custom
was disappearing, and what was coming was not visible. She was
certain that women would be ultimately victorious in achievement
of a redefined status in British society and sharers in its responsibilities and duties. She enunciated a hypothesis which if accepted
made any comparison of male and female intellectual ability tentative and not fully reliable—women's abilities had not been cultivated to the same degree or in the same areas, so that making
generalizations was illogical. She noted the mental similarity of the
sexes in early life and the gradual divergence in late childhood and
adolescence when girls were conditioned to be submissive and
gentle, clearly shaping their subsequent productive intellectual
lives.[14]

The Shirreffs, however, sought not merely female liberation and
fulfillment; they were devoted to the social regenerative ethic of the
Victorian era. An equitable male-female intellectual partnership
Maria saw as the condition *a priori* to "the elimination of moral
cesspools, the conquest of civilization over barbarism or the brute
in human nature, and the triumph of the divine and immortal over
that which perishes in the using." For more than thirty years the
sisters clearly tried to avoid bitter controversy centered on the issue
of male versus female intellectual capabilities. Since they acutely
needed allies in their several projects, they sought accommodation
with men who placed women in a subordinate place intellectually
but at the same time demanded for them an expanded educational
and cultural life.

The Shirreffs faced stereotypes which had become affixed to
women involved in the liberation movement. Lynn Linton marked

out the two prevalent demeaning images: women freed from the binding moralities and women who had abandoned clinging affections. She described the liberated woman as an enemy of man and at the same time as a plagiarist, a man hater yet a man imitator. The liberated women, she said, saw manhood as the incarnation of pride, gluttony, selfishness, and wrath. The Shirreffs endeavored to counteract such caricatures by drawing distinctions between, on one hand, personality, emotions, maternal feelings, and familial ties, and on the other, intellect which they believed transcended sex but was not independent of its demands.

The sisters described in a perceptive manner and sometimes in chilling detail the vacuous life-style and hedonism of women of the upper and middle classes which often led to frustration and even despair. The Shirreffs sketched problems and offered realistic means to respond to them. But they presented no quick solutions because the difficulties were deeply rooted in the fabric of society. Indeed Emily observed that nature was a stepmother to women.[15]

As society is constituted...I see no relief from without to a condition which in many or even in the majority of cases is hard to bear; therefore it is that I think it wiser to bid women look for resources within, and learn to infuse the excitement and vigor of intellectual activity into their inactive lives, than to look beyond to one small opening or another from the massive wall that hems them in.[16]

She listed the difficulties: childbearing, a myriad of family cares which arose periodically in the lives of married and single women, the refusal of the professions and business to admit women to their ranks, the social opprobrium which many women were unable to accept if they engaged in learning patterns and public activities not sanctioned by convention. The solutions offered by the Shirreff sisters in the mid-Victorian years were neither dramatic nor socially disruptive. They urged women to cultivate their minds and direct their emotions and energies to an ongoing system of self-development. They believed liberation for women depended upon access to the mental and psychological resources which had sustained men throughout the ages but had been almost entirely closed to women.

The Shirreffs had several immediate goals at mid-century which they pursued actively: (1) creation of viable educational patterns, formal and informal, for women of all ages, (2) analysis and revitalization of the several roles of women as wife, mother, and "old maid," (3) the opening of public life to those women who had the ability, education, and time which a vocation required, and (4) an exploration of the contributions which women were able to make to the advancement, happiness, and moral righteousness of society. This program was in accord with that of Mary Wollstonecraft at the end of the eighteenth century and also the outlook of the Shirreffs' contemporaries, John Stuart Mill and Harriet Taylor.

The Shirreffs gave a profile of women of polite society in the mid-Victorian years. They saw women faced with a number of difficulties, first, a painful sense of inconsistency between life as it existed and the religious theory upon which it was supposedly based, second, a confusion of ideas, and third, the want of some comprehensive principle by which to regulate thought and action, a real aim for their exertions. Maria and Emily concluded that in large measure the faults of women were traceable to the atmosphere in which they grew up and lived out their days. Women's position, they said, did not relate to their own merits nor any acknowledged rights, but on the character of the men they happened to be dependent upon. Usually women, according to the Shirreffs, met with kindness and indulgence on one end of the scale and on the other harshness and ill usage but seldom justice; the caprice of husband and father was the sole arbiter of a woman's happiness. The Shirreffs believed that women had been raised from household drudges not because their just claims had been recognized but because concessions had been given by indulgent and civilized masters. They charged that men fostered in women the habit of yielding to feelings which was at the core of the criticism of extreme partiality leveled at them. Men's definition of the ideal woman as a creature of feeling, the Shirreffs claimed, often led to their designation of strength of mind, judgment, and decisiveness, which were ingredients of intellectual independence, as unfeminine. The sisters called upon women to raise their estimation of their sex. "When women shall have generally a keen sense of justice and a contempt for the petty arts which wheedle a man into granting as an indulgence that which ought to have been conceded as a right, much else around them must also be changed."[17]

But despite the inferior status they so pointedly outlined, the Shirreffs impressed upon Englishwomen that they possessed a power that men could not cast off or abridge because it sprang from their natural position toward men which could not be altered, whatever the outward forms of society. That power was based upon the passions and affections of man. The Shirreffs saw the power as a divine gift which gave women the means to counteract any passivity which was imposed upon them. Whatever men impressed upon females, either good or evil, they received back through the instrument of the family circle. They announced that men could not achieve a permanent advance except by the willing cooperation of women.

History accordingly shows us too often the most depraved periods are those in which female influence has been most prominent and active. But the fact, so often commented upon by the satirist, only proves the general truth, that influence exercised without the restraint of moral principle is dangerous in proportion to its power....Whenever men sink into mere lovers of pleasure and creatures of intrigue, they necessarily become the tools of those who can flatter their vanity and play upon their passions.[18]

Thus the Shirreffs conceived of women as the major source of moral strength exercising greater potential power than professors and ideologues. The sisters, however, regretted that in the nineteenth century women's moral impact had not kept abreast of the advance of knowledge and progressive social changes which had occurred.

The ineffectiveness of women of polite society Maria Grey saw summed up in the "idols of society—gentility and femininity." They seemed to her degraded symbols of once noble ideals. Gentility like Buddha, she said, had many incarnations and resided for each class in the class above it. There were, she noted, genteel neighborhoods in every town as well as genteel religious denominations, and the gate to them was money. She set forth a number of regulations which guided the genteel. (1.) Do no useful work, for it was the necessity of the vulgar and idleness the privilege of the supremely genteel. (2.) If one was unable to keep the law of idleness for oneself, it had to be enforced with double severity on daughters because work for them was both ungenteel and unfeminine. (3.) Do all things your neighbors do who are above you in rank and fortune, and those who depart one jot from the formula will not enter into the kingdom of gentility. (4.) "Fret not yourself about what you are, only about what you seem."[19] Maria considered such interpretations of gentility an inversion of traditional ideals. Serious study by women incurred the stigma of singularity and strong will and so was thought not to be genteel. Maria Grey observed that husband hunting was the only acceptable vocation for women. "If unsuccessful in that, the daughters remain weary and too often in sound and disappointed idleness in their father's house, eating their hearts out, if they have any vigor or character or intellect in the enforced dependence and vacuity of their lives in fastness, sometimes, in some form of pietism, ritualistic or evangelical."[20]

In contrast to gentility Mrs. Grey offered the attributes of motherhood as the ideal to be emulated. The qualities did not necessarily depend on actually undertaking the contract of marriage and the physical act of motherhood but were rather qualities of character and personality; they were in fact the essence of womanliness—tender, strong, just, self-controlled, idealistic, and orderly. She rejected habits of life or methods of education which tended to repress such attributes. But doubtless of extreme import at that juncture in the women's rights movement was Maria Grey's insistence that men should possess the same characteristics. "On examination they appear to be the same as we have already enumerated, differing only in the manner and circumstance of their exercise."[21] But throughout their long lives they endorsed the traditional view of the sex roles of parents: women cared for the needs and shaped the development of the infant and young child, and men in large measure were the observers at that juncture. However, the Shirreffs called upon men to take time from their occupations to shape the minds and personalities of their sons and daughters in late childhood, and particularly in adolescence the sisters considered the male impact crucial.[22]

The Shirreffs in their various writings traced the causes of female degradation. Emily described perceptively the restricted code of action and narrow social milieu which held in their grip young women of comfortable material circumstances. Parents motivated by kindness, Emily said, kept daughters in needless dependence.

She compared the situation to a fully grown creature trying to take exercise in a go-cart or find rest in an infant's crib. Girls paid a high price, she thought, for care and protection; all details of life and domestic arrangements came under parental care.

It is common to see young women, and women no longer young, kept dependent in every movement, with a moderate allowance for dress, from which not infrequently they hardly dare to economise for any other object. They are without the power of making a journey,—of asking a friend to stay with them,—of making acquaintances,—of engaging in any undertaking, unless it is to cost nothing beyond their own trouble, and to square exactly with the most trifling arrangements of the rest of the family,—without even a quiet room of their own in which they may if they choose enjoy solitude and their own pursuits.[23]

Emily thought it only natural that women in such a colorless existence found flirtation exciting; where there was no active life of thought, fancy and feeling were easily stirred and simple novelty had unspeakable charm. And women unfortunately, she pointed out, had no adequate educational background to make judgments on suitors. She concluded that the overriding factors in young women's lives which drove them to snatch at an offer of marriage were fear of poverty, undue constraint, and want of a definite occupation and station in society. Decisions of young women on marriage were made, Emily thought, on a series of hypotheses in which love was not the essential consideration—firstly, the expectations of parents, and secondly, the conviction that the only honorable and useful life for women was the married state.[24]

The sisters felt that the plan of marriage in Britain was as debilitating to the human spirit as the continental *mariage de convenance*.[25] They claimed that the latter was not hypocritical; it was a mercantile transaction and carried on in calm businesslike manner and at least guided by parents who were deeply committed to the welfare of their children and to saving them from some of the illusions of vanity and ignorance. "In our system it is the young themselves who learn to make a trade of the warmest feelings of their nature, to try to excite affection which they neither respond to nor value, and who in the excitement of this game of artifice are much more likely to lose sight of all that makes married life dignified and happy."[26]

Maria Grey examined the status of the "old maid" in the circles in which she moved. She commented on the definition given by Mr. Bonverie, MP, who called old maids social failures.[27] He implied thereby that female existence was nonutilitarian when it did not directly minister to the male. Mrs. Grey judged that such a frame of mind led to female infanticide in certain societies. She observed that women of meager income were often designated "old maids" while those with large independent means had a respected and honorable place in society. She regretted that people viewed the old maid as a social failure or a social superfluity or a social laughing-stock. In contrast St. Paul had seen the old maid as a virgin dedicated to God and hence possessed of social dignity. Yet Mrs. Grey criticized that view of the single woman because it related solely to her sexual function.[28] Indeed, Mrs. Grey felt that Christianity had more often focused on Eve, the temptress, than the humane group of women who gathered at the foot of the Cross.

In the decades when the sisters examined the problems and outlook of single women of the middle class, and particularly their needs and areas of service, that sector of the national community rapidly increased in numbers. The percentage of British single women rose 16.8 percent between 1851 and 1871. There were in 1851 2,765,000 single women over fifteen years of age; there were 2,956,000 in 1861 and 3,228,000 in 1871. The increase was probably due to different mortality rates between the sexes as well as to male emigration.

The Shirreffs deplored middle-class parents' lack of serious attention to the education of their daughters. They felt parents hesitated to give daughters the type of education which would equip them to enter the professions or public life because such livelihoods brought their daughters into contact with chance companions. Yet, by and large parents were not able to provide sufficient income for daughters when they died. The Shirreffs were knowledgeable about a tragic group of middle-class mature women who had to earn a living by some means. They had only two options, needlework, which led to a life of drudgery, and service in a household as a governess. The latter occupation Maria Grey considered to be stifling as constituted. She said that governesses hung like Mahomet's tomb between the earth of the vulgar and the heaven of gentility, yet were excluded from the pleasures of either world. They had to eat the bread of dependence which was as bitter as dust and ashes to the taste. "From the first to the last they are the victims of gentility."[29]

Maria Grey feared that the position of single women in the last third of the century would remain on the whole a confined and inactive one, and the remedy for their somber outlook had to come from intellectual self-development for the purpose of personal pleasure. "Mental resources, and energy to use them without external stimulus, are the surest safeguard against the depressing influence of circumstances we cannot control." She suggested as the first step an education to give girls the frame of mind that marriage was not the only acceptable option for them.

There is little fear that the young creature full of warm affections should form too bright an anticipation of a lonely life; but it is well that she should feel that no evils that life can bring can equal the humiliating misery of a wife's dependence without perfect esteem; or even—with some natures at least,—the cares and sufferings of married life, without that earnest love in whose fullness is abnegation of self.[30]

Maria Grey criticized mothers who talked to their daughters of marriage as an inevitable necessity in which if one form of suffering was avoided, another had to be endured. She said mothers depicted marriage as a lottery in which no one could know her lot but also made in Heaven which meant that all earthly prudence was needless. Objectionable attitudes seemed to Maria prevalent among young women who approached marriage; they were often worldly or rash. She claimed that women lived in a milieu where two conflicting streams of thought operated—a low opinion of men but a servile submission to the fault-ridden husbands, whom they ridiculed in private, together with an exalted opinion of the married state.[31]

In their early writings the Shirreffs actually offered no panacea for single women beyond simply the development of self-dignity, a life of the mind which brought self-satisfaction, and if financially desirable or indeed necessary the legitimate right to pursue a public career. They focused attention on a neglected and at times reviled segment of the female population, gave a realistic profile of its problems, and then examined in doubtless an overly prudent manner the options of single women.

The Shirreffs castigated the preparation women received for marriage and motherhood within the family circle and in social life. Prior to marriage girls rushed from one giddy round of pleasures to another without any solid education.[32] Motherhood, they pointed out, required knowledge, vigorous understanding, acute perceptions, and moral power. They agreed with the commonly accepted point of view that a woman without tender and active sympathies and affections was a rebel against nature. Indeed the Shirreffs asserted that it was impossible for women's feelings to be too warm, their affections too tender or too strong, "but the greater their intensity, the more unfit they are to be our guides; and the more indispensable they are for women's usefulness and happiness, the more necessary is it that some other power should be brought into action to control and regulate their exercise." And Maria and Emily complained that the logical power, a relevant and comprehensive system of intellectual development, had not been available to females. Indeed the sisters believed that a sort of tragic-comic educational and cultural schema had evolved for women of the middle and upper classes. They described the simplistic pattern which held sway, schoolroom discipline of superficial book learning, needless repression of childish pleasures, idleness, pursuit of worldly vanity, the lottery of marriage, or single life with its neglect. Attention to dress, devotion to trifles, and gossip filled the idle hours.

The Shirreff sisters' concern for women's personal and household lavishness was based on an accurate appraisal of social life. They observed the situation firsthand. Wealthy upper-middle-class and aristocratic women who enjoyed a myriad of social engagements connected with the London season expended large sums of money; an effuse life-style required a household to sustain it. One writer has called the years 1866-1880 the golden age of the dressmaker. The growing prosperity of the upper middle class allowed the lady of the household from that class to be removed from useful domestic enterprise; servants took care of most household affairs, and child care became relegated to the nursery and its staff.[33] The lady of the family, less needed in these areas, engaged in visiting, shopping, adorning her person, and partying which made her more and more dependent on her husband for funds. Such a life-style also increased the necessity to spend her time and efforts to please him and further his social aspirations and business or professional goals. Maria and Emily noted that a series of social objectives were affixed to female education, and they centered on the goal of marriage; females learned skills to please men and in particular to pander to their fancies, caprices, and vanity. The applause and homage of men had become the chief object of female education in the home, school, and society, and wealth, rank, and artifice were held out as desiderata.

The Shirreffs decided that women of the middle class had more time on their hands than their husbands, and their overriding sin was frivolity which led to trivial occupations, petty cares, and waste of time and talent. The Shirreffs saw even moral and religious training, so often central to female education, as so unsystematically structured and the connection between its abstract principles and their bearing on daily life so little or carelessly developed that it had only a minimal impact on character. In the educational process morals seemed to the Shirreffs disconnected from religion and the latter from secular life, and intellect regarded as completely separate from all. The Shirreffs wanted married women to participate in the quest for knowledge but did not expect them to become scholars. Nevertheless, they urged women to acquire knowledge, the mental habits which study gave when followed in the right method and spirit.

The sisters saw no validity in the commonly stated view that love of knowledge was totally useless to women. They maintained that thinking and knowing were the life of the soul and knowledge the food of the spirit and thus as vital to women who lived quiet and retired lives as to men who engaged in public affairs. The pursuit and love of knowledge created a spring of mental energy for women who the sisters insisted were deeply in need of such resources because they had social positions marked by trial and privations, sorrows and the suffering which came from dependence, helplessness, and an almost total recourse to affections for sustenance of the spirit.[34] Moreover, the Shirreffs felt sure that love of knowledge would add zest to the lives of indolent and active-minded women as well as another all-too-prevalent group, "women with crushed and wounded affections."[35] The Shirreffs warned that knowledge could not give happiness or harden the spirit against the touch of sorrow because such functions were beyond its scope; the life of the heart and intellect were different, and food for one did not nourish the other. "But the soothing and elevating influence of the love of knowledge may steal over the wounded spirit and win the thoughts from self, from regret or anxious brooding.... The value of that mental refuge which the love of knowledge affords... is a sanctuary open to her, where evil shall not follow, and whence she will surely return refreshed and invigorated."[36]

The sisters contrasted love of knowledge with the solace of religion. They defined the latter as the chief resource of the human being in times of sorrow; its hopes led away from the world. Intellectual exercise in which emotion and self-contemplation held only a minimal place they saw in contradistinction to religion; it gave the mind "a healthy tone" and prepared the human being for a struggle with life which was necessary and an almost constant process.

That religion had become a form of escapism to some women just as marriage had to others made Emily Shirreff uncomfortable. "What but the vacuity of life I have been complaining of makes so many young women fall a prey to superstitious devotion?" If women fell under the sway of evangelical preachers, they were often, Emily said, sent forth to distribute tracts and teach Sunday school. On the other hand, if they lived within the rule of the High Church, its clerics directed some of their hours to religious exercises and devotions and others to the embroidery of altar cloths. The church extended itself to those sickened by leisure and idleness who desired occupation and excitement. "The Church provides the occupation and dispenses with the labour of self-regulation,—the weak, the enthusiastic and the timid naturally fall under its dominion."[37]

The Shirreffs designated the transmission of love of knowledge to children as one of the chief functions, and in fact a natural by-product, of the joyous involvement of women in a mature intellectual life. They told women that love of knowledge could be infused by them into the minds and hearts of children, and they characterized it as an ennobling affection. "Let a high appreciation of the fruits of knowledge and the gifts of intellect by which those fruits are won, be shown to their sons in their conversation, and teaching and pursuits, and they will do more than all the eloquence of philosophers to prevent those gifts being offered up on the altars of Mammon."[38]

All in all the Shirreffs urged women to undertake the long-range rehabilitation of their sex by recasting their own intellectual lives and then educating their families, especially their sons, to be sensitive to the suffering of the weak and to propagate justice for all. The Shirreffs advised women to inculcate in their daughters self-control in place of self-indulgence and caprice. The reason why women had not exercised a more profound impact upon society seemed to the sisters to be defective education in home and school which they described in some detail, together with their inactive existence determined by the strictures of society and their natural role of home keeper and mother. The sisters labeled mental vigor as a necessary adjunct of moral power and said that unless women undertook their own reform program, they could expect very little aid from the powerful and free in a world of mixed and selfish motives.

John Morley, Liberal political leader, social commentator, and man of letters, in a popular periodical presented an essay on what he judged to be a national catastrophe—want of social responsibility among the educated and materially comfortable citizenry.

Of course the young lady, wrapped in soft clothes and fragrant odours, is very sorry for the half-clad, famished wretches whom she passes in her carriage, on her way from the opera or the circulating library. . . . The first of all social responsibilities is, to have an intelligent set of convictions upon the problems that vex and harass society, and continually keep a wide margin of miserable anarchy about her skirts. This is the point at which the well-to-do classes break down. It is not that they are cold hearted so much as they are slow-headed. Their inaction is the result not of moral apathy but of lack of intellectual energy. Active as we are, and keen-sighted in adjusting means to ends, in commerce and mechanical inventions, we are amazingly slow and shiftless in carrying on a similar process with reference to the impalpable concerns of society. . . . It is the shirking of this plain social duty, of having clear-sighted convictions of some sort on social subjects, which keeps all the most terrible questions of today—pauperism, prostitution, profound and widespread indigence—open and unsettled, and, worst of all, in no fair way of being settled.[39]

The Shirreffs, who were concerned about the same deficiency, held firmly to the belief that an adequate educational system for females in conjunction with a reorientation of family values would enliven the social responsibility upon which human progress depended.

The female characters in the novels written by the Shirreffs in the 1850s and 1860s, when they also wrote their polemical works, dramatized the complex nature of women and the overwhelming impact upon them of social conventions and familial burdens. The message about women in their novels was similar to that in their tracts and articles. Life was a challenge to women even under what appeared to be favorable conditions. By means of their fiction they asked women to reexamine the character and parameters of the role of wife and mother.

Interestingly the novels of the Shirreffs contain several of the qualities which Lynn Linton saw in fiction written by women in the nineteenth century: (1) their heroines often were not physical beauties—perhaps even plain girls with plenty of soul, (2) the female novelists protested the theory that man was automatically a more powerful being than woman, and she at best a domestic appendage of the husband, and (3) their heroines were often strong, able, and intelligent, and some of the key male characters appeared secondary to women. Miss Linton believed that heroines in the work of female novelists were not the type of heroines women admired in real life. She felt that such a condition was not explainable by women's lack of perception but by the fact that the female novelists at some stage in their careers had been thrown back upon themselves and isolated in feeling from the world. "Women heroines, except in the case of the best artists, are conceptions borrowed, not from without, but from within."[40] Miss Linton described the social milieu which shaped their outlook.

It is the lot of many girls to pass their childhood or youth in a somewhat monotonous round of domestic duties, and frequently in a narrow domestic circle, with which, except from natural affection, they may have no great intellectual sympathy. The stage of intellectual fever through which able men have passed when they were young is replaced, in the case of girls of talent, by a stage of moral morbidity. At first this finds vent in hymns, and it turns in the end to novels. . . . They know the sensation of social martyrdom, and it is a little sort of revenge upon the world to publish a novel about an underrated martyr, whose merits are recognized in the end, either before or after her demise.[41]

The sisters collaborated in *Passion and Principle* (1853), and Maria wrote *Love's Sacrifice* (1868). Women characters in the novels are the dynamic focal points. In *Passion and Principle* the husband of Ellen, Lady Cardwell, had "poisoned her life by his falsehood and treachery, and then had despised and trampled upon his victim." An exploration of that relationship gave the Shirreffs an opportunity to present the hidden suffering endured by a segment of women of the upper classes at the hands of their husbands who exercised a dictatorial sway in the domestic circle. Despite maltreatment Lady Cardwell returned to her husband, cared for him during a desperate illness, and remained with him. She displayed the forgiveness, charity, and self-sacrifice which the Victorian age venerated in women and which the Shirreffs endorsed. The sisters saw women as the custodians of morality, and their liberation was not to be at the expense of that role. A destruction of their mission of morality, the Shirreffs believed, would destroy the society of which they were a part.

Louisa Conway, the other heroine in *Passion and Principle*, spoke of the Shirreffs' concern for the women of intellect. Her life of the mind combined with spiritual faith sustained her during a life of privation and threat. "She poured on every subject she handled the light of a clear and powerful intellect—that by her hand the ponderous weapon of close and logical arguments, and the lighter arms of wit and satire, were wielded with equal ease."[42] The Shirreffs catalogued the special difficulties of mentally intrepid women who endured poverty.

Not the least of the sufferings she [Louisa Conway] had to endure was the utter solitude in which she lived. . . . It is only women who can know such solitude as hers, which her conventional position converted into a dreary prison house. No ties of business connected her with her fellow creatures—

no community of interests, such as a man, however abject his poverty, might rejoice in as he discusses public news in the resorts of his fellow men.[43]

Perhaps the greatest burden which Louisa bore was the mental suffering which came from her inability to bring to fruition her God-given desire for intellectual fulfillment, "the conflict of an aspiring mind struggling in vain against its invisible but galling chains—the wild longing of a spirit, full of energy and consciousness of power to find scope for its exertion, ere it could sink within its cage and be still."

Maria Grey also dealt with the special difficulties which resulted from women's almost total absorption with domestic affairs, in particular their involvement with the unseen battles of life.

Hers was not the martyrdom accomplished by one heroic effort to which the soul is braced by lofty faith, by the sympathy of noble minds. It was, as that of women generally is, a martyrdom of small things, the perpetual pricks of pins and needles, with no grandeur in its self-sacrifice to stimulate or support endurance, no pathos to invest it with poetic beauty.[44]

Maria Grey also drew vivid portraits of selfish and malevolent women who appeared in *Love's Sacrifice*. The mother and wife of Henry Hardcastle fell into such a category. The former was depicted as more pathetic than evil, "narrowness of heart and mind, bigoted attachment to a religious creed joined to worldliness of practice" made her a repellent figure. The latter, Melanie Hardcastle, a beautiful woman, schemed to manipulate people for her own advantage. She destroyed the happiness and prosperity of others and betrayed her husband with many lovers. She represented the wealthy woman who had no motivation but self-gratification, and certainly Maria saw such women in her own social circles. In a very real sense they were victims of family, social, and educational patterns of upper society from which the Shirreffs hoped to rescue the next generation of women by opening the life of the mind to them. Selfishness, the salient quality of Melanie's character, led to an unfulfilled life in her mature years.

But indolence, and the love of good eating, which now divided her affections with the love of dress, had favoured the tendency of middle age to *embonpoint,* and the graceful roundness of her youth was fast turned to rotundity. Her power of fascination had long been on the wane, and being obliged to abandon her cruel game of coquetry, she had taken to tormenting her maid instead of her lovers, and to eating instead of flirting.[45]

Emily Shirreff's apprehensions about democracy and her criticism of the irresponsible social, moral, and intellectual attitudes of young men and women of the middle and upper classes and their indifference to national values appeared in "Our Modern Youth" in *Fraser's Magazine* in 1863. She felt that youth of her era possessed an overweening self-assurance, but their excitement with life turned quickly to ennui. Moreover, she charged that among young people self-indulgence prevailed, accompanied by a disregard for the accumulated wisdom of their society and a shallow approach to life. Emily ascribed the objectionable qualities to defective education, desultory reading, and an independent spirit encouraged by the democratic movement.

Yet, four years before the Reform Bill of 1867 Emily realistically recognized that her country was moving inevitably to full democracy. She agreed with critics who said that a narrow veneration of the wisdom of custom had perpetuated abuses, but she did not wish to cast out that false idol for a new one—wealth. Emily claimed that the evolutionary political pattern which had produced freedom in Britain had been created by men who were socially secure. Thus, political principles had been in large measure kept free, she believed, from petty social jealousies with the result that freedom had priority rather than equality. Indeed she maintained that inequality of some sort always existed in society.

Knowledge she considered to be the force which could produce both stability and progress. She quoted Henry Buckle. "Wonder is the product of ignorance; admiration is the product of knowledge. Ignorance wonders at the supposed irregularities of nature, science admires its uniformities." Emily wanted the spirit of inquiry to be the guide of youth. Possibly her acceptance of the inevitability of democracy came about by discussions with Henry Buckle. In *History of Civilization* he wrote that in countries educated to freedom all systems would collapse if their governments opposed the march of public opinion and held to views that were repugnant to the spirit of the age. Success in politics, he wrote, depended upon compromise, barter and concession. "Innovation is the sole guard of security."[46] At the passage of the Reform Bill of 1867 by the House of Commons Robert Lowe set forth as a national imperative education for the working class. "I believe that it will be absolutely necessary that you should prevail on future masters to learn their letters." For her part Emily Shirreff issued a challenge at that juncture to the middle- and upper-class parents who already had political power to provide their children who so often lacked social responsibility with an adequate education which they seldom received in existing systems.

If, according to Emily, the democratic spirit had encouraged a rebellious mood among youth, it had also brought about the liberation of women which she described in compelling and also realistic terms.

Women caught the direction of freedom.... It was no longer here and there a wronged woman claiming justice against her tyrant; it was the multitude of women standing up to claim that tyranny should no longer be a favoured institution.... And steadily, with perseverance against difficulties, and patience against ridicule, have they worked their onward way, till views, deemed visionary and dangerous a few years ago, are accepted; and the warm sympathy of men has often been enlisted in favour of what at first was supposed to be subversive of their interests. Never, indeed, can their objects be fully attained; for never, we fear, will might cease to be right, nor law be able to reach the abuse of power screened from public cognizance by all that makes home sacred.[47]

At the opening of the last generation of the century Emily was in the midst of her work for the Froebel Society and the Women's Education Union. At that time opportunities for women to participate in economic life were far greater than they had been in the 1850s when she had made cautious appraisals of what the future held for women. In 1881 she observed that three types of human labor had been present in society: labor for subsistence, labor for distinction, and labor for chosen objectives. She pointed out that labor for subsistence had been the only legitimate one for women; the second had been completely denied them and the third so hampered by conventional difficulties that nothing was available to them except a narrow charity field. Emily demanded that it be universally accepted "that the mere right to live is not all that women may justly claim, that the desire for a chosen field of activity and the desire for distinction being deeply rooted in human nature, belong legitimately to women as to men, and till it is so recognised, there is no chance of a rational consideration of the subject in its wider bearings."[48] The attempt to repress the natural motives for work in women, she claimed, led simply to useless and frivolous activity. "As regards work as with so many things, she has been deliberately trained, not as a full and responsible human being, but as the creature intended only to help man when and in the manner in which he demands her help."

Accordingly Emily judged that civilization had developed through the ages in a one-sided and imperfect manner. She also concluded that women had been so cramped and confined that in many ways "we hardly know the real tendencies of their nature." With fervor she wrote, "I have boldly maintained that ambition is legitimate for women and that the impulse of activity is as strong in them as men." Emily saw as women's right full participation in public service tasks that had been monopolized and guided by men.[49]

By the 1880s Maria Grey recognized that she had been a participant in a revolution.

The ideal of the lady . . . was that of the woman daintily dressed, and daintily lodged, all her wants provided for by some male care, with no occupation taking her out of her home circle, having no necessity for exertion laid upon her independently of her own choice and inclination; shielded from all the rough work-a-day world. . . . But I need not fight this battle over again. It has been fought and won.[50]

Lady Stanley, her close ally, believed that Maria Grey's Women's Education Union had been a crucial factor in bringing about the change. Lady Stanley observed that the button-and-slipper argument was no longer raised, and women could use their time and intelligence on something beyond the comfort of their families. But Maria Grey was not satisfied with what had been accomplished and urged women to new efforts. In *Last Words to Girls on Life in School and After School* (1889) she broadened dramatically the focus which she had taken forty years earlier concerning women and political and social action. Her message was moderate in tone but radical in content and set forth a mission which a group of women at the end of Victoria's reign and in the new century followed energetically and which is briefly discussed in the following chapter.

Maria believed that the most significant challenge which faced modern society was to combine stable order and free growth in a viable formula; both qualities of life were indispensable to a healthy political system. She judged that Britain had made remarkable strides in the previous two centuries in forming a political system which encompassed both. She described briefly and in a rather simplistic manner conservatism—the value of tradition and institutional continuity to human society. However, she directed her major attention to the philosophy of change. She noted that change had to occur or decay resulted, but to be healthy it had to be developmental rather than disruptive. The strength of liberal or progressive thought she designated as sympathy with human beings, in particular with their wants and rights. She quoted Frederick Denison Maurice, a Christian Socialist on the point. "It expresses the worth of each single man. It counteracts the monarchical and aristocratical tendency to set up certain persons' authority on any formulas and decrees against human beings who form this nation."[51] The liberal philosophy, she contended, was the philosophy of hope for the toiler.

Maria admitted that inheritance, association, education, and temperament decreed how a person began political life. But she felt that wider knowledge, reflection, and experience modified or indeed reversed judgments. She accepted as normal and beneficial shifts in political life on a somewhat regular basis from conservatism to liberalism or progressivism. "Motion and resistance are the very elements of life, of free action."

Maria called upon women to become involved in politics. She felt that logically women ought to be on the side of the weak and helpless because they had been in that status for so long, and therefore inclined to the liberal cause which sponsored reform for their group. She pointed out that in fact large numbers of women embraced conservatism which she explained by the fact that society had excluded them from participation in public life and confined their sympathies. "We sympathise only with what we understand or can realise through imagination, and imagination is of all our faculties, the one that most depends for its range and power on cultivation and training."[52] Secondly, Maria observed that the weak and ignorant clung to the settled order which they knew. She told her readers that the first fruits of the education of women and their emancipation from "old world trammels" would be their fullest sympathy with every struggle for equal rights and privileges for all human beings.

They will recognise all the arguments against the enfranchisement and leveling up of the masses the precise arguments that were and are still, as regards political life, used against their own. Their indefeasible sense of weakness should make them sympathise with the weak while their trained moral sense should make them bold to fight for better things, instead of cowardly shrinking from possible disagreeable incidence of the change on themselves.[53]

Maria expanded the concept of social duty beyond the traditional Christian imperative to embrace legitimately any theistic faith or secular altruism. She rejoiced in the growth of human brotherhood. She assigned as an appropriate motto for women the cry of the French Revolution—liberty, equality, and fraternity. Under the banner of freedom she called for an arduous battle against all indirect and subtle invasions of human freedom, to struggle for freedom of person, freedom of work, freedom of conscience for all men and women alike. She observed that in theory and in the common law of the land all rights were secure, but in actuality were limited and sometimes completely lost by the pressure of opinion and social custom. Maria was heartened that one of the last major legal religious disabilities had been wiped away by the elevation of Baron Rothschild, a Jew, to the House of Lords, but she pointed out that social disabilities existed that inflicted penalties for opinions and beliefs. Educated women she called upon to strive to remove old social penalties because they had been active in imposing them. Maria said that women had a mighty position in the social sphere and could prevent its severest penalties from falling on the political and religious deviant. "When they have done this, they will have done their part in making liberty of conscience a reality in our social habits as in law."

Maria reminded her readers that by law the persons and labor of all adults were free but then asked them to consider if laborers were really free who worked from morning till night for a wage that barely kept body alive and did not provide even a pittance for refreshment or recreation.

Is the "sweater" who buys them of their own necessities at a much cheaper rate than the slave dealer bought his cargo of slaves very different from the latter except in the form of his dealings? Has not the Socialist some right on his side when he declares our boasted freedom to be a hollow mockery, while such slavery as this binds hundreds of thousands in its chains? There can, I think, be but one answer to this in just and thoughtful minds. The fact is there in its terrible, undeniable truth. The practical question is where to find a remedy?[54]

But Maria made it clear that in her schema revolution was not a remedy; the solution rested in better education, effective organization of the working class, and fairer distribution of the products of the economy. She urged women to seek solutions and not remain passive.

In a full exploration of the meaning of equality Maria probed in a serious manner the discrepancy in wealth in Britain. She contended as she had in earlier writings that no true equality existed among human beings; organized society decreed some sort of hierarchy of power; complete equality of material goods could only be achieved by prohibiting private property (an idea she rejected), but a fairer distribution of wealth seemed to her advisable and feasible. Despite the fact that fortune, education, habits, and manners led inevitably to social gradations, Maria said that equality in a number of areas could be effectively pursued as a realizable goal. She concluded that equality before the law was not a reality in Britain even though it was enshrined in the statute books.

How much remains to be done by the social reformer before the poor suitor can be said to stand on an equality with the rich one—the waifs and strays of the world with those who have the security of settled means and position. . . . We cannot and ought not acquiesce in such monstrous inequalities as those between the rich and the poor in the great cities; between the agricultural labourer earning his 9s. to 12s. a week and with nothing but his strength to do the work and his chance of keeping it to do, between him and the workhouse, and the country gentleman on whose land he works, and who thinks the times horribly bad which leave him only all the comforts of life without its luxuries.[55]

Maria observed that political economy of the past dealt only with the production of wealth. She insisted that it had become evident that the production of wealth was but one, and indeed an elementary, problem of the health and prosperity of any human society, and the maldistribution of wealth was as important and much more difficult to deal with. Maria stated that socialism in various forms and cooperation, productive and distributive, were offered as solutions, and although she did recommend a specific one, she asked women to study them carefully and make a decision without prejudice.[56]

Maria judged that perhaps the greatest change in her lifetime was a general recognition of human brotherhood; it had been laughed at by Whigs as hollow and impractical and condemned by Tories as revolutionary. She rejoiced in the fact that it had become the keynote of legislation. Extension of the franchise, adequate educational patterns, diminished hours of labor together with improved working conditions, and amusement for the people at low cost she saw as practical fruits of recognition of a common humanity. Maria condemned those who said that the masses would remain untrained, ignorant, unruly, and controlled only by the rod of authority, and thus fated to do the rough work of the world. She had confidence that automation relieved human beings from the most onerous tasks, and human labor depended increasingly on the greater use of intelligence and skills of all kinds.[57]

Possessed of such a conviction, Maria demanded that educational planners give attention to the cultural life of the general population. She believed that one of the major progressive developments of the nineteenth century was a widespread recognition that all people had a right to play and pleasures. She ascribed rejection of play and pleasure for working men and women to the Puritan philosophy of the seventeenth century. She wanted for all people not simply rest but "the brightening, quickening effect of

amusement." Human pleasure she defined as necessarily incorpo-
rating the active exercise of the body and mind.[58] Other middle-
class female intellectuals held that position. Her contemporary
Anna Swanwick, writer and translator of German classics, advocated people's concerts, informational and entertaining lectures and
courses, excursions to the country, and free access to art exhibitions
for workers and their families.[59] But in fact, even at the opening of
Victoria's reign, a number of middle-class women had brought that
theme to the fore including Mary Leman Gillies, niece of Lord
Gillies, who moved among the intellectuals of Edinburgh—Scott,
Erskine, and Jeffrey; also Eliza Meteyard, Catherine Barmby, Mrs.
A. J. Hippisley, and Mary Howitt. William and Mary Howitt's
circle at their home in Regent's Park in 1850 included Tennyson,
Mrs. Gaskell, Joanna Baillie, and members of the Pre-Raphaelite
Brotherhood.[60] These women presented their views in the *People's
Journal* and *Howitt's Journal*.

Maria, who had been concerned for forty years about the issue of
female involvement in economic life, came to the conclusion that
every effort had to be made for women, including married women
who had economic needs or wanted personal fulfillment by such
activity, to have access to careers.

I am inclined to think that the answer to the question whether or not a
married woman can carry on professional work without detriment to her
family depends on whether her work adds enough to the common income
to enable her to proper care and service for her children and household,
leaving upon her only the task of supervision. This places her in exactly the
same position as the woman of the leisured and wealthy classes, and it may
be doubted whether any profession absorbs a mother's time and thoughts
away from nursery and schoolroom as much as the life women lead in
society. It may be doubted also whether the woman returning home when
her professional day's work is over is not better fitted by its training in
patience and steady industry, and by practical discipline of faculty, to
exercise wisely her home office of general superintendence and government, than she who has spent her day, and a good part of the night before
it, in the exhausting idleness of society.[61]

In her last public testament Maria called for women's intellectual
development in conjunction with a familial one and urged that it be
integrated to the responsibilities and joys of domestic life. She

explained that the process could not be standardized in a simplistic formula; it had to be achieved by each individual through a slow maturation of her cultural life. Moreover, Maria defined intellectual growth in a flexible manner. She insisted that the goals of women with varied personalities and abilities had to be met; some did not respond to books but rather to observation of external things and personal experience; still others found the objects for exercise of mental faculties in art and music. "The pursuit for which nature has given you a capacity is a legitimate one to follow; all I ask is that you will make it a serious one, not follow it fitfully and in dilettante fashion, as a matter of no moment beyond the fancy of the hour."[62] The advantage, she insisted, was that such activities provided a shape to character. "The steady concentration of energy upon an ideal object, the constant aiming at excellence, the exercise of will, of reason, of conscience, in keeping action steady to the chosen course, are the very elements of trustworthy character, the prime requisite for good service in any capacity."

Maria asked women to embrace joyfully the duty of service, what Emily had urged a few years earlier in her essay *The Work of the World and Women's Share in It* (1881). For women of education and leisure Maria sponsored all sorts of activities with young children, guidance to family, and involvement in programs of philanthropic and charity agencies. She believed that because of the newly won place of women in society their various missions needed to be reassessed. The purposeful work that she advised them to undertake was not, by and large, new. However, she urged that more dynamic approaches and attitudes be adopted. Social service work she saw as an appropriate activity; indeed it had already become a major trend. "Certainly at no previous time of our history, has there been such an amount of practical, voluntary, zealous unpaid work done in every direction, philanthropic and educational, for the relief of distress, and improvement in the conditions of life, the general 'leveling up,' in short, material, mental and moral, of the poorer classes."[63] She asked women to conform to the role of a Sister of Mercy rather than Lady Bountiful, that is, a superior being affably providing for the bodily wants of inferior beings and patronizing the clergymen's efforts to save the soul of the latter.[64]

Maria Grey, in agreement with her sister, called for charity programs that would remove causes of distress and pauperizing influences as well as merely relieve them; she wanted to raise the status of the poor by encouragement of the spirit of independence, and provide aid in a form that would lead to self-help. Such charity required sympathy which could relate to troubles wholly foreign to one's own experience, and the process of aid, Mrs. Grey insisted, had to be framed so as to involve no loss of respect to the recipient or interference with personal independence. Education of the right sort, she said, created the frame of mind appropriate to carrying out this mandate; by cultivation of imagination one's sympathy became livelier, and by training of reasoning power one's judgment attained dimension. However, Maria warned, not all women were fitted to undertake work with the poor and problem sectors of society. Hence, she decried the engagement in such activities merely for fashion's sake and wanted only the prepared and the dedicated to make such commitments.

In sum Maria Grey found intellectually and politically liberated women indispensable to any real advance of humanity. The hope and safeguard of democracy, she said, depended on the construction of a truly cohesive society. "I have not written utterly in vain, you will, all of you, feel that work such as this for our fellow creatures, the work of removing the unnecessary and arbitrary inequalities of human life; is preeminently women's work, and to do it any purpose will require the training and discipline of the moral and intellectual faculty which you have received."[65]

# 4

## Organizations for Justice and Equality

In the last half of the nineteenth century, when the Shirreff sisters formulated their philosophy of female intellectual development and engaged in a variety of educational programs for females from early childhood through the adult years, the place of women in British society in political, social, and economic affairs underwent reevaluation. A corps of women and their male allies launched determined efforts to give females a more equitable place in the national community.

Undoubtedly the suffrage movement, in which the Shirreffs were peripherally involved, gained the greatest public attention. With the death of Lord Palmerston in 1865 and the resultant political realignments that made practical a new male franchise bill for which there had been considerable agitation, the female suffrage movement also came to the fore. In 1866 a London committee for women's suffrage formed and the following year became the Society for Women's Suffrage led by John Stuart Mill, president, and Mrs. Peter Taylor, secretary. Also in 1866 a petition for women's suffrage, containing signatures of fifteen hundred women, was presented to Parliament, and attendants at the annual meeting of the Social Science Association heard a plea for political enfranchisement of women.

A national female suffrage movement prospered in the late 1860s; almost simultaneously with the activity in the British capital, societies formed in Manchester, Birmingham, Bristol, Edinburgh, Glasgow—indeed in forty towns. Public meetings on the subject came in the wake of the establishment of organizations, and women became platform orators, formerly a rare feature of English community life. At that juncture a number of male intellectuals and politicians had joined the cause, including John Bright, Sir Charles Dilke, John Morley, Richard Monckton Milnes, Lord Amberley, Russell Gurney, Professor Cairnes, and Dean Alford of Canterbury. In May 1867 an amendment to include women offered to Disraeli's male franchise bill failed in the House of Commons, but eighty members supported it. Defeated in the legislative halls, the activists tried to gain their objectives by judicial action. They claimed that in fact the enfranchisement legislation of 1867 applied to females, and in several areas—Manchester, Salford, and Scarisbrick—women tried to be registered as voters. In November 1868 the Court of Common Pleas rejected their claim.

Suffragists, thwarted in Parliamentary action and judicial interpretation, moved to other paths. The Manchester Society started the *Women's Suffrage Journal* in 1870. The following year the town councils of Manchester, Salford, and Barnley passed resolutions for removal of the disabilities on women's service on town councils and forwarded them to Parliament. In a number of towns groups sponsored public meetings and drawing-room assemblies to enlighten the citizenry on the desirability, indeed the necessity, to enfranchise women. In 1869 under the auspices of a Liberal government women householders gained the right to participate in municipal elections (Municipal Franchise Amendment Act).

The Shirreffs enthusiastically endorsed women's suffrage. However, it is clear that their devotion to the intellectual and cultural liberation of women somewhat diverted them from taking the lead in the political struggle. A letter from Emily to Helen Taylor in 1872 dealt with that point. "I wish I could interest you in our educational work. We are fairly launched now, only wanting support and influence more than ever, for the work grows and foolish prejudice declining."[1] She noted that she had in the main restricted her focus to education and avoided deep involvement in questions of women's political rights because the subject had no popularity at the time and she could not afford to rouse party hostility.

Maria wrote a pamphlet *Is the Exercise of the Suffrage Unfeminine?* (1870), which in fact examined in large perspective the place of women in public affairs rather than merely female political rights. She attacked the stereotyped view of women as simply queens of the domestic hearth. She assessed the place of women in society and concluded that their opportunities to shape affairs did not match their responsibilities. To those who said women had no place in politics because public life dealt with areas in which women had little interest or knowledge, she asked, How about women's relationship to laws that dealt with marriage, guardianship of children, education, taxation, and the home with which even the opponents of female franchise admitted they had a primary concern? Maria also asked, Was patriotism purely a male virtue? She attacked with humor observers who charged that women would lose the charm of modesty and the grace of dignified reserve if they entered the political arena and became active in public life. She felt that it was strange to hear such an argument when all over Europe in public places Englishwomen were found in abundant numbers. "It has even been said that no portion of the crowd is so rude, so recklessly pushing, as that composed of English ladies, and that rudeness is so very often in proportion to their rank. Is it unfeminine for an Englishwoman to enter a crowd only when she goes to perform a duty, but not in the pursuit of pleasure?"[2]

Maria Shirreff Grey moved beyond the franchise question and probed the deeper issue, What was women's work? She pointed out that two and one half million women earned their own livelihood in England. Moreover, some of them did hard manual labor, field and barge work, and early in the century served almost as beasts of burden in mines. She wanted to know why it was acceptable for a woman to be a nurse in a male ward but unfeminine to practice medicine as a physician in children's and female wards. She maintained that custom and social arrangements had assigned tasks as legitimate for women without any reference to their essential qualities but simply by an arbitrary standard adopted by a particular country, class, or era. Mrs. Grey said that often the word "unfeminine" meant "unladylike," and the latter meant to do nothing gracefully. The tradition of genteel helplessness and dependence, she insisted, kept middle-class parents and poor gentry from giving their daughters an education to fit them for an honorable liveli-hood. "It will be well for all parties when the idea of ladyhood changes, and the true lady is recognized not by what she does, but by the spirit in which she does it." Maria Grey saw the franchise as the *sine qua non* for the construction of an educational system for females. "Then in God's name give them the suffrage quickly, for not till then will men see the necessity of educating them."[3]

At the rejection of the Women's Suffrage Bill of 1877 by the House of Commons, a member stated that none of the pioneers of female education were in favor of women's suffrage, and indeed the speaker made particular reference to the founders of Girton College and Newnham. At a suffrage meeting shortly thereafter Mrs. Grey challenged the assertion and stated, "All the women who had been active in any cause for the benefit of their sex were strong friends to suffrage."[4] In 1879 the National Society for Women's Suffrage issued *Opinions of Women on Women's Suffrage* (1879). Among the educational leaders who presented forceful endorsements of the cause were Maria Grey, Emily Shirreff, Mary Gurney, and Miss Manning.[5]

In 1870, when women gained the right for the first time to serve on school boards, a group of public-spirited citizens asked Maria Shirreff Grey and Emily Shirreff to seek election to the London School Board as representatives from the Borough of Chelsea. Initially in October 1871 both sisters declined, but after attendance at a religious service conducted by the Reverend Stopford Brooke who preached on duty and some later reflection, Maria changed her mind.[6] She concluded that since she had no home duties but did have an independent income and disciplined intelligence, undertak-ing nonpaid work for people's education seemed reasonable. Miss Garrett and Miss Davies also stood for election.

Maria engaged vigorously in a six-week campaign in a hotly contested election. She lost by a few votes.

But I gained much which was worth all the hard work; first a knowledge of the bona fide working man, for the mass of my supporters were working men, who had grasped the idea their superiors seemed slow to understand, that they had girls as well as boys to send to school and therefore, that women were wanted on the School Board to look after the girls, and who, having grasped it, gave me (I might almost call it) chivalrous support and help throughout my canvas. Secondly, I learned to know how much thoughtful reading and real gentleness of breeding—I can use no other term—there was among the shopkeeping class, several of them my own tradesmen, with whom nothing but the equality of an election committee room could have brought me into social intercourse. Thirdly, besides these and many amusing experiences of all sorts and conditions of men, I gained friends who proved invaluable helpers and colleagues to Emily and me in all our own later work—Mr. William Barber, a barrister in large practice, who spoke and worked for me as none of my idle friends could find time to do; Mr. William Stebbing, co-editor of the *Times*; Mr., now Rt. Hon. Sir James Stansfeld; Sir Henry Cole, Director of the South Kensington Museum, and his son-in-law Mr. G.C.T. Bartley.[7]

Indeed, Maria considered the election a turning point in her own life and that of her sister Emily in that it led them into educational activity of an organizational nature. Before it dissolved, the election committee which had supported Maria urged her to form another association to develop female education of all types. She was asked to deliver a lecture on female education at the Chelsea Vestry Hall in early 1871. These developments stimulated her to set down specific proposals for female education. In April 1871 she presented a plan for an organization to a committee of the Society of Arts, and on the eighteenth of April the council of the Society, in which G.C.T. Bartley had considerable influence, resolved to form such an organization. They commissioned Mrs. Grey to read a paper on the subject on May 31. Thus the preliminary steps to launch a new organization had been taken. The work of the Shirreff sisters and their allies in the field of education is presented in the succeeding chapters of this study.

The Shirreffs' enthusiasm for organizational life was in accord with farsighted women of the era who desired change for their depressed sisterhood. Women placed faith in organizations to enlighten the public of their situation and sponsor viable programs of reform. Clearly the success of men with organizations in the previous sixty years, in particular the antislavery associations and Anti-Corn Law League, provided a stimulant to women.

In the generation from 1860 to 1880 organizations conducted largely by women to deal with problems faced by females prospered. The new associations sought to protect women from a variety of harsh features of life and to give them a more equitable place in the national commonwealth. The Married Women's Property Committee wanted for married women the same legal control over their own property, as well as freedom to make contracts, that males had. Mrs. Elizabeth Elmy and Mrs. Jacob Bright headed the organization which saw a majority of its goals attained in legislation in 1870 and 1882.

Previous to the nineteenth century English law had taken very little notice of women's needs nor had it responded to the numerous injustices which they suffered. But with some vigor various legal inequalities which afflicted British women came under scrutiny in the middle-years of Queen Victoria's reign, leading to amendment of existing statutes and, more often, new legislation. And women's organizations gained some action in a few areas to which they directed their attention. Parliament passed the Married Women's Property Acts in 1870 and 1882. Both houses of Parliament accepted with very little controversy Lord Selborne's bill of 1882. At its passage the *Spectator* said, "The English married woman is, in fact, legally reenvested with her own money." And the journal considered that the legislative enactment of 1882 was in accord with the mood of the times. "They [women] are hungry for more education, for more independence, for more individuality, and they will keenly desire to retain some, at least, of their own money, to manage it for themselves, to spend it for themselves, to enjoy it, if they are to give it to their husbands, the luxury and the grace of giving."[8]

The Custody of Infants Law of 1873 and the Bastardy Law Amendment Act of the previous year extended mothers' rights in the crucial area of child guardianship. The former relaxed the crude and rigid rules which assigned a child to his father unless he could be proved an unmitigated brute and moral leper, and the latter allowed an unwed mother to sue the father of her child for support, although the amount she could gain was minimal. The Matrimonial Causes Act of 1878 dealt with cases of husbands convicted of aggravated assault on their wives. The ground had been prepared for official action. Sergeant Pulling presented a paper on wife abuse to the annual meeting of the Social Science Association of 1876. Frances Power Cobbe in the *Contemporary Review* in 1878 wrote a well-documented report on the wide incidence of what she called wife torture. Alfred Hill of Birmingham prepared the bill in 1878 which gave wives the protection of judicial separation and custody of children when husbands were convicted of violent acts against their wives.[9]

The social morality laws of the Victorian era discriminated in flagrant ways against women; divorce laws required a more aggravated offense by the husband and a less aggravated one for the wife; a girl under-age for all other offenses was regarded as above age in the matter of seduction; and the statutes pertaining to prostitution made it difficult for women to escape from vice and easy for men to seek it. It was no violation of law for a man to solicit a woman in the streets, but it was a legal offense for a woman to solicit a man. The Contagious Diseases Act of 1864 recognized prostitution as a calling and gave police and public authorities wide discretionary power over prostitutes in garrison towns and seaports. For the next generation Josephine Butler worked to amend the 1864 legislation which deprived women of basic legal rights; it had been loosely framed and placed inordinate power in the hands of the police.

The Vigilance Association for the Defense of Personal Rights and for the Amendment of the Law upheld the principle of the perfect equality of all persons before the law, regardless of sex or class. In fulfillment of that goal it sought repeal or amendment of all laws which violated that principle and opposed any new restrictive legislation. Second, the organization supervised the execution of laws in order to prevent administrative, judicial, or police action detrimental to the principles of equality. Lastly, it publicized the rights and liberties which English citizens enjoyed and the moral foundation upon which they rested. To this end the association published monthly *The Vigilance Association Journal*. Josephine Butler, a leader in the higher education movement for women, became honorary secretary of the national association and of the Ladies National Association for the Abolition of State Regulation of Vice.[10] Harriet Martineau, Florence Nightingale, and Mary Carpenter insisted on equality of treatment of sexes in the matter of elimination of venereal disease which involved medical inspection. "The question is whether the two sexes are entitled to equal rights, or whether one is created for the use of the other. This once settled, the next follows easily. Granting medical necessity for stamping out disease, then any law to effect this must affect sexes equally."[11]

The Women's Peace and Arbitration Auxiliary established in April 1874 affiliated with the London Peace Society which had existed since 1816. The former organization maintained that war was inconsistent with Christianity and the interests of mankind, and it promoted peace by publications, speeches, and contact and understanding of foreign people.[12]

The National Health Society, with offices at Berners Street, London, had Miss Lankester as secretary. It diffused sanitary knowledge concerning pure air, proper ventilation, food, cooking, prevention of diseases, and so forth by lectures at workingmen's clubs and mothers' meetings, tracts and papers, and prizes to students and teachers for spread of health information. It sought by various means to secure open spaces for recreation for the people.[13] The Ladies Sanitary Association, allied to the National Health Society, published tracts on sanitary and domestic subjects and established lending libraries.[14]

The Metropolitan Association for Befriending Young Servants, established in 1875 on a plan by Mrs. Nassau Senior endeavored to meet some of the needs, first, of females sent into domestic service from the Metropolitan Pauper School, and second, other young women who became domestics and lacked home protection and solace. It had branches in various parts of metropolitan London and in 1880 assisted 740 females in the first category and 2,000 in the second.[15] It constructed a home in Bloomsbury and another in Fulham. Louisa Twining became secretary of the Association for Promoting Trained Nursing in Workhouse Infirmaries and Sick Asylums which at its foundation in 1879 obtained the cooperation and sanction of the Local Government Board for its activities.[16]

The Women's Temperance Association of 1876 sought to forge an effective union of women's temperance societies in various parts of the United Kingdom. In 1880 there were forty-eight affiliated societies; Edinburgh had twelve and Belfast forty-five. In total 136 societies were connected to the central association.

Women also enrolled as full-fledged members of dynamic new organizations which aided all members of society, men, women, and children. Indeed they moved into the inner councils of some organizations. The Charity Organisation Society (the Society for Organising Charitable Relief and Suppressing Mendacity), founded in 1869, was one of the first to appoint women to such positions; Maria Grey and Octavia Hill served on its council. Mrs. Grey also became honorary secretary and chief organizer of the Charity Organisation's branch committee in Chelsea. The society made possible cooperation between poor law authorities and private relief agencies. It had thirty-nine local committees in the greater London area that consisted of poor law guardians and representatives of local charities and a paid employee in each committee. The society focused aid on those groups whose character and circumstances made probable a permanent improvement in their lives by means of the benefit given. It gave loans and grants, supplied letters of recommendation to hospitals and convalescent homes, sought employment for applicants, and kept a labor exchange for temporary jobs. Diverse charities cooperated in the venture including night refuge centers, soup kitchens, and public day nurseries. Its medical committee prepared rules to guide provident dispensaries. In 1873 the society investigated causes of public distress and gave attention to improvement of the dwellings of the poor, employment opportunities, migration, emigration, and means to encourage provident habits.[17]

Octavia Hill presented the ideology of the Charity Organisation Society in *Macmillan's Magazine*. She contended that if the poor were to be raised permanently to a condition of economic self-sufficiency and moral strength, they had to be dealt with as individuals by individuals. She envisioned the ideology carried out by hundreds of dedicated workers who made personal contact with the depressed members of the community and established a rapport with them. The organization utilized part-time workers whose activities were coordinated and supervised by a professional in the social service field. Miss Hill considered that two benefits resulted—the aid furnished and also advancement of social harmony and class understanding.[18]

Maria Grey's interest in the economically and socially depressed members in the community, which had been evident in her devotion to the Charity Organisation Society, caused her in the mid-eighties to take the lead in founding the Women's League. The league reached out through volunteers to problem areas of society, trying not simply to be remedial but also to create an apparatus which experimented with patterns to improve community life.

Women emerged as a decisive factor in the university extension movement. The North of England Council for Promoting the Higher Education of Women and Anne Clough and Josephine Butler wanted educational enlargement in conjunction with liberation of women politically and economically. Academicians Henry Sidgwick, James Stuart, Henry Fawcett, James Adam, Arthur Cayley, Frederick Denison Maurice, and Thomas Morley worked to bring women into an official if not organic association with Cambridge University. And James Bryce, Sir John Seeley, J. W. Hales, Sir Henry Roscoe, and Charles Pearson willingly lectured to women's groups. The first university extension course at Nottingham in 1873 had a large number of women in attendance. At Norwich the coalition which made possible the establishment of a university program had the same complexion as that found in other towns— clerics, public officials, and feminine leaders—the Reverend James Wilson, vicar of St. Stephen's Church, first honorary secretary of the Norwich Extension Society; Mary Hinds Howell; Alice Day; E. Lucy Bignold, treasurer, chairman and finally president of the society; and Laura Colman who married Professor James Stuart.

In the last quarter of the nineteenth century Cambridge University and then Oxford University, which entered the field in 1885, established nearly fifty extension centers in Yorkshire. The three-year university extension experiment at Leeds showed several of the basic qualities of the program found elsewhere in the nation. The number of students enrolled did not fulfill the hopes and expectations of its founders. Attendance at programs varied greatly, determined of course by the time when a lecture was offered, its subject matter, and the skill of the instructor. Members of the working class did not form the bulk of the student body. Edward Carpenter, who taught in the Leeds extension service as well as at Halifax and Skepton from 1874 to 1876, said that women made up the great majority of the student body in the afternoon sessions. He placed the female participants in three categories: scholars from girls' schools in the area, young women in comfortable material circumstances living at home with much leisure time, and finally mature women in the latter category. The evening sessions he described as also heavily attended by women, and in addition elderly clerks, shopkeepers, and a lesser number of manual laborers. Cambridge University favored—and other centers adopted—three subcommittees operating as a coordinating agency for the program, one subcommittee for women, one for men, and one for laborers. In 1875 sixteen major towns had extension courses in operation, including Leicester, Derby, Lincoln, Chesterfield, Liverpool, Stoke, Newcastle, Burslem, and Henley, as well as five towns in the West Riding: Leeds, Bradford, Keighley, Halifax, and Sheffield.

The London Society for the Extension of University Teaching started in June 1875 under the presidency of the Lord Mayor. Maria Grey served on the council of the society. In the first term of the 1878-1879 session the society had six centers, eight courses of lectures and classes, and 284 entrants. In the first term of the 1879-1880 session they had thirteen centers, thirty-six courses, and 1,224 entrants. At that juncture centers in suburban areas prospered: Hampstead, Camden Road, Brixton, Crauch End, and West Ham.

Although a few women engaged in a sporadic fashion in political activities by attending public meetings and participating in clubs and discussion societies in the late eighteenth and first half of the nineteenth centuries, they were not officially affiliated with the major parties until the last generation of Victoria's reign. At that time Milicent Garrett Fawcett, active suffragist, noted that opportunity for political work by unenfranchised women, short of the vote itself, was one of the most vital political instruments for change which they possessed.

The Women's Liberal Federation formed in 1887; it was a support organization for the Liberal Party and was conducted by women for women. In 1890 the federation had 51,300 members of whom only 3,950 were men; in 1891, 66,721 of whom 14,987 were men. It had been immediately preceded by the London Confederation Central Union with Mrs. Theodore Fry as honorary secretary, which merged with the federation. William Gladstone and the key leaders of the Liberal Party refused to press for female suffrage and so did not include women in the provisions of the Franchise Bill of

1884. Mrs. Pankhurst left the Liberal Party in the preceding year. Despite the attitudes of the Liberal leadership, many of the rank-and-file members of the party were sympathetic to the enfranchisement of women. The Women's Liberal Federation officially endorsed female suffrage in 1890.

In 1888 the Liberal Unionist Women's Association formed. Its executive committee within a half dozen years recruited women devoted to a wide range of social causes and enlargement of economic and educational opportunities for women, including Miss Anstruther, Lady Frances Balfour, Lady Arthur Russell, and Milicent Garrett Fawcett. In a lecture at Newcastle in 1870 Mrs. Fawcett said "the remedies which the condition of women needs are self-reliance and education; and the latter is the sole remedy if understood in its widest sense."

The Primrose League (1883) was an *omnium gatherum* for women with commitment to the Tory cause. Female suffrage was simply one topic of interest to female members of the league and indeed not the most important after 1890. The league in 1889 ordered branches not to become involved in discussions about votes for women; it sought to avoid the sharp divisions on the issue which had arisen in the Liberal women's organization. Yet both Disraeli and Salisbury had endorsed in a somewhat oblique fashion female enfranchisement. Other issues of a purely female nature, such as female wages, the Contagious Diseases Act, and development of higher education for women, rarely surfaced in official gatherings of the league.

The Dames of the Primrose League, especially in rural areas, did much grass-roots political work. Their political activity was often an outgrowth of their social and religious lives. "Political work, and especially house-to-house canvassing, came naturally to many middle-class women accustomed to church visiting and volunteer charity work, which by the end of the seventies had almost become a fashionable necessity."[19] Primrose League members, however, did not by and large stand for municipal or school board posts or study local budgets; they did the humble work. Janet Henderson Robb saw the lack of participation in the new education by middle-class women in rural areas as responsible for their docility in political affairs.[20]

In 1857 a group of men of liberal outlook who wished to study the major facets of community life, expose defects, and frame remedies in order to bring the nation into a progressive pattern of action, founded the National Association for the Promotion of Social Science. The organization attracted to leadership positions in the several subdivisions—health, education, jurisprudence and amendment of the law, and economy and trade—the energetic and humane leaders in politics, academia, and the church, such as Lord Brougham, Lord Shaftesbury, Lord Lyttleton, J. Shaw Lefevre, Professor Fawcett, Charles Kingsley, J. Kay Shuttleworth, Edwin Chadwick, Sir Charles Hastings, Edwin Lankester, and Nassau Senior. Isa Craig Knox served as assistant secretary of the association for several years. Advocates of an expanded and redesigned educational system for females in the late 1860s and 1870s utilized in an effective manner the forum offered by the association. Moreover, women's rightists found of much moment to them other topics which came within the purview of the association: equality before the law, female employment and industrial training, juvenile delinquency and detainment, preventive medicine, hygiene and nursing, and child rights (in particular custody of infants in 1883-1884), as well as patterns of charity. The association, in order to further its goals, framed petitions, memorials, and resolutions, and forwarded them to Parliament, ministers of the government, and other appropriate bodies. Of course it also served as a public information agency and published transactions. Major periodicals and journals analyzed its sessions and the programs it advocated for improvement of British society.

The Shirreff sisters during the 1870s attended its annual meetings and appeared on its programs. In 1871 at Leeds Maria spoke on "What are the Special Requirements for the Improvement of the Education of Girls?"[21] In 1872 at Plymouth Emily gave a paper, "What Public Provision Ought to Be Made for the Secondary Education of Girls?"[22] In 1873 Maria at Norwich again took up the question of female education, "Lectures and Classes for Women."[23] The following year Emily probed at the Brighton meeting, "Is a Fair Proportion of the Endowments of the Country Applicable to Female Education?"[24] In Liverpool Maria read a paper prepared by

Emily, "On the Training of Teachers."[25] In 1878 at the annual meeting at Cheltenham Emily gave attention to the area of early childhood education which became her chief focus, "On the Kindergarten and Froebel's System of Education."[26]

During the annual meetings the Shirreffs came into contact and formed professional alliances and warm personal relationships with feminine activists of the era—Dorothea Beale, Emily Davies, Mary Carpenter, Mary Gurney—and the male leaders in the cause—Professor Hodgeson, Joseph Payne, Cooke Taylor, and Brooke Lambert. The activities of the association also brought the sisters into a personal rapport with public men who aided them in their causes. At the 1871 session, Maria formed a friendship with Lord Frederick Cavendish, whose wife served on the council of Maria's new organization and interested Princess Louise in honorary headship of the new venture. At the 1873 meeting of the association at Norwich, Maria found warm sympathy from Richard Monckton Milnes, Lord Houghton, and Sir Willoughby Jones who chaired a conference in the city which established a local branch of Maria's National Union.

Women became most often involved in the educational and law and jurisprudence sections and to a lesser extent in those dealing with repression of crime and with economy and trade. A special women's conference was held as a part of the annual general congress in 1870 at Newcastle and at a few earlier meetings but was subsequently discontinued.[27] Successful enactment of the Married Women's Property Bill in 1882 resulted, in a considerable degree, from the continuing efforts of the association. In 1867 at the Belfast meeting of the organization, George Hastings read a paper on the subject. A memorial from Mrs. Butler, Miss Boucherett, Mrs. Glyn, and Miss Wolstenholme was circulated; a committee was formed under the auspices of the association which worked with J. Shaw Lefevre, J. S. Mill, and Russell Gurney who brought forth the legislation in August 1882. A number of women in addition to the Shirreff sisters brought various facets of women's educational needs to the attention of the association for consideration. As previously noted, Miss Cobbe opened up the issue of higher education for women in 1862, and six years later Miss Davies described a proposed higher education establishment for her colleagues at the annual meeting. Mary Carpenter presented female Indian educational needs at meetings in 1867 and 1871.

Paucity of employment for women was another concern brought before the members of the Social Science Association. In 1859, the year that Jessie Boucherett founded the Society for the Employment of Women, she presented a paper on "Industrial Employment of Women" to the association, and Miss Parkes spoke on "Market for Educated Female Labour." In 1868 Miss Boucherett came again to the association to urge proper education in technical fields to prepare women for adequate employment. A recurring theme at sessions was the moral issue of employment of married women in factories.

In 1859 Jessie Boucherett and Adelaide Proctor established the Society for the Employment of Women at 15 Prince Street, Cavendish Square, London. The society sought work opportunities in fields that had been closed to women. Its first undertaking was a commercial training program for women that developed into a small school which prepared women to be bookkeepers and copiers of law papers. The course lasted fifteen weeks, and students were given certificates at its completion. An employment bureau was maintained for them. The program was broadened to embrace plan tracing and shorthand as well as typing. Of equal significance, the society publicized an increased array of positions and training opportunities available for women as nurses, cooks, wood engravers and carvers, art and house decorators, proofreaders, lithographers, compositors, upholsterers, hairdressers, gilders, linen makers, pharmacists, and library workers. Indeed it endeavored to get women positions in twenty-five occupations.[28] In 1888 it estimated that more than one hundred women were engaged in the library field.[29] A decade after the foundation of the society, the Queen became its patron as did her two daughters, the crown princess of Germany and the marchioness of Lorne who also strongly supported the Shirreff sisters' educational ventures.

The Women's Protective and Provident League, established in 1874, promoted protective and benefit societies among women who earned their own living. It tried to prevent undue depression of wages, equalize hours of work, and encourage sickness and unemployment assistance; in addition it acted as an employment bureau and engaged in arbitration between employers and employees. Mrs. Emma Paterson founded the league; she had been secretary of the Women's Suffrage Association for the previous two years. Members of the league by and large were men and women of the upper middle class. (Mrs. Paterson was the daughter of the headmaster of schools in St. George's parish, Hanover Square.) She edited the organization's monthly publication *The Women's Urban Journal*. The league helped to form the London Women Bookbinders (1874), a trade union which also drew to its activities Mrs. P. A. Taylor and the Honorable Mrs. H. F. Ponsonby; other women's unions which it encouraged included the Shirt and Collar Makers (1875), Tailoresses (1877), and Dressmakers.[30] Edith Simcox, who gained a place on the London School Board in 1879, attended several international labor conferences on the continent as a delegate from Britain, took the lead in the establishment of the Shirt and Collar Makers Union, and served as its secretary.[31]

At Emma Paterson's death in 1886, leadership of the league passed to Emilia Strong Dilke, an art historian of note, of upper-middle-class origins, daughter of a military officer and widow of Mark Pattison, rector of Lincoln College, Oxford.[32] At the time she became head of the league she married Sir Charles Dilke, a distinguished Liberal politician whose involvement in an unsavory divorce case thwarted his hopes, and indeed expectations, of leading his party.[33] The headquarters of the league, which became the Women's Trade Union League in 1889, was in an alley off Shaftesbury Avenue, London. Mrs. Paterson had been the first female delegate at a Trade Union Congress. Women presented their cause at the annual Trade Union Congresses but were not heeded. It took eleven years, from 1879 to 1890, to get a Trade Union Congress to demand women factory inspectors even though 100,000 women belonged to unions.[34] The success of the match girls' strike in 1889 and the laundresses' a decade later brought public attention to women's trade unions. The league sought extension of the Factory Acts and from 1889 tried to get men's societies to admit women as affiliates. By the latter year the general labor unions (Workers, General Workers, and Transport) admitted women, but craft unions like engineers continued to exclude them. By 1905 over sixty unions had women affiliated with them, including the great textile associations. But in traditional women's trades—sugar, confectionary, food preserving, wax making, laundry and millinery work, domestic, hotel and restaurant service—unions hardly existed. Unless women's trade unions were attached to men's organizations, they found survival almost impossible.[35] Jessie Boucherett and Helen Blackburn considered that the National Federal Council for Women's Trades, which supposedly represented the interests of 93,000 women, was dominated by men. "It is certain that the management of the Federation is in their hands."[36]

In the last third of the century, by and large, middle-class women led the female labor movement as they did the female franchise and education movements. There is evidence, however, to suggest that prior to the middle of the nineteenth century a consciousness of women's needs and aspirations had appeared among working-class adherents, male and female, of Chartism. Its emphasis on universal suffrage and sex equality in education had a special appeal to women who were an identifiable and vocal sector of the agitation.[37] But by the late decades of the century those rumblings had not produced a clearly defined female working-class leadership elite. An essay by a contemporary historian which dealt with British working women explored their status at the close of Victoria's reign.

One thing is certain: If British workingmen had added some middle class notions about women to their own culture, working class women were not able to join their wealthier sisters in complaint. Long deprived, they were demoralized further by the changes in their lives at the end of the Victorian era. Though no longer traditionally resigned, they were far from possessing the ability to protest as women.[38]

Lady Dilke's two secretaries, May Abraham Tennant and Gertrude Tuckwell, carried forward their mentor's mission. Their circle included labor leaders Tom Mann and Ben Tillett as well as Keir Hardie, Sidney Webb, Miss Llewellyn Davies, Norman MacColl, editor of the *Athenaeum*, and Joseph Knight of *Notes and Queries*. May Abraham served as one of the assistant commissioners of the Royal Commission on Labour headed by the duke of Devonshire.

In 1893 she became the first female factory inspector. Gertrude Tuckwell edited the *Women's Trade Union Review* and presented a program for child assistance in *The State And Its Children* (1894).[39]

Margaret Gladstone MacDonald was a daughter of Dr. John Gladstone, a prominent scientist, a founder of the YMCA and an educational innovator. She engaged in the activities which Maria Grey at the end of her professional life had envisaged as necessary components of the next stage of women's liberation. Margaret Gladstone attended Doreck College. Tragically, she lived only forty-one years but had a very full and socially productive life. She married J. Ramsay MacDonald and had six children. The Mac-Donald apartment in Lincoln's Inn Fields was a social center for reform activists. Its hostess engaged in a surprisingly varied public life in the cause of women. Margaret MacDonald gave dedicated service to the National Union of Women Workers which was established to bring together women working in all fields so that they could deal with problems that were common to their sex. It recruited women of different ideological commitments and social classes, and it was the latter program which Mrs. MacDonald sought to expand. As a member of several of the union's committees, she delved into a number of familial and societal problems: rural housing, registration of midwives and nurses, courts for children, medical inspection and feeding of children, restaurants for women workers, and early closing of shops. She combined concern for the physical welfare of human beings with devotion to expansion of all sorts of education for them. She belonged to the Anti-Sweating League and the Charity Organisation Society and for nine years edited the industrial section of *The Englishwomen's Yearbook*.

Margaret MacDonald was a founder of the Women's Labour League; its preliminary organizational meeting was held in March 1906 in rooms which she provided. The Railway Women's Guild had urged creation of the new association. The gospel which she preached for the league was in accord with the hopes of Maria Grey who died that year.

The League was making special efforts to get in touch with the wives and mothers, sisters and daughters of the men in the movement, with the women trade unionists, and all women wage earners, with the women school teachers who recognized that the children could not have full opportunities under our present system, with the women of leisure and education who wanted to share their advantages with all their sisters. . . above all with the great majority of women whose first duty and responsibility is to their home and their children, but who are learning that they cannot thoroughly fulfill their charge without taking part in the civil life which surrounds and vitally affects their home life.[40]

In the *Women's Labour Day Souvenir* (1909) Mrs. MacDonald described the basis of the ideology of the league as the fusion of the Christian injunction "Thou shalt love thy neighbour as thyself" with the French revolutionary concepts of liberty, equality, and fraternity. In memory of Margaret MacDonald, who had served as its secretary, the league opened the first baby clinic in Britain.

In the last decade of the century the Women's Industrial Council under the guidance of a large committee headed by the countess of Aberdeen and Clementine Black, novelist, established several committees on investigation, on education, and on legal and statistical affairs in order to bring into sharp focus needs of various groups in society. Margaret and J. Ramsay MacDonald were key members of these committees. An examination of one of the areas of interest of the council—children—reveals the dimensions of its organizational life. In 1902-1903 the special Committee on Wage-Earning Children headed by Nellie Adler sought memorials from members of Parliament, religious leaders, and university settlements in order to secure legislation to control more closely the employment of children; subsequent legislation embodied many of the council's suggestions. The organization sponsored lectures dealing with separate courts for children, adequate milk supply for children, and female training to enrich family life. It launched a variety of investigations, and sponsored in 1908 the National Conference on Industrial Training of Women and Girls.

Beatrice Webb was a member of the National Union of Women Workers but resigned within a year after she failed to get the organization to abandon prayers at the opening of their meetings. Margaret Cole, her biographer, noted that she was probably not fully comfortable in an entirely women's organization.[41] Nevertheless, when she moved to the forefront of the Fabian Society in the after-

math of her service on the Royal Commission on the Poor Law and
publication of the minority report which was largely her work, she
established the Half Circle Club for the wives of labor leaders.

Although women, in particular Mrs. Pember Reeves, had been
active in the Fabian Society, there was no separate women's organization within the society until 1908. In that year Mrs. Charlotte
Wilson formed the Women's Group which included Mrs. Pember
Reeves, Mrs. G. B. Shaw, Miss Murby, and Miss Emma Brooke.
The women's group had its own office at 25 Tothill Street, London,
with a paid assistant secretary, and published a series of tracts,
including an analysis of women's work in seven professions, edited
by Professor Edith Morley. The group joined with other women's
organizations to further female interests.[42]

Maria Grey's suggestion that women explore the cooperative
movement was reasonable in light of the nonvirulent approach to
the ideology by the women associated with it in the last generation
of the century. In 1884 the Women's Cooperative League became
the Women's Cooperative Guild. Miss Llewellyn Davies served
devotedly as secretary. The league had been founded the previous
year by Mrs. A.H.D. Acland and Mrs. Lawrenson. By 1892 it had
one hundred branches and gained many adherents from the working class. Both Arthur Acland and his wife Alice Sophia Acland
combined interest in the cooperative movement with educational
work. In 1892 he served as vice-president of the Committee of
Council of Education in the last Gladstone ministry. Mrs. Acland
told the founders of the guild that women's influence had to be
quiet. She did not want platform oratory or advertising, "no going
out of women's place." But the unobtrusive approach gave way as
membership of working women increased. Virginia Woolf wrote of
the development.

The women who had crept modestly in 1883 into Mrs. Acland's sitting-
room to sew and "read some Co-operative work aloud," learnt to speak
out, boldly and authoritatively, about every question of civic life. Thus it
came about that Mrs. Robson and Mrs. Potter and Mrs. Wright at Newcastle in 1913 were asking not only for baths and wages and electric light,
but also for adult suffrage and the taxation of land values and divorce law
reform. Thus in a year or two they were to demand peace and disarmament
and the spread of Co-operative principles, not only among the working

people of Great Britain, but among the nations of the world. And the force that lay behind their speeches and drove them home beyond the reach of eloquence was compact of many things—of men with whips, of sickrooms where match boxes were made, of hunger and cold, of many and difficult childbirths, of much scrubbing and washing up, of reading Shelley and William Morris and Samuel Butler over the kitchen table, of weekly meetings of the Women's Guild, of Committees and Congresses at Manchester and elsewhere. All this lay behind the speeches of Mrs. Robson and Mrs. Potter and Mrs. Wright.[43]

At the end of the century the Central Bureau for the Employment of Women, 9 Southampton Street, Holborn, and similar bureaus in Edinburgh, Manchester, and Liverpool acted as clearing houses and information agencies to women. Louise Creighton, wife of Mandell Creighton, bishop of London, who described the mission of bureaus, suggested the need to expand the general public's view of what was suitable employment for women.[44] Clearly, the problem of expanding employment of women into new areas remained acute.She urged work for women in the higher echelons of industry and aid to them to establish their own business ventures.

Housing for the young woman engaged in gainful employment arose as a concurrent issue. The establishment (by Disraeli's former secretary) of the Rowton Houses for men possibly stimulated women to explore the problem. The Women's Industrial Council in London launched a survey to get accurate information on the dimension of the need. A few experimental residences opened. The Ladies Residential Chambers of flats opened at Chenies Street and also at York Street, London. Sloane Garden House and Holborn House also served women. The Town and Gown Association of Edinburgh built a residence.

In 1874 Mrs. Nassau Senior received appointment as poor law inspector, and the next year the first woman won election as guardian of the poor in London. Enactments and judicial decisions made women eligible for a number of posts—overseer, church warden, governor of a workhouse, medical officer of a workhouse, surveyor of highways, inspector of factories, and member of a parish council—but implementation remained a serious issue. The public mind had been prepared somewhat for the assumption of quasi-public offices by women in the previous decades. Florence Nightingale's work in the nursing field led to establishment of a band of nurses who regularly came into contact with the general public. In 1866 Dr. Elizabeth Blackwell took an MD degree in Switzerland, and at the same time Miss Garrett began her medical studies in London. In 1876 Parliament passed the Medical Qualification Act (the Russell Gurney Act) which removed restrictions on medical registration of duly qualified people on the basis of sex.[45] In its wake the Royal Free Hospital, Grey's Inn Road, London, opened its wards to women students associated with the London School of Medicine in which the Shirreffs took an interest and, indeed, aided. In 1880 there were twenty-one registered female physicians.[46] But within a generation women activists charged that tokenism had become the order of the day. Mrs. Nassau Senior occupied a lonely pinnacle; in fact her effectiveness was reduced because in addition to her post, inspector of poor law schools, she received an additional task—inspection of workhouses. Louisa Twining demanded employment of more women as inspectors and managers in workhouses and supervisors of hospitals, prisons, and mental asylums as well as more substantial female analyses and direction of the nursing profession.[47] Some departures occurred at the opening of the last decade of the century as previously noted. A woman became inspector of factories and also sanitary inspector, and the borough of Kensington appointed the first woman guardian.

In retrospect the women's rights movement of the late Victorian era seems moderate. But to contemporary observers activity, challenge, and change seemed the immediate consequence of the earnest examination of the place of women in British society. A review of *Women of the Day: A Biographical Dictionary* (1885) presented that viewpoint. "These are times of great feminine activity, the sphere of women's labour is continually being enlarged, quite an army of workers is engaged in the emancipation of the sex, with results that are among the social phenomena of the age.... The soul-sustaining literature of fiction, for instance, has known a fortyfold increase, and the authors of the prodigality run advocates of women's suffrage and rights exceedingly hard for first place in regard to numbers."

The foundation of female clubs in London in the last third of the nineteenth century was a corollary of the advancement of women to a more prominent place in British national life. A few clubs had a sexually mixed membership: the Albemarle Club (1874), composed of six hundred women and two hundred men, and the Bath Club, founded a generation later, which offered recreational activities and physical exercise such as swimming for its membership that included twelve hundred men and three hundred women.

Clubs exclusively for women served a number of needs. The Alexandra Club (1884) by the end of the century had about nine hundred women on its roster. It was a convenient gathering place for ladies and provided a needed London address for residents of the provinces. It stated as the norm for membership eligibility to attend Her Majesty's drawing rooms. The Victoria was an in-town residence facility as were the Empress and the Victoria Commemorative founded at the end of the century. The University Club opened its doors to women who had been at college. It required from members a university degree or diploma from a higher educational institution or registration as a medical practitioner of some sort. It limited membership to three hundred. The Writers Club also had a restricted clientele, female journalists and literary women who developed a camaraderie within its walls. The Green Park Club had a mainly musical and social orientation.

Several clubs served the educational needs of women and provided forums to explore issues relevant to them, that is, areas associated with their own political, social, and intellectual advancement and service to the community. The Somerville Club (1878) followed in the tradition and focus of the Women's Club and Institute. It gave women the opportunity to discuss in a serious and disciplined manner topics of a political and social nature. Indeed it required such an interest for membership and recruited a thousand women within a relatively short period. In 1892 Mrs. Emily Massingbird, temperance leader and social reformer, launched the Pioneer Club which examined regularly a variety of topics of the era, ranging from vaccination and vegetarianism to women's suffrage and home industries. The Sesame Club (1895) also focused on all areas of contemporary British life of concern to women: education, child studies, theater, literature, music, and foreign languages. The Grosvenor Crescent Club, closely allied with the Women's Institute, examined similar topics.

Eva Anstruther, who analyzed women's clubs in 1899, gave primacy to the social-educational organizations. "It is not to detract from the value of the less ambitious institutions to say that it is before clubs such as these that our future lies." She admitted that women's clubs still were in their seminal stage or, as she said, their "young bridal stage." She felt that women had not developed the clubbable spirit, the intangible but significant ingredient in male clubs.

A woman uses her club to eat in, or to learn at, or to entertain her personal friends; she does not yet look upon going to it as a means of passing time in a place which is congenial to her among people who are very good comrades while she is thrown with them. Women's social attitude to each other in the majority of clubs is not such as to make club life attractive or give a spirit of unity to the club.[48]

*The Englishwoman's Year Book* of Emily James contained three hundred pages filled with material about institutions, societies, and organizations directed to and managed by women. Female characters in novels written at the end of the century reflected the more diversified and complex position of women in real life. The working woman of independent character who shaped her own life-style appeared in a number of works including Evelyn Sharp's *The Making of a Prig* and Noel Ainslie's *Among the Thorns* and *An Erring Pilgrimage*.

The Shirreff sisters were sympathetic to and indeed at times participants in the work for equality and justice carried forward for their sex by the organizations discussed in this chapter. The friendship of the Shirreffs with women who led the various endeavors to broaden responsibilities, opportunities, and rights of females drew them into a coalition dedicated to moral rearmament of society, cultivation of a personal ethic of charity and social responsibility, faith in the efficacy of education, and above all an optimism about human potential. The middle-class women who sought by organizational means to improve their society, and specifically the patterns of life for their sex also sought a union of women rich and poor and of various social classes dedicated to a search for human dignity and individual fulfillment. In retrospect the organizational effort was most limited in relation to need, the heavy reliance on self-help unrealistic, and a patronization of the less fortunate in evidence. Despite such shortcomings, leaders of the women's movement established an imperishable heritage—a sisterhood that transcended class based on intellectual, cultural, and economic ties of enlightened self-interest. Of doubtless even more significance, conditions changed; women by collective action were able to reshape major features of their lives and in the process relate that change to the mainstream reform movements of their society.

Significantly, Maria Grey, in her campaign for the London School Board, affirmed that regardless of class or condition, the great hope for society rested on the spaciousness of common humanity which could become the relevant force in the community if directed to full potential by educated, dedicated, and mature leaders.

Starved, distorted, degraded as it may be by all the neglect, by all the vices of what one calls civilization, it is still to the eye of him who knows how to look, the same nature which was created in the image of God, which was endowed with the God-like privilege of choosing between good and evil, made capable of battling for the true, the just.... It is on this common humanity that the educator must build. Let him find the true touch, that "one touch of nature makes all the world of kin," and he will master the whole instrument and harmonise to the grand march of human progress. ... I venture to think that I have some help towards finding that true touch. I have lived much, read much, and through all these ways, have learnt something of human nature and human life—have gained some of that power of sympathy which is as the eye of the heart and gives insight into other hearts.[49]

# 5

# New Educational Opportunities for Women

During the decade from 1850 to 1860, the Shirreff sisters were in the middle stage of their lives. They had spent many years in serious study, purposeful travel, and careful observation of the society in which they moved. They were cosmopolites in manner and taste who had achieved intellectual sophistication, and it seemed to them a propitious time to present their philosophy of education and basic curricula for females. The existing educational system in Britain, by and large, was antithetical to that sponsored by the sisters. A few educational reformers of similar outlook had established what at that time were experimental ventures, but the vast majority of girls and young women had no opportunity to attend reputable educational institutions which met their needs. In a reflective mood in 1884 Maria looked back to mid-century and observed that then the question of women's education had barely surfaced. However, during the generation between 1860 and 1880 it had come to the fore with amazing vigor. "Perhaps no movement of equal importance and involving such far-reaching consequences ever developed so rapidly, or obtained its object so completely, within a fraction of the life time of one generation."[1]

The first major effort in the nineteenth century to provide middle-class and upper-class girls quality education occurred in 1846-1847 under the aegis of enlightened academicians, clerics, and women, including the Reverend Frederick Denison Maurice, Kings College, London; the Reverend R. C. Trench, later archbishop of

Dublin; and Lady Stanley of Alderley. Their creation, Queen's College, affiliated with the established church, initially educated governesses, a pressing need, but then broadened its focus. It opened in Harley Street in 1848 and five years later received a royal charter.[2] In addition to regular day classes the college offered free evening classes exclusively for governesses in arithmetic, mathematics, geography, Latin, history, theology, and mental and moral philosophy. Frances Mary Buss and Dorothea Beale, two future leaders in girls' education and allies of the Shirreffs, attended classes at Queen's College. The institution recruited an able faculty: Maurice, Trench, Dr. Plumptre, Dr. Laing, Thomas Cock, and John Pyke Hullah. In 1849 Bedford College, the project of Mrs. Elizabeth Jesser Reid and Miss Elizabeth Bostock, came into existence; it had the same cast as Queen's except that it had no religious connection.

Female education developed no new directions until more than a decade later. In 1862 Emily Davies took the lead in formation of a commitee to obtain admission of girls to the Local Examination of Cambridge University.[3] In December 1863 an experimental examination was held in London with the cooperation of the syndicate. Female students received only six weeks' notice of their eligibility for the examination. Forty senior and forty-three junior girls took the examination, and six senior and twenty-seven junior girls succeeded. The following year Miss Davies drew up a memorial signed by a thousand men and women connected with education; it requested the official inclusion of girls in the Cambridge Local Examination. In 1865 Cambridge University agreed, and six centers opened. By 1881 there were eighty-seven centers, and in that year 1,554 junior female students and 1,139 senior students took the examination. Of the juniors 57 percent passed, and of the seniors, 57½ percent. Oxford followed the lead of Cambridge but went further in regard to equality of the sexes in that girls were not classified separately; their names appeared on a general list of results.

A Royal Commission, the Schools Inquiry, or Taunton Commission (1864-1867), investigated conditions in schools. It probed the area left untouched by the previous commissions, the Newcastle Commission which gave attention to elementary schools and the

Clarendon Commission for the seven public schools. The original charge to the Taunton Commission did not specify the parameters of its assigned tasks, and women educationalists utilized the memorial which had proven successful in opening the Cambridge examinations to women to persuade the commission to consider girls' education. Emily Davies and Elizabeth Bostock of Bedford College drew up the document for presentation to the commission. Several assistant commissioners had a sincere interest in female education: J. Fitch, James Bryce, T. H. Green, and D. R. Fearon. The commission agreed to include girls' education within its purview. Leading women educators who had made significant contributions in the mid-century generation testified: Emily Davies, Frances Mary Buss, and Dorothea Beale of Cheltenham. In addition men who did not have a professional connection to female education but had national stature and desired a reputable education for girls presented evidence to the commission: J. S. Mill, Professor Huxley, and Dr. Mark Pattison.

The report of the commission gave a psychological lift to the women's educational movement by a stirring affirmation of the need for extensive expansion of educational facilities for girls and young women. It quoted John Middleton Hare, journalist and assistant commissioner on popular education in 1858, that an educated mother was of more importance to the family than an educated father. It also agreed with Ralph Lingen, secretary to the Committee of Council on Education (1849-1869), who noted that large numbers of women of the middle class had to earn their living. For that reason, as well as many others, the commission announced that widespread indifference among middle-class parents about education for daughters had to be combatted together with the long-established prejudice that girls were less capable of mental cultivation and less in need of it than boys. It concluded that many parents' concern about female education centered on providing their daughters with accomplishments and superficially attractive personal qualities.[4] However, it noted that female education doubtless would always have to take into account certain primary considerations—in particular preparation for marriage which required of young women gentle graces and winning qualities of character and personality. The commissioners, nevertheless, wished to deal with obvious deficiencies and shams in female education that were clearly traceable to a preoccupation with the latter facets. Their report included Emily Davies' indictment of the chief goal of female education—the creation of an individual who was amiable, inoffensive, always ready to give pleasure and to be pleased. Another simplistic dictum Miss Davies said served as an unofficial guideline was that girls' schools should be places of moral rather than intellectual training. The commission took a sober view of female education; it predicted that educational planners would have to expect a larger proportion of failures in achievement of goals than in educational programs for males. A survey compiled at the previous census disclosed 547 endowed grammar schools with an enrollment of 31,528 boys and 3,374 girls or almost ten times as many boys as girls. Moreover, 2,179 female students were in just a few areas: York, Lancashire, Cumberland, and Westmoreland.

All members of the commission agreed upon the general deficiency of female education. Their report listed the flaws: want of system, slovenliness and showy superficiality, inattention to rudiments, undue time given to accomplishments which were not taught intelligently or in a scientific manner, and lastly want of organization.[5] The commissioners concluded that girls' schools were inferior to boys' schools. They probed the effectiveness of instruction in various subjects and general curricular deficiencies in girls' schools. They decided that by and large English, history, mathematics, geometry, and algebra were not mastered in a thorough, or indeed basic, way by students at girls' schools; arithmetic and grammar appeared to them especially poorly treated by teachers; physical science had been introduced to the curriculum in a haphazard manner and had not been developed coherently by experimentation; and Greek was so little taught that it did not merit any serious assessment. Instruction in the French language, a popular subject in girls' educational institutions, the commissioners believed to be weak by any standards, with grammar neglected and its fine points rarely attended to. Music, another subject which drew large numbers of students in girls' schools, the investigators also judged to be handled by teachers without the expertise which its wide popularity certainly warranted, and instrumental music, the area of greatest interest, tended to be approached as the acquisition of a manual skill and not dealt with in any depth.[6] Needlework occupied too much space in curricula and was of a purely ornamental sort in the judgment of the commissioners who recommended that it should be developed elsewhere, primarily in the home. They regretted that physical education was in large measure neglected.

The commission felt that Inspector Norris presented the main areas to be attended to.

We find, as a rule, a very small amount of professional skill, an inferior set of school books, a vast deal of dry uninteresting task work, rules put into memory with no explanation of their principles, no system of examination worthy of the name, a very false estimate of the relative value of the several kinds of acquirements, a reference to effect rather than to solid worth, a tendency to fill or adorn rather than to strengthen the mind.[7]

The commission recognized that some of the criticisms leveled were applicable to male education, though not to the same degree. However, it declared that a reformation of boys' education had commenced with certain goals and methods agreed upon, and the urgent issue was whether similar methods of improvement with similar objects in view should be applied to female education.

The commission announced that weighty evidence existed that "the essential capacity for learning" was the same, or nearly the same, in the two sexes. It referred to the evidence presented by several inspectors—Fraser, Bompas, Fitch, Gifford, and Fearon—as well as what could be ascertained from observers of American education. Yet it hedged somewhat on the concept of the intellectual equality of the sexes; it noted equality meant balancing one quality against another. "Many differences such as the tendency to abstract principles in boys contrasted with the greater readiness to lay hold of facts in girls—the greater quickness to acquire in the latter with the greater retentiveness in the former—the greater eagerness of girls to learn—their acute susceptibility to praise and blame—their lesser inductive faculty and others."[8]

The commissioners felt that the University of Cambridge system of Local Examinations for girls below the age of eighteen, started experimentally in 1863, had demonstrated the mental abilities of girls. The Eighth Report of the Syndicate, they said, gave a valid profile of the situation, but it also dealt with the mental differences of the sexes. The most intelligent boys, it decided, wrote with vigor and precision, the best girls with ease and vivacity. "The boys were for the most part content to relate information derived from books, or to describe the process of some branch of manufacture; the girls were eager to express their own views and were most successful when they endeavored to trace their own intellectual phases or to depict the trifling incidents of everyday life."[9] The commission approved a system of examinations for girls in the pattern set forth by Cambridge University—candidates not arranged in order of merit and candidates' lists not publicized. In such a framework the commission decided that girls were not forced into the stimulation of individual competition and public exhibition. It also favored a regular inspection of girls' schools on the same basis as boys' schools; the commissioners suggested that inspection of private institutions be optional but under the aegis of a recognized agency. The commission rejected totally the assessment that the health of girls would be impaired by increased and more systematic intellectual exercise and attainment. Indeed it said on the basis of scientific evidence at hand and past experience it would have the opposite impact—a bracing one.[10]

The commission estimated that female education cost about the same as that for boys. In regard to the quality of education provided by girls' boarding schools versus that of girls' day schools, it gave a higher rating to the latter because they combined beneficial home influence, which was a marked feature of middle-class life, with breadth of curricula and discipline. The Report of the Schools Inquiry Commission contained a number of recommendations regarding female education: (1) full participation of girls in endowments but allocation of a smaller proportion of funds to female education than to male because a smaller number of girls attended schools, and they terminated their education at an earlier age than boys, (2) opportunities for a liberal education for all young women of the middle class who desired it, (3) establishment of colleges for ladies on the model of Bedford College which would be analogous to universities and a necessary adjunct to girls' schools, (4) schools for middle-class girls rather than schools of mixed social classes because many parents objected to the latter type.

The commission concluded that a large number of female teachers in girls' schools were not equal to the academic tasks assigned them due to lack of breadth and accuracy of scholarship and want of knowledge. In sum it decided that teachers had not been well taught, and in turn they did not know how to teach. The official investigators decided that the main obstacle to a reformation of female education was the dominant social values of the era; many parents were apathetic, uncooperative, and indeed hostile to the steps that needed to be taken. "Here as elsewhere we hear that they look chiefly for immediate pecuniary results; that they will not pay for good teaching when they might have it; that they oppose what is not showy and attractive; that they are themselves the cause of deterioration in competent teachers; that their own want of cultivation hinders it in their children."[11]

Dorothea Beale edited the section of the Schools Inquiry Commission's Report which dealt with girls' education.[12] The commercial publication received wide circulation among the devoted band of educationalists. Maria Grey said about it, "To this volume the present writer has often referred as the Doomsday Book of women's education—recording, however, not its possessions but its deficiencies."[13] The message of the commission had great relevance for the Shirreffs. During the previous generation they had studied and then documented the inadequacies of female education and the social ethic and familial patterns which perpetuated ignorance among British women. The commission substantiated the position which the Shirreffs had developed in some detail.

Women of all ages in the nineteenth century did have access to informal educational agencies. Middle-class women attended open meetings of a vast array of literary and philosophical societies founded by males in the late Georgian and early Victorian periods in all parts of the country. Moreover, females gained official membership in a plethora of specialized scientific organizations including natural history clubs and botanical field clubs as well as provincial antiquarian societies. The East Kent Natural History Club, founded in Canterbury in 1857, within its first year had 163 members, 32 of whom were women.[14] The Manchester Field Naturalists' Society recruited 170 members during its first year, and 30 were women.[15] The Botanical Society of London (1837), which urged women to undertake botanical research, made a special appeal to women to join. A number of women wrote botanical material for the general reader including Ann Pratt, Margaret Plues, and Margaret Scott Gatty.[16]

In London the Royal Institution, London Institution, Russell Institution, and Surrey Institution offered women of polite society opportunities to attend all sorts of lectures as well as short courses presented by leading scientists and men of accomplishment in the humanities.[17] But certainly such learning was haphazard and often superficial in character, encouraging a dilettantism that the Shirreff sisters felt was extremely evident among women of their era. Robert Southey made comments on the social character of learning in regard to women, and in the process disclosed his own attitudes. He charged that women attended lectures and scribbled on pads in order to have some topics for use at conversation parties.[18] Louis Simond, a French visitor to Britain in the first decade of the century, noted that large numbers of fashionable people, including many women, flocked to popular lectures. He believed that public lectures were useful primarily to those who knew little and aspired to little. "Real learning is only acquired by solitary studies; but a taste for the arts and sciences although superficial is, at any rate, very desirable in all those to whom fortune gives leisure."[19]

In the latter half of the century, when a corps of British women had embarked upon various efforts to open up avenues for education as well as employment and public service, they established intellectual organizations to further those efforts. In the provinces, one such organization was the Malvern Discussion Society which operated in the 1870s. It had about one hundred members who probed a variety of social, literary, and educational questions. The society published a magazine.[20] The Victoria Discussion Society of London focused on topics of relevance to the women's movement in the last third of the century. It had two purposes: to provide a forum for the exchange of ideas by those concerned with women's work and role in society, and secondly, to give women an opportunity to develop the art of oral presentation that was a vital skill for those who sought to advance their cause. At that point a few women like Miss Becker, Millicent Fawcett, and Lady Amberley, had become effective platform orators. Emily Faithfull commented on the organization, "It brought together a number of earnest people who would never otherwise have met, and it encouraged many leaders to express valuable opinions, who, under other circumstances, would probably have been too nervous to afford help to other workers, but 'would have died with all their music in them.' "[21] Many leaders of the women's movement or spokesmen for social issues of most concern to females appeared before its membership. Dr. Elizabeth Blackwell and Dr. Elizabeth Garrett Anderson discussed medicine as a career for women; Edward Jenkins, MP, the need to improve the condition of working-class families; Herbert Mozley on women's property rights; and Chunder Sen on female educational needs in India.

The mechanics institute and then the lyceum movements, which appeared in the generation that followed Napoleon's defeat, recruited in the main lower-middle-class people and skilled artisans. The new adult education centers offered basic courses in science, English, and mathematics but also entertaining lectures and cultural activities of a diverse sort; the latter grew in scope and popularity as the years passed. Samuel Greg, Manchester industrialist and philanthropist who supported adult education programs, described the purpose of the latter: education consisted not merely of the learning provided in schools nor even in the acquisition of literary and scientific knowledge but of all that had the tendency "to form the character, enlighten the mind, soften manners, refine taste, enlarge the views and improve and civilize the whole mind."[22] In Lancashire in 1859 there were about one hundred mechanics institutes with eighteen thousand members. Lord Stanley estimated that there were perhaps one thousand adult education centers in the county attended by possibly one hundred thousand people. At that juncture there were mixed feelings about the goals of such organizations. James Hole, who headed the Yorkshire Union of Mechanics Institutes, wanted them to sponsor disciplined education.[23] Robert Hunt at the Educational Exhibition of 1854, sponsored by the Society of Arts, pleaded for serious scientific educational programs at adult centers.[24] Lord Stanley in mid-century also believed that an adult education program to be successful had to be nonsectarian and financially supported by its participants; its courses had to be disciplined and serious. Yet James Stansfeld, Liberal politician, at an annual soiree of the Halifax

Mechanics Institute in the early 1860s said that institutes had to become effective social centers as well as schools. The London *Times* agreed with Stansfeld that they should be comprehensive, catholic, and popular. Although mechanics institutes had been founded for males, women slowly found a place in their programs. Mechanics institutes drew attention to the absence of any regular program of education for large numbers of females at the lower end of the social spectrum, but like other male-dominated institutions, they actually made only minimal efforts to accommodate women until rather late in their development. Nevertheless, spokesmen for the movement and officers of individual institutes often expressed approval of female intellectual development.[25] Women's attachment to the institutes varied; initially, they often attended lectures, participated in social gatherings and excursions, and joined vocal music and dance classes.

The lyceums, which were much concerned with the social side of education, welcomed women. The Yorkshire and Lancashire Union of Mechanics Institutes in the late forties encouraged a number of its member institutes to establish women's classes. The three major institutes at Liverpool, Manchester, and Leeds launched women's programs; Liverpool had 667 female members in 1845, Leeds, which admitted women in that year, had 280 female members in 1851. In Manchester more than two hundred women attended classes at mid-century, and as early as 1839 probably one-fifth of the audience at most lectures was women. Women's classes were formed in at least thirty towns in Lancashire and Yorkshire.[26] Indeed some towns, such as Keighley and Huddersfield, established separate women's institutes. At mid-century approximately twelve hundred women belonged to Yorkshire institutes, and six hundred were affiliated with Lancashire centers. Women members seemed to be recruited in large numbers from the lower middle class. Indeed the Annual Report of the Manchester Mechanics Institute stated that it formed classes for daughters of shopkeepers and respectable mechanics.[27]

Females who participated in systematic courses in basic subject matter or enrolled in the mini-schools maintained by some of the mechanics institutes were initiated into the structure and indeed ritual of the British educational system. Typical was the regimen utilized by the East Lancashire Union of Institutes. Its annual examination of 1860 was an event of considerable ceremony. An examination for 169 people, 146 males and 23 females, took place on a Saturday morning and afternoon; the students took tests in mathematics, grammar, reading, recitation, geography, dictation, letter writing, and domestic science. The president of the union, Sir James Kay Shuttleworth, presided. At the noon hour refreshments were served, and he addressed the candidates. Henry Moore, leading employer of Burnley, lectured the students on the value of education as a means to improve their work opportunities. At the conclusion of the second series of examinations in the afternoon the students again received refreshments and listened to speeches. Certificates and awards were presented in a formal ceremony.[28] Students who attended mechanics institutes were simply on the fringes of the educational world, and yet they were drawn by a variety of steps into the fraternity of the diligent and civic-minded citizenry.

In 1859 at the annual gathering of the National Social Science Association, which met that year at Bradford, Fanny Hertz asserted that relatively small numbers of females had participated in the mechanics institute movement. She ascribed the situation to "the prejudice that woman has neither the same powers nor the same aspirations as man." She said society was paying a frightful price for the neglect of the mind of the working woman.

What a multitude of evils exist here, mainly traceable to the uncultivated condition of our working women, "the greatest part of whose humanity sleepeth a deep sleep." No thoughtful person can walk through our streets, or perchance enter our people's homes, without reaching this sad fact on every side. He will read it in the physical type of the population, deficient in stamina, from long continued disobedience to physiological laws; deficient in beauty for want of the impress of thought and noble emotion. He will read it in the numbers of neglected, unhealthy children, doomed to pass from the cradle to the grave diseased in body and mind because their mothers have become mothers without one single qualification for so holy a charge.[29]

Fanny Hertz listed the impediments to recruitment of working women to educational programs—first, the drabness of their lives which discouraged all thoughts of beauty, refinement, and self-development, secondly, the small amount of leisure allowed them, and thirdly, the large floating population of female labor in the textile industry. She examined two mechanics institutes for women, Huddersfield, founded in 1847, and Bradford. The fair amount of success in the educational programs at Huddersfield she ascribed to the large numbers of students who worked as milliners, dress-makers, or domestic servants or who lived at home which led to a stable membership and attendance at comprehensive courses. The Bradford Institute had been founded a decade later. Although 600 females had contact with that institution between 1857 and 1859, only about 150 were regular students. It offered courses in reading, writing, arithmetic, geography, history, grammar, needlework, singing, and an advanced class in natural science.

Fanny Hertz believed that to be viable, educational programs for working-class women had to utilize skillful teaching and subject matter which tapped the reasoning and imaginative powers. She wanted elements of physical science and physiology developed as essential features of curricula for female workers. She suggested that history, geography, and other subjects be taught when possible by illustrations, visual aids, and models. "By means like these we shall best accomplish our object of raising our young working women to the dignity of human beings, and of awakening them to a sense of the beauty and preciousness of life."[30]

During the 1860s the women's educational world was alive with organizational activity; new agencies came to the fore which affirmed the ideas of individual reformers. Indeed their membership consisted of men and women who had broken educational ground for women. The North of England Council for Promoting the Higher Education of Women that had a seven-year life span (1867-1874) and its offshoot, the Ladies Council of the Yorkshire Council of Education, had a representative cast. The former had as leaders women educators and social reformers like Josephine Butler, Anne Jemima Clough, Miss Wolstenholme; education officials like J. G. Fitch, Thomas Markby (secretary of the Cambridge Local Examination Syndicate), and academicians from various colleges of the prestigious universities. The relationship of the council to the university extension movement is discussed elsewhere in this study as is the council's direct impact on Maria Grey's Women's Education Union and the Girls' Public Day School Company. The council in 1871 invited her to present her ideas at one of its meetings and arranged to have her bring the message to towns represented in the organization.[31]

The leaders of the council, in particular its secretary, Anne Jemima Clough, gave the campaign for female education publicity and forged a broad-based coalition, and such a dimension made it easier to build the educational agencies like the Women's Education Union, the Girls' Public Day School Company, and the Froebel Society sponsored by the Shirreffs without years of preliminary musing.[32] Miss Clough called for a wide range of educational offerings and institutions to serve the needs of members of her sex of all ages. In *Macmillan's Magazine* in 1866 she pointed out (1) a want of standard, and (2) lack of a clear academic pattern as the catastrophic deficiencies in female education. "In the education of boys there are a series of steps which serve as guides to teachers. The preparatory schools look to the great public schools and the more advanced private establishments to Oxford and Cambridge examinations and both public and private schools to the universities and the various civil, military, and naval examinations."[33] Educationalists, men and women, utilized organizations to give a sense of urgency and breadth of support to their pleas for a complete system of education for females.

If the educationalists used organizations to authenticate their message, they also saw the value of creating organizations of diverse types to carry forward educational plans of all sorts. Anne Clough asked devotees of women's educational rights to consider the desirability of a permanent central educational board to supervise female education, its members, appointed by the government, to be drawn from various interested groups and empowered to administer the distribution of government funds. She envisaged it carrying out a number of functions: the reception and evaluation of educational schema but also construction of its own proposals, sponsorship of cheap editions of school publications, and guidance to school libraries.

Anne Clough also suggested an educational association in each district to improve elementary schools, its guiding council composed of school inspectors, educational volunteers, teachers, and parents. She asked for attention to the methodology used in Prussia, in particular Berlin, to impart reading and writing skills in a short period. At the secondary school level she wanted, under associational guidance, a central school in each district provided with extensive educational facilities of all sorts, both physical equipment and learning materials of all kinds where many kinds of educational programs could be instituted and evaluated.[34]

Advocates of female educational renewal, by and large, recognized that the government had a viable role to play in its development. The extent and areas of the government's contribution were controversial, and often points of view on the issue were not refined to any degree. Individual effort, philanthropy, and private associational activity together with government financial aid, which meant regulation, had become the order of the day. However, the exact relationship between the private sector and the government was difficult to define because the dominant social ethic of the era had an ambivalent approach to the whole topic. The Shirreffs to a considerable degree approached the issue of government association with education in a pragmatic fashion.

Helen Taylor, stepdaughter and confidant of J. S. Mill, asked in 1866 for experimentation to reign supreme in women's search for their full liberation.

It is the commonest thing in the world to hear even educated people, who, on other topics, pride themselves on having some foundation for what they say, confound together in one group millions of women, of different races and different religions, brought up in different climates and under different institutions, and predict, with quiet security, how all these would act under utterly untried conditions—such as perfect political and social freedom— of which the history of the world has never yet furnished even a single instance whereon to ground a sober judgment.... From all these workings of imagination there is no final appeal but to facts. Experiments must be tried before we can hope to arrive at trustworthy conclusions. They can be tried cautiously if we fancy, as many people do fancy, that in dealing with women, we are dealing with very explosive material. But, until we are willing to try them in some way, we cannot deny that those who are willing to appeal to facts are more candid, and those who desire to have recourse to experiment are more practical than those who are content to defend the present state of things by vague predictions of possible evil while they refuse to put their own predictions to even the most gentle test.[35]

Women educators and their allies sought to launch or make more visible effective educational institutions for women which they considered to be paradigmatic, but in actuality paralleled in many fundamental areas male institutions at the secondary, collegiate, and university levels.

The North London Collegiate School for Girls provided Maria Grey the operational model for the network of secondary schools she wished to establish throughout the country. In 1870 the school had been in operation a generation under the guidance of Frances Mary Buss, at that time a woman of forty-three. Previous to the launching of the Camden school, her mother, with her assistance, operated a school on Pestalozzian principles in Kentish Town. Frances Mary Buss in the spring of 1850 launched the North London Collegiate School with thirty-three students. The entire Buss family took part in the academic venture. Mrs. Buss taught younger students until her death in 1861, Alfred Buss (her son) Latin and arithmetic, another son, Septimus, drawing and scripture, and her husband, Robert William, science, drawing, and elocution. The Reverend William Laing, honorary secretary of the Governesses Benevolent Institution, gave solid support to the venture. The Buss family provided a purposeful and rigorous education for middle-class girls and daughters of materially comfortable families who, for the most part, lived in Camden Town. Frances Mary endeavored to minimize social gradations in the school and stressed a liberal religious spirit; parents had the right to withdraw their daughters from instruction in the catechism of the Church of England or sectarian religious classes.[36]

She testified before the Endowed Schools Commission and enunciated the position to which the Shirreffs subscribed—a girl's education should not differ substantially from that enjoyed by boys. She forcefully presented the case for more girls' schools and better ones with revamped curricula and effective instruction validated by qualifying examinations.

In the wake of the Endowed Schools Commission, the opening of the Tripos examination to girls, and the foundation of Girton College, Frances Mary Buss imparted new vigor to the academic

life of the North London School because she was eager for her girls
to engage in the whole examination program created for boys.
Mary Gurney in a publication of the Women's Education Union,
*Are We to Have Education for Our Middle-Class Girls, or the
History of the Camden Collegiate Schools* (1872), described the
educational complex which had emerged under the Buss family's
guidance. In 1871 the North London Collegiate School for Girls became a public school, the property vested in a board of trustees
with a governing body. The North London School moved to new,
commodious quarters at 202 Camden Road, and a second school
opened in its old quarters, a lower school which offered a simplified
education at a reduced cost. One group of students received instruction in the morning and another in the afternoon. The annual
fees amounted to 4.4 shillings, and the leaving age was set at sixteen. The Lower School had its own headmistress, but Miss Buss
remained superintendent. At the end of the first year of operation it
had a student body of 220.

The new quarters of the North London Collegiate School, a converted private home, had adequate but certainly not luxurious
facilities—a schoolroom which could serve 120 pupils, another
large classroom on the second floor, and on each floor two smaller
classrooms. Two hundred girls attended; their ages ranged from six
to eighteen years and the fees from 9 to 15 guineas per annum, and
for resident students there were two boardinghouses close by with
different fees. In 1872 the school publicized its academic standards
as reflected by the achievements of its students. In the entrance hall
of the school Miss Buss posted the names of 112 students who had
passed various official examinations, those of Cambridge University, the College of Preceptors, and the School of Arts. In 1871
eight students obtained honors in the Cambridge examinations and
two in the London University examination for women.

A letter of Frances Mary Buss revealed some of her basic curriculum ideas. She advocated the range of courses found in boys'
schools but also special subjects suitable for girls. "After many
years of work for what might be called the middle section (and,
indeed, the upper sections also of the middle class), I should include
all that I have mentioned, viz., English thoroughly, with Elementary Science in courses such as I have alluded to, French, Latin,

bold outline drawing, careful part singing, plain needlework and thorough arithmetic, with geometry and algebra in the higher class."[37] Miss Buss demanded that students delve deeply into the subject matter of the curriculum and not be satisfied with an easy acquaintance. "I want to train up girl students in science; I want to teach music grandly—thoroughly in class...making each girl understand...as if she were reading some passage of poetry, teaching her to find out the musician's thought; his mode of expressing it; other ways of expression of the same thought, viz. words." She did not include instrumental music in the regular curriculum, feeling it could be learned privately if desired. She said that physical education was a necessary part of the educational pattern. "Our system, an American idea called musical gymnastics, is excellent. Easy, graceful and not too fatiguing, gently calling every part of the body into play by bright spirited music, which cultivates rhythm of movement, it has become popular, and has wonderfully improved the figure and carriage of the girls."[38]

She sponsored schools with large enrollments not merely to keep tuition and fees fairly low but also to expose girls to a more realistic view of society and thereby eliminate narrowness.

Concurrent with the expansion of the educational foundation headed by Frances Mary was a financial campaign to raise sufficient funds to defray the cost of a new building and its equipment. She hoped to raise 6,000 pounds, 5,000 for the Camden venture and 1,000 for the North London establishment. Maria Grey and Emily Shirreff enlisted in the volunteer effort. A public meeting at the end of 1870, presided over by Lord Lyttleton, did not bring in any appreciable funds. It took three years for her and her corps of workers to raise a meager 700 pounds. Maria Grey wrote to the *Times* that 60,000 pounds had been raised for a middle-class boys' school; she requested but one-tenth of that amount. Two additional meetings, one presided over by the Lord Mayor, did not raise the desired monies. Maria Grey wrote a second letter to the *Times* and observed that her own appeal had gained only 47 pounds, and of that amount 20 pounds would have been given regardless of her public appeal. As a result of that second appeal approximately 100 pounds came in. In a third letter to the *Times* she urged the Reverend William Rogers, who had solicited 60,000 pounds for the boys' foundation, to aid the girls' venture. She asked the editor of the *Times* to make a statement on the subject.

Will you, Sir, not raise, in the name of the nation, a protest which cannot be so easily set aside? Will you not at least make it clear to the public that this is not a woman's question, but a man's question, a national question and that to leave uneducated one-half of the people—and that the half that moulds the associations, habits and life of the other half—is a course so suicidal to the nation which deliberately follows it we are tempted to exclaim in bitterness of soul, "Quem deus vult perdere prius dementat?"[39]

In November 1871 the Princess of Wales agreed to become patroness of the North London educational complex. In her letter of acceptance she noted it would serve as a model for similar schools elsewhere. Maria Grey made known the royal patronage in another letter to the *Times*. Small contributions followed.

Maria Grey, however, in that period initiated her own project, the Girls' Public Day School Company, and Frances Mary Buss showed some irritation because the proposal led to establishment of a school in fairly close proximity to her own, which she thought interfered with her fund raising.

Several people have written to me about the £5 shares in the Brompton School, and my ire was rising. Mrs. Grey handed over all Mr. Morley's £500 to purchase shares in the new school shows pretty clearly—in addition to the Goldsmid gift—what chance do we have of help in that quarter. There can be no doubt that the new school movement is leaving us high and dry. I do not feel aggrieved by the Union in the least. It only makes me more determined to act. Miss Davies shuts herself into one bit of work; Mrs. Grey into another; I into a third.

However, a letter from Maria Grey in the same period showed a basic good feeling between the two women. "Several people have told me that your meeting yesterday was a complete success. I congratulate you heartily and sincerely regret not having been able to attend. I wonder whether I shall see similar success won by the Company's schools. If we could but get a duplicate of you, I should feel very sure of the success whether I live to see it or not."[40]

A supporter of Miss Buss's educational foundation in a letter urged her to aid the St. John's Wood School established under the auspices of the Girls' Public Day School Company. She commented that if Frances Mary subscribed to the effort, she would demonstrate that she felt the school in no way interfered with the success of her own institution. Frances Mary took shares in the company, and indeed served on the council of the Women's Education Union, its parent organization, as a representative of the Schoolmistresses Association.

Financial concerns about the North London educational venture slowly receded, and within a decade the school had become financially sound. An endowment by the Brewers' Company was of major assistance. In the early 1880s the upper school had a student body of five hundred and the lower, four hundred. In the mid-eighties Miss Buss established another link to the work of the Shirreffs by becoming a member of the council of the Maria Grey Training College. She had been deeply interested in teacher training and as a temporary expedient had articled student teachers at her school. She hoped to establish a training college in conjunction with her school but gave up the plan when Mrs. Grey took the lead. However, Frances Mary and Anne Jemima Clough were instrumental in the foundation of the Cambridge Training College.[41]

In the seventies and eighties a number of women's professional educational organizations emerged which often cooperated with each other on issues dealing with strengthening or expanding educational opportunities for girls. Of course they had separate goals which they also pursued with energy and with varying degrees of success. Their members included the alumnae of the various women's educational foundations which had been created in the previous two generations and faculty members of the institutions. The Schoolmistresses Association (1866) owed its existence largely to Emily Davies, who was the honorary secretary for twenty years, and Frances Mary Buss, who became its president in 1867. However, ferment and new developments in the field of female education led Frances Mary to suggest a new organization. The Association of Headmistresses was formed in 1874 at Miss Buss's home on Primrose Hill. Nine women attended the first meeting, and in its aftermath they issued invitations for membership to heads of schools in various parts of the country. At the first general session of the new organization the participants approved the principle strongly advocated by the Women's Education Union—examination and certification for men and women teachers. Members also sought to clarify their own powers and rights, in particular the extent and areas of control they exercised over the institutions they directed. Frances Mary became president and served in that office until her death in 1895. Dorothea Beale succeeded her and held the office until her death in 1906, when the organization had a membership of more than two hundred fifty. A decade later the Association of Assistant Headmistresses formed. The Teachers Guild, launched by Frances Mary Buss as a provident scheme at the Headmistress Association conference of 1883, sought to bring together teachers in a single association of fellowship and material benefit and yet not take the place of their separate associations.

Dorothea Beale became the lady principal of Cheltenham Ladies College in 1858 at the age of twenty-seven. By the time the Shirreffs engaged in their varied educational activities, Miss Beale had made the institution into a prestigious educational facility which was housed in 1873 in an impressive new Gothic building. In subsequent decades it was enlarged to accommodate the growing student body that reached nine hundred by the opening of the new century. Miss Beale in the mid-seventies, in sharp but largely behind-the-scenes struggles, gained full internal control of the college, and thus it mirrored her educational objectives. Mrs. Grey met Dorothea Beale in 1871 at the annual meeting of the North of England Association for Promoting Women's Education. Thereafter Dorothea Beale became her ally in the educational movements in which the Shirreffs held a premier place, the Women's Union, the Girls' Public Day School Company, and the Teachers' Training and Registration Society. Miss Beale established at Cheltenham a kindergarten division and three departments for training teachers at the secondary, elementary, and kindergarten levels. In 1885 she tried to get the council of the college to establish a girls' public high school in Cheltenham. The council did not approve of the plan, since the school would not primarily provide students for Cheltenham College. But at the end of the eighties, Miss Beale opened

Cambray House, the old home of the Cheltenham Ladies College, as a day school with a small boardinghouse close by, with low student fees. Miss Beale conducted it for eight years.[42] When she was in the midst of her effort to gain firm control of the ladies college, she conferred with Maria Grey about the powers of the councils of the Girls' Public Day Schools.[43]

Miss Beale did not recruit daughters of tradesmen for her school; many of her students were offspring of military officers, colonial civil servants, and clerics. In contrast, the Shirreff sisters sought daughters of tradesmen and indeed wanted a student body drawn from a cross section of society in their public day schools. Miss Beale was the prototype of the dynamic and imposing headmistress who came to the fore in the late nineteenth century. "The great headmistress of that late Victorian period had something of a film star quality. Supplied with a ready-made audience of respectful admiring young maidenhood; they were perpetually acting a part and successfully 'putting over' their own idea of themselves to others."[44]

On several occasions Miss Beale gave evidence of her high regard for the work of Maria Grey. In 1878 Maria received a silver casket containing an illuminated address of warm acknowledgment of her services to education. It was the project of all the headmistresses of the Girls' Public Day Schools and Miss Buss and Miss Beale. In the fifteenth anniversary volume of the National Educational Association just before her own and Maria Grey's death, Dorothea Beale gave a glowing appraisal of the Shirreff sisters' contributions to education. "The two sisters had worked in faith and gradually the mountain of prejudice yielded; their high intellectual endowment, their power of expression, their gentleness and strength, above all their lofty and unselfish character lifted the workers into a region too high for the ignorant and worldly to climb or for the arrows of ridicule to touch them."[45] Maria and Emily brought to their several educational programs for girls a cooperative spirit and thereby formed a rapport with educators who had won attention and acclaim.[46] In the last third of the century, the sisters stood in the vanguard of an effective educational coalition.

Emily Davies, born in 1830 the daughter of a clergyman, became deeply committed to the cause of women's rights. Influenced by

Barbara Leigh Smith, Madame Bodichon, and Bessie Parkes Belloc, she contributed to the *Englishwoman's Journal*. She formed a close friendship with Elizabeth Garrett who struggled in the early sixties to gain a medical degree from the University of London and get her name entered on the British Medical Register. Emily Davies' dedicated work for admission of women to university examinations was based on a concept strongly endorsed by Frances Mary Buss and the Shirreff sisters—women should fulfill all the examination obligations placed on men. They wanted equality of academic opportunity and said such considerations required equality of performance.[47] They felt that girls did not have to pursue the curriculum set forth for boys but had to have equality of standard ascertained by examination.

In 1869 Emily Davies opened a college in a converted dwelling, Brownslow House, on the chalk cliffs above Hitchin; she initially had only five students. Mrs. Manning served as headmistress at the opening of the college. At the end of the first term Emily Shirreff was prevailed upon to assume the duties of headmistress in Lent term. Cambridge University academicians including E. C. Clark in Latin and Greek, Professor Seeley in English, and Dr. Hart and Professor Stuart in mathematics, gave weekly lectures at the college. Emily held her post at the college less than a year. Maria Grey explained why Emily did not remain there: she encountered a persistent opposition to her influence and views concerning governance of the institution. She felt that the sacrifice of her time and freedom of action was useless in that the objects which she had in view did not seem possible to accomplish.[48] Emily Davies retained the decision-making power even though she was not in residence at the college. A letter of Emily Davies confirms Maria's evaluation. She wrote, "No doubt she [Emily] would prefer to have the whole internal management including the direction of the studies in her hands, but nothing was said to justify her expecting it."[49] Emily Shirreff felt that she should sit on the executive committee of the governing board of the college, a privilege that had been accorded to Mrs. Manning, the first headmistress, but denied to her successors.[50]

Evidently Emily had been an effective guide and mentor to students during her short tenure. J.W.B. Herschel in 1881 informed

Emily that his daughter Constance had married a widower with several children and was most happy. He reminded her that he had enrolled his daughter at Girton when she headed the institution. "I wish that words were not so weak, that I could convey to you my own deep conviction that she owed her happiness to you, and my own veneration for you, in all that you and your sister have so nobly done for your countrywomen."[51]

Despite her resignation Emily remained a staunch supporter of the college and a member of its council. The institution faced the difficult task of raising funds for its adequate maintenance. Close friends of Emily Davies contributed the sizable amounts the college needed, 1,000 pounds from Madame Bodichon and 1,000 pounds from Mrs. Manning. In 1873 the college moved to Girton. Lady Stanley reported, "The teaching has been Cambridge teaching; and the Girton students have been yearly examined from the same papers and under the same conditions as the undergraduates."[52] Within a generation of its foundation Girton emerged as a dynamic focal point of female higher education and something of a symbol of women's campaign to play an enlarged role in public life. In *Utopia Ltd.* by Gilbert and Sullivan Princess Zara, the chief female character, returned to her homeland to reshape it into a progressive state. She had studied at Girton:

> Oh maiden rich
>    In Girton lore
> That wisdom which
>    We prized before,
> We do confess
> Is nothingness,
> And rather less,
>    Perhaps, than more,
> On each of us
>    Thy learning shed
> On calculus
>    May we be fed
> And teach us please,
> To speak with ease
> All languages
>    Alive and dead!

Indeed the women's colleges at the famed universities became a vogue among the intelligentsia. William Gladstone sent his daughter to Newnham. One student at that college recalled the stream of visitors who came to see the new experiment including Turgenev, Ruskin, and George Eliot.[53]

The establishment of Girton College provided Maria Grey with the opportunity to endorse strongly university work for young women. "But this much I must say that no organization of education for girls can be complete without the College to supply the higher knowledge when the school training has prepared the mind to desire and receive." However, Maria made clear that she did not advocate that all girls attend college or pursue university work. "I should be sorry, indeed, to see it become the fashion for young women, as it is for young men of a certain station in life, to go to College, whether they cared for its intellectual advantages or not, and pass through a three-year course not of culture but of very expensive idleness." She said that university work then in operation was certainly not ideal, but she saw definite signs of reform. Despite all curricular shortcomings and other dificiencies, she valued the official attachment of female students to universities because they provided intellectual maturation of a basic sort, concentrated students' attention on selected subjects and demanded a thorough foundation in them. Moreover, universities subjected the acquisition of knowledge to valid and recognized examinations.

Maria Grey believed that mixed education, both on intellectual and moral grounds, was best. She considered that women's colleges and local examinations for women served as preliminary steps that would lead to integrated education at the university level. They established the capacity and desire of girls to follow the same course of study as boys and accustomed the public to the idea of both sexes working toward common objectives and tried by common standards. The various schemes of advanced education for young women then in operation, Maria maintained, did not compete with one another but engaged the energies of different constituencies. Educational programs in post-adolescence she justified as valid in creating a framework to delay marriage beyond seventeen or eighteen for girls, so that they could become mature and cognizant of the responsibilities of married life.

The small Kensington Society which held sessions in the late sixties drew together the most dedicated people in the cause of female education, Mrs. Manning, her stepdaughter, Miss E. A. (Adelaide) Manning, Miss Davies, Annie Ridley, Frances Mary Buss, and Sedley Taylor, to discuss a variety of issues. In 1867 they examined the topic "A Proposed Woman's College."[54]

Certainly Girton with its strict collegiate organization, high standards of matriculation, and demanding curricula was an appropriate higher educational path for only a limited number of young women. A more experimental pattern also emerged at Cambridge. In 1870 a system of lectures for women was sponsored by a committee of men and women; the men had an association with Cambridge University and included Professor and Mrs. Fawcett, Henry Sidgwick, F. D. Maurice, Adam, and Cayley. The experiment led Anne Jemima Clough to open a residence hall for women participants of the program, only five in 1870 but by 1876 twenty-six students. In 1873 the Association for Promoting Higher Education for Women in Cambridge formed and built Newnham Hall for women students by means of a limited liability company which sold shares. Although it had been launched to afford students an adequate preparation for the Cambridge Higher Local Examination, it offered more advanced instruction and the privilege granted Girton of informal examination in the Tripos subjects. In 1880 the association and Newnham Hall merged to produce Newnham College.

And so the Girls' Public Day School Company of the Shirreffs had a dual function: it launched a national movement to provide schools for girls who wanted a sound terminal education above the elementary level, but its regimen was also a foundation for a variety of higher educational opportunities which its graduates were prepared to pursue.

By the late seventies women moved to broaden their higher education by full participation in the existing university structure. They made a serious assault on the coveted citadel of male privilege; university examinations available to women in the early seventies were especially designed for them with the exception of the informal Tripos examination offered to students of Girton and Newnham colleges. In 1878 the senate of the University of London proposed to convocation a supplement to its charter—to open to women all degrees of the university. The motion passed by an almost two-to-one vote, 241 to 123. Maria Grey said that it was a date to be ever remembered in the history of women.[55] In 1882 women graduates of the University of London gained the right to vote in convocation. In 1881 Cambridge University received memorials, one from resident members of the university, to admit women formally to the Tripos examinations. The suggestion received overwhelming approval, 258 votes to 26. Cambridge, however, did not recognize women as members of the university, nor could they take the examination for the ordinary degree. The rationale seemed strange to Maria Grey—a prejudice existed against following a course of education for its own sake and admittance to the honors examination for any reason except that it would confer benefit in professional advancement. But she perceptively commented, "We may, however, be satisfied with this partial result knowing well that the wedge already inserted so deeply will not fail to be driven home before long."[56]

A few months after the Cambridge University reform the University of Durham opened to women its public examinations and its first degree in the arts on the same condition of residence which applied to males. However, the liberal step did not have relevance immediately because a female residence facility and means of instruction did not exist. Prior to the University of London's action the University of St. Andrews had opened its degrees and examinations to women on the basis of complete equality with men. Maria Grey had one reservation about the step taken by St. Andrews: she feared women would be ridiculed if they used the designation Licentiate. They were called by the university Lady Licentiates, LLA. Maria maintained firmly that academic distinction transcended sex and simply marked levels of learning.[57]

Maria Grey surveyed the steps taken to open existing higher education to women with much satisfaction. "The privilege is won; the door so long closed is open wide, and the ways and means of knowledge abundantly provided." But she presented a challenge which women's rights advocates as well as members of the general public often placed before the generation of women who had achieved advances. "It remains only that women shall prove themselves worthy of the freedom which they have gained; that they throw off the mental and moral defects contracted during long ages of irresponsible dependence."[58] A springtime feeling of expectancy arose among feminists who by and large felt that new educational opportunities meant moral renewal for their own sex and also the rest of society. In that spirit advocates of female enfranchisment who had been temporarily thwarted were often buoyed by the expectation that its eventual realization would be accompanied by a new social dynamism based on ideals and ideas evolved in the temples of education peopled for the first time by women who had access also to major occupations which shaped the development of national life.

# 6

## The Shirreff Sisters' Educational Philosophy and Regimen

The Shirreffs, in accord with the other dedicated leaders, Emily Davies, Anne Jemima Clough, Dorothea Beale, and Frances Mary Buss, who worked tirelessly to establish a viable pattern of education for females in their country, defined education as preparation for life and not for a special position in society. The Shirreff sisters maintained that the principles upon which any effective system was based had to be applicable to all human beings, men, women, artisans, professional men, peers, and commoners. Maria Grey subscribed to the traditional goals of humanistic education. "It is intellectual, moral, and physical development, the development of a sound mind in a sound body, the training of reason to form just judgments, the disciplining of the will and affections to obey the supreme law of duty, the kindling and strengthening of the love of knowledge, of beauty, of goodness, till they become governing motives of action."[1]

The Shirreffs felt that undue emphasis had been given to the useful which elevated professional over liberal education. They freely admitted that liberal knowledge had no practical knowledge in the sense commonly used of money value. "So long, therefore, as education is tested by the amount of knowledge acquired at a certain age and needed for certain purposes, female education may be tolerated as a harmless fashion, but it has no real purpose or importance." Emily said that in the quest to open avenues of education to women and workingmen, wrong questions had been posed. Instead of asking What is taught? How much knowledge does the system impart? had the questions been Why is it taught? To what does it fashion minds subjected to its influence? the results would have been different.[2]

Emily Shirreff designated as the priority of education to rouse minds from a passive to an active state. "It is only when that change is effected that the knowledge really becomes mental nurture." She sought substantiation for her position from John Henry Newman in his famed lectures *Idea of a University.*

It is not mere application, however exemplary, which introduces the mind to truth, nor the reading many books nor the getting up many subjects, nor the witnessing many experiments, nor the attending many lectures. All this is short enough; a man may have done it all, yet be lingering in the vestibule of knowledge; he may not realize what his mouth utters; he may not see with his mental eye what confronts him; he may have no grasp of things as they are, or at least he may have no power of advancing one step forward of himself in consequence of what he has already acquired, no power of discriminating between truth and falsehood, of sifting out the grains of truth from the mass, of arranging them according to their true value, and, if I may use the phrase, of building up ideas. Such a power is the result of a scientific formation of mind; it is an acquired faculty of judgment, of clear sightedness, of sagacity, of wisdom, of philosophical reach of mind, and of intellectual self-possession and response, bodily eye, the organ for apprehending material objects is provided by nature; the eye of the mind of which the object is truth, is the work of discipline and habit.[3]

If the purpose of education was the systematic and harmonious development of the person's whole moral and intellectual nature, then it followed that the elementary principles had to be the same for all. It was the failure to accept such a position that the Shirreffs said caused Britain to halt between different systems of school and university education, and as a result women and the working class suffered.

If we argue upon grounds of mere worldly utility, we can never get rid of petty squabbles as to the amount of arithmetic, grammer or history which may or may not turn out profitable to them, and it must even remain an open question whether industrial schools are not better than those of a more intellectual character. But if we take our stand upon the ground that the human being remains a mutilated creature, if the capacities of his mind are left dormant, or if, when awakened by circumstances, he has no command over them, then it becomes apparent at once that every study which tends to exercise those powers is useful in the highest sense of the word, and that the only limitations to this mental discipline, and to the knowledge which it is good for all human beings to acquire, are those imposed by time and means. The education of women has no firm standing on other grounds.[4]

The sisters decided that two evils flowed from the prevailing attitude toward education. First, the necessary connection between moral and intellectual cultivation had been forgotten, so that the development had been one-sided. Secondly, the increase of the external or money value of knowledge obscured its intrinsic worth, and love of truth had not kept pace with progress of knowledge. Intellectual training which society acknowledged to be necessary for boys, the Shirreffs felt, took up the greatest share of their attention while moral development was left almost unheeded and thus shaped by chance and circumstances. In contrast, the Shirreffs observed that female intellectual cultivation in their own era had no purpose and so was regulated by caprice or fashion; girls received moral training, but since it was linked to narrow views and undisciplined intellects, the benefits were minimal. In both situations there had been a failure of the necessary action and reaction upon each other of intellectual and moral culture.

The Shirreffs rejected the generalization that moral culture was synonymous with religious teaching. They noted that true religious feeling would not save one from doing mischief amidst the complicated conditions of social existence by exercising a wrong influence or failing to exercise a right one. The mind had to be strengthened by exercise of thought and judgment; mental discipline braced the moral system with a clearness of view and strength of conviction. The Shirreffs reminded their constituency that truly excellent persons in regard to religious practices were often narrow-minded and prone to make poor judgments. The sisters deplored the widespread belief that moral training was synonymous with religion and religion with theology. Moral culture meant to them practice in everyday activities of truth and justice toward fellow human beings, avoidance of selfishness and ill temper; they believed that a cultivated intellect was essential to attainment of positive moral values. Another area to which they called attention was the general indifference to knowledge except as a marketable commodity which often led to the unfortunate assessment that leisure was synonymous with idleness.

Although the outlook for engagement of women in professional life seemed uncertain to the Shirreffs and they could not predict where and how women could be adequately brought into public life, they said that women's need for education was not therefore diminished but indeed expanded. Women had to achieve, they claimed, the self-motivation to pursue learning for its own sake, which was the essence of true education. However, the Shirreffs pointed out a difficulty faced by girls in pursuit of education which boys did not encounter—victimization by social position and mores imposed by civilization. Thackeray's poignant narration of a girl's life illustrated the situation. "This is the condition of young ladies' existence. She breakfasts at eight, she does Mangnall's *Questions* with a governess till ten; she practices till one; she walks in the square with bars round her till two; then she practices again; then she comes down to play to papa because he likes music whilst he is asleep after dinner."

The Shirreffs keenly perceived the frustration together with social opprobrium which accompanied the divorce of a woman by means of her education from the goals and standards set for her by society. The sisters presented the dilemma of parents who charted the course of education of their daughters if they heeded the dictates of society.

They may form a resolute character, but they must enforce diffidence in conduct and opinion; they may inspire generous and lofty aims, but they must beware of kindling ambition; they must train the energy that overcomes difficulties, but they must teach the bold spirit and strong will that generally accompany energy to be content with submission. They may teach love of truth and scorn of the world's baseness and folly, but they must inculcate deference to that world's opinion; they may earnestly strive to train the spiritual nature to that full development of all its powers which is its indefeasible right, but they must fit the women for a career of dependence, of narrow aims and repressed action.[5]

In spite of all difficulties, the Shirreffs claimed that a well-designed liberal education could satisfy the desires of women, allow them to pursue public careers when possible, create a richer family life, and through the latter contributions bring about a reformed and equitable society within a few generations.

In methodology the Shirreff sisters followed the path of earlier educational progressives, such as Rousseau and Mary Wollstonecraft. The sisters urged parents and educators to be cognizant that physical health, environment, and personal relationships between learner and instructor had a crucial impact on attitudes toward learning and the successful utilization of any educational regimen. They advised guides of children to consider the possibility that violent temper, withdrawn and morose attitudes, indeed an entire spectrum of what might be considered negative personality traits to the observer, could well be related to physical dysfunctions of various sorts.

The Shirreffs believed that the child should not be subjected to the regular system of schoolroom education until twelve years. Emily wrote on that point, "In my opinion such progress is not only impossible in most cases but undesirable in all. It is a crying sin against childhood to cut short the careless healthy idleness, to substitute books for play." When children reached the age for classroom work, Emily advocated that they rise at 6:30 and engage in pleasurable pursuits and physical play before beginning lessons at 8:30 AM. During the day she suggested that students devote three hours to classroom study interspersed by regular intervals of play and other forms of recreation. When students reached adolescence, Emily asked that the classroom regimen be increased to four to five hours.[6]

Emily wanted students introduced to the techniques of scientific investigation and reasoning.

We want especially to learn them because the same principles, although not precisely the same method, must be borne in mind when considering the subjects we daily and necessarily deal with. That is, although we cannot use experiments to ascertain truth in moral or social questions, nor obtain the same accurate observation, nor make the same analysis of phenomena, nor venture to generalize so boldly from ascertained facts, yet the principles are alike.[7]

She noted that caution, close reasoning, freedom from any motives except the desire for truth, patience, and accurate observation were required. But clearly the Shirreff sisters did not conceive of educational development as simply the application of a packaged methodology but rather the artful and flexible use of methodology by the educator—either parent or professional. "Means, situations, ability, health, all bring in a variety of considerations that tend to modify in each family the adoption of any system of education."[8] Emily set forth the desirable mindset for the instructor—a number of master educational principles wedded to a spirit of method in development of the learner's thought processes and humanistic and moral values within the framework of several knowledge areas. The success of the scheme depended on a personal rapport between learner and instructor. "Habit influences action, association influences thoughts and wishes, both are indispensable instruments, but the power the parent possesses of moulding the mind through associations is the highest power one human being can exercise over another."[9]

Thus, despite the detailed curricular plans which the Shirreffs drew up for female students, they placed priority on the quality and emphasis of instruction. "In a word to repeat once more the golden rule of all teaching, it is not what we teach but how we teach that stamps value upon the lesson and raises instruction to the rank of education." Emily branded girls' education *terra incognita*, but she willingly ventured into that area to offer advice.

She stepped into the fray between the linguists and scientists. The former advocated the centrality of languages, ancient and modern, in curricula because they advanced the power of thought and gave accuracy and clarity of expression. The latter took the position that the same qualities were better advanced by mathematics and science. Emily insisted that school studies had to be directed to valid educational goals—intellectual training for future work, not simply proficiency in knowledge but fitness to pursue advanced study and command of faculties for the general plan of life—in short, effective mental activity and the power to direct that activity aright. With such groundwork she thought that a mind so equipped would pursue with zest several fields of knowledge.

Emily advised teachers to have a distinct purpose of mental discipline which accompanied the acquisition of knowledge by their students. She told them that in every discipline there were basic principles to be secured upon which intellectual growth and maturity depended. She believed that several conditions facilitated the attainment of a mature intellectual life: individual character, home associations, and education. She decided that the course of study in schools possibly had more significance for girls than boys. Unless women achieved an inner motivation, the world offered them little outward motivation and no real reward for pursuit of knowledge; in contrast she argued that the world led men to mental exertion. Emily set forth for female educational schema a task of great magnitude—to define in a specific manner the varied needs of females and then to meet those needs as they pursued traditional life-styles, which were all that were open to them, and in many instances militated against a dynamic intellectual life. "It is infinitely easier to educate for the world than for the home; for future work than for future leisure; for the continued tutelage of a profession or an office, than for simply responsibility to God and our own conscience for the worthy use of faculty, leisure, and influence."[10]

The Shirreffs described the task of education as twofold—to cultivate moral and intellectual habits and to inspire love of knowledge which could be accomplished by a program of study, association, and influence. Effective education, they said, made formation of habits the first object to which attainments of every kind were subordinate.[11] They suggested that subjects of study be selected for the purpose of mental discipline rather than knowledge imparted. They divided areas of study into essential and nonessential. The former had a character of their own, and their primary goal was not to enrich the memory with information but to cultivate habits of mind without which mental exertion would always remain feeble and almost worthless. If any study tended more than another to exercise patience, observation, or judgment, it fell within the category of essentials, "for pupils must still, by whatever means in our power, be taught to observe, to compare, to reason, to work with accuracy and patience and method."[12]

In female education the category of essentials also included what would cultivate interests and excite that desire for knowledge which exercised that same beneficial influence over women's lives that active and professional employment exercised over men's. In cases where the means of education were small that design had to be accomplished by influence and association alone. Since the Shirreffs contended that subjects to be included in a study regimen for women could not be closely defined, they asked teachers to give careful attention to the interests and capacities of pupils, and advantageously utilize them to bring about love of knowledge as well as to awaken that lively concern for truth which led a student to delve below the surface and exert herself mentally. Thus, whatever led to these goals the sisters considered to be essentials of education.

Intellectual education they placed in two classes, culture of the reason and culture of the imagination. The proportion in which the two were combined determined, they said, the direction and distinctive quality of mental maturation. In the education process they desired to balance the two divisions. In *Intellectual Education* Emily asserted that educationalists had given almost their entire attention to culture of reason. The cultivation of linguistics defined in broad terms she declared to be vital to both classifications. Emily Shirreff called culture of the imagination the loftiest power of the human mind and the most ennobling pleasure. She felt that the moral impact of want of imagination was constantly overlooked. "The coldness, the want of tact, the want of sympathy of the unimaginative make them as unlovable as they are uninteresting, and peculiarly unfit them for holding a position of moral influence, such as that which belongs to women."[13] Emily defined imagination as "all that gives a spiritual charm to the daily intercourse of life, all that gives generosity to benevolence, and a soul to love and heroism to self sacrifice... all that makes the human heart flow with rapture." In learning it was associated with poetry, art, music, and the beauties of nature.[14]

For girls Emily Shirreff advocated a broad basic education. She sought to familiarize them with a number of areas of knowledge rather than an in-depth exploration of one or two. She felt that knowledge was not small if it was solid. She desired to open many fields and provide basic principles which females were able to use as a foundation for future intellectual exploration. She decided that the vast majority of women, because of family obligations and social restrictions, were unable to pursue knowledge into profound realms. "Where much depth is out of the question, it appears evident that we cannot be gainers by limiting the surface."[15] In 1858 Emily Shirreff claimed that realistically hardly any gentlewoman gained the independence to follow the bent of her own mind till she had reached an age when her interests and habits were difficult to alter. Furthermore, the few openings for them in the professions and upper echelons of business did not offer hope of high distinction or a reward for severe mental labor for the vast number of females. Unmarried women, she explained, did not have time or money at their disposal; their movements, their companions, and their activities were regulated by others. Marriage offered only minimal increase of freedom and actually often made them more dependent and restricted in their life-style.

Emily Shirreff justified a broad liberal education for a number of reasons. It provided women cultural latitude; because of a narrow pattern of life a particular interest could not often be followed, but if other interests had been cultivated, they could be pursued as substitutes. Secondly, in lives absorbed with domestic affairs of all kinds it was desirable to establish breadth in order to exchange "worthily exciting human thoughts and enterprise and link the person with the hopes and endeavors of those who labored actively in a field of accomplishment and research." Thirdly, the surest bond of friendship between a man and a woman, she said, was mental sympathy, the understanding that grew out of similar interests and happiness which flowed from them, so that an adequate educational foundation for women enriched the male-female cultural relationship. On the latter point Emily was able to speak with feeling; she had such a relationship with Thomas Henry Buckle. "Such friendships, which vulgar minds may deride, and to which vulgar gossip may often give another name, is a truly precious treasure, and in a different manner beneficial to both."[16]

The Shirreffs, who placed the mother in the preeminent position in infant and early education, also gave her centrality to the whole panoply of female education. Emily wrote on the subject. "I have said before that in speaking of education of girls synonymous with mother, at least that the latter must inevitably exercise a degree of influence which makes any other nugatory."[17] She acknowledged that the tuition of the girl could be left to others, but the mother had to give basic motivation and method to the education. In fact in their generation the Shirreffs saw the educational process as a sort of closed and somewhat vicious circle in regard to women. "Till women, therefore, are better prepared for this portion of their maternal office—till they are more often sufficiently educated to feel at least an equal interest in the duties of the schoolroom as in those of the nursery, we can hope only for partial improvement."[18]

The Shirreffs' work in the seventies, in particular Maria Shirreff Grey's use of the Women's Education Union to bring into existence a viable secondary school system throughout the country, had been based on a serious analysis of curricula appropriate for girls of the middle and upper classes. In 1858 Emily had given a clear outline of her ideas on the content of education. She divided female adolescent education into three stages: twelve to fourteen years, fourteen to sixteen years, and lastly, sixteen to eighteen. In the first period her plan of study had three main divisions, science which embraced mathematics, languages which consisted of logic, literature, and composition, and history including geography. Moreover, she wanted the achievement of specific competencies and mastery of certain knowledge areas prior to entrance on the first phase of adolescent education—a basic grasp of the rule of three, fractions, decimals, and by the age of thirteen the first book of Euclid together with a sound understanding of grammar.[19] She advised that the student be introduced to modern languages— French and German—at an early age, so that by twelve years a girl could be fluent in one or both.[20] The study of Latin and Greek or both seemed to Emily to be appropriately undertaken at the age of twelve, and five years of study would prepare a girl for either university examinations and/or advanced work in those languages during her years in a university. She preferred such a pattern to study of the ancient languages at an early age.[21] Emily, however, did not give priority to ancient languages in curricula for women; she described their value to women as being primarily in development of accurate and sophisticated use of English grammar. During the first stage of education for adolescents she proposed that facility in the basics of modern foreign languages previously gained be advanced by study of history and geography and note taking in those languages.

In the students' native language, English, she sponsored exercises in grammar and composition and selections from a variety of prose writers and poets for careful analysis. She believed that German and Italian provided a useful adjunct to a serious exploration of English grammar, and yet she pointed out that the French language probably had more practical value to girls of the era. She sought to have the student express opinions on prose readings and poetry of all sorts. "Young people are seldom sufficiently accustomed to the free expression of their thoughts and difficulties and imaginings. . . . There is often more value in an hour's conversation with young people than in many hours reading."[22] In historical study she advocated extensive use of maps, chronological tables, and other materials supplemented by geography in order to avoid a fragmented approach to learning.[23] Emily rejected any total reliance on memory training in historical study in the first stage of adolescent education. On the other hand she warned about any deep exploration of philosophical or moral dilemmas or issues in history in that stage of adolescent education because the student was immature. By the end of the first two-year period (twelve to fourteen years) she expected that the student would have a basic understanding of ancient history and the national histories of major European countries.

Emily maintained that the core of education was development of the art of reading at a mature level. She insisted that reading assignments should never be imposed upon students as a punishment because such a procedure created negative attitudes about the essential ingredient in the learning process. She called upon teachers and guides of children to treat their charges, who had a wide range of abilities, in an evenhanded manner so that students of limited abilities would not feel inferior or the bright child conceited.[24]

Emily maintained that children should not be isolated on sex lines and so advocated a healthy mingling in the informal educational experiences which she highly valued. In the seventies she spoke on the subject of mixed classes. Because education prepared the student for life, she observed that the more the habits of the early years taught men and women to know one another, the more both the vain prejudices and false glamor born of ignorance would be dispersed. The equal and free companionship of school life, she contended, would direct the outlook of children toward a normal and wholesome adult relationship. She described school experiences of all sorts as preparation for the mature relationships that led to marriage and a happy family life. She judged that young women and men did not have a realistic view of the qualities of the opposite sex. "We may venture to assert that more foolish marriages would be prevented and more corrupting literature be stopped by this reform than by any other that has yet been proposed."[25] Yet Emily Shirreff approached the topic of full coeducation with cautious realism displayed time and time again in her varied writings and activities. She accepted the fact that mixed education had to be worked for "gradually and cautiously" because it struck at time-honored custom as well as prejudice, and it could be accomplished only by the success of individual experiments which would serve to change minds and introduce new attitudes. She decided that any mass movement which resorted to overt pressure to gain mixed education would be counterproductive.

In the second stage of education, from fourteen to sixteen years, Emily withdrew history from students' course plan because they had a rudimentary knowledge of the subject, but their minds at that age had not sufficiently developed the ability to deal with historical works in an interpretive manner which was necessary in a mature study of the subject. Emily gave a preeminent place in the curricula in phase two of adolescent education to grammar and composition and elementary areas of science.[26] If geometry had been started earlier, she included for study the first three books of Euclid; if begun at fourteen, the Euclid material plus algebra carried to quadratic equations in order to give some knowledge of the nature of symbols and the mode of working with them.

Natural history seemed to Emily a desirable basic study for girls in the early teens, in particular zoology because of the diversity of understandings and insights it gave to animal life and physiology. She added geology to the curriculum in the second stage; astronomy she left to the third stage, so that it could benefit from mathematical studies which had been covered and so make possible a serious exploration of the subject.[27] Emily also recommended attention to the history of science, even if it had to be studied in a somewhat superficial manner.

There, especially, we have unfolded to us the value of method, when we see that after men had groped in the dark for generations, or caught now at one, now at another brilliant conjecture, a new light seems poured in when the right method of investigation is discovered, and soon ordinary minds are enabled to reach what before eluded the grasp of genius. These are the great lessons which make the history of science so valuable a contribution to mental discipline; it must be the task of the teacher to enforce them.[28]

Emily insisted that in science education as in all branches of learning the expertise of the teacher took precedence over the materials used. One example of the centrality of the teacher, she said, was the ability to develop interrelationships among the various branches of science, such as the association of laws and facts of astronomy with the principles of mechanics by which some of the major laws in astronomy had been established, together with the history of the earth and its condition influenced by other parts of the solar system, and finally with the various forms of animal life evolved under differing conditions of climate, geographical, and geological foundations and atmospheric conditions.

Grammar became a primary focus in the second stage of adolescent learning in Emily's curriculum because mature usage of language, she believed, was of utmost value to young women. Works of criticism she considered of vital importance to students, but much of their value also depended on the skill of the teacher in utilizing the material. The study of foreign languages, she felt, also provided an enriched dimension at that juncture to the study of the native tongue. Dedicated attention to composition gave the student mastery of both written and spoken English.

To possess the power of language in its full form and delicacy, is perhaps as rare as to possess the finer qualities of thought or imagination; these are given to very few; but all may learn to clothe their thoughts in simple, accurate, well-chosen words, and so to express themselves so as to run no risk of being misunderstood by others, or what is more important still, of leaving an undetected confusion in their own minds, for want of being able to bring clearly out, what they do and what they do not understand. It is very common with young persons to answer to any question testing their knowledge by saying that they understand clearly enough but cannot explain themselves. This may or may not really be the case, but at any rate, it points to a defect which is within reach of cure.[29]

She charged that in England the art of writing and speaking had not been carefully cultivated. "It is strange to say...that so many parents should spare no trouble or expense to make their daughters sing like angels, while they are content to let them talk like fools."[30] Emily judged that the French superiority to the English in conversation was explainable not by depth of material utilized but by habitual attention to linguistic skills.

In students' adolescent years Emily Shirreff believed that the ability to take notes became a crucial process in their education. Of course she advised utilization of the rudiments of that learning technique earlier in students' careers. Because of its paramount place she suggested a pattern to follow: an outline of basic points, another section for views of the author, a third section for the reader's reactions and/or ways to utilize the material. In writing of any sort Emily urged students to avoid excess verbiage and stress analysis and conclusions in their prose compositions.[31]

Miss Shirreff maintained that the essence of secondary education was formation of a mature intellectual regimen. She called it the "conversion of routine into principle and the habit of obedience into the power of self-guidance."[32] The latter she considered to be the ultimate object of all education, and without it the best-disposed human beings were creatures of impulse or outward circumstances. With fervor she urged women to reject the traditional values imposed upon them by society—pliancy and docility—and replace them with decisiveness and vigor.[33] Indeed she concluded that half the follies and lack of influence of womankind could be ascribed to deficiency in these areas. "They want determination, they want energy and clearness to enable them to see a course and pursue it." Education to submission she saw as education to nullity.

Miss Shirreff made a sharp distinction between submission demanded of the student by the intellectual regimen of school and the pernicious sort imposed in the home. The former did not meddle with thought or feeling, and the moral nature was not under subjection. Furthermore, it had a purpose and a time sequence and was not a scheme for life. "In a school the master teaches and commands, but it is public opinion of the young community which sways feeling and principle."[34] Too often she saw in families the domination of parental authority which claimed the heart, will, and conscience of the daughter and had no natural limit; at no age did a daughter have the simple exercise of natural freedom, "and from these nursery trammels, one step places a girl amid the cares and responsibilities of marriage; never having ruled her own life for a day; she undertakes duties involving the happiness of one she loves and the comfort of the many."[35] The free spirit of self-regulation Emily saw as the necessary foundation for vigorous mental activity, independent action, and a lively moral nature. To support her position she quoted Novalis (Frederick von Hardenberg) and J.S. Mill. Since women's social position imposed subjugation on them, it was essential, Emily thought, to cultivate in the educational process during the early mature years the independent mind which was desirable for all human beings.

Miss Shirreff felt that some observers confused feebleness with gentleness; she claimed that in truth gentleness and tenderness were completely compatible with great force of character. She judged that one of the chief difficulties in education was to determine when to relax authority, when to sink the absolute ruler in the guide and the guide in the counselor and friend. Thus the young had to be assisted in forming views and opinions for themselves. The impossibility of keeping young men under restraint, she noted, made parents relax their control over sons but the same conditions did not operate for girls. The parental power of the purse she designated the last resort that effete authority exercised as a tyrannical sway over daughters.[36]

Miss Shirreff wanted young girls taken into partnership in the education process, to plan it, set its goals, and examine its basic philosophical foundation in order to cultivate the independence of mind and spirit which she believed of supreme importance. In addition she urged those who guided girls, whether parents or teachers, to give their charges social freedom, the right to spend money in the fashion desired, select amusements, and undertake the type of service to others which appealed to them. Emily advised young women to create a system of methodical self-regulation that she considered an intrinsic part of a constructive daily life in contrast to one given over to the shifting rule of circumstance. "In the former, although every semblance of regularity be forcibly broken, perhaps for weeks...the moment the cause of disturbance ceases, the accustomed order is spontaneously resumed; progress in a given pursuit has been retarded, but the mind has preserved its equilibrium; nothing has been unsettled in the inner life."[37] She sought a mind receptive to study, possessed of observational and judgmental skills and the ability to draw correct inferences and infused with moral virtues, self-control and a sense of responsibility for self. In truth Miss Shirreff summarized the frame of mind that she and her sister had been able to establish amidst many distractions, domestic burdens, and illnesses that had arisen in their lives.

She asked that amusements be a significant part of the education of young women, including gardening, sports, nature walks, art and music, and reading for pleasure. "I would not have it supposed for an instant that I write in a spirit of ascetic opposition to pleasure and amusement. Far from it, I do not, as I have said before, think the capacity of youth for enjoyment is even sufficiently considered. Let us cherish every joyous impulse—every innocent manifestation of the lighthearted careless spirit."[38] She contended that it was living for pleasure that she criticized, systematic frivolity and laborious idleness that were imposed by social convention and the necessity to make a marriage.

In the educational process Emily Shirreff placed in a central position the search for happiness which she sharply differentiated from pleasure and amusement. She judged that one group in society of her era tended to live for pleasure, and at the other end of the scale another group concentrated on duty. Very little attention, she believed, had been given to serious exploration of what happiness in education meant and how it could be achieved. "Men may perhaps wring theirs from fate, by the strong arm, and the stout heart, and the dauntless will; but women must win theirs in the power of a cheerful, hopeful spirit; knowing they will have more to bear than to do; they must have the art of making means that are thrust upon them minister to their own purposes."[39]

Emily regretted that moralists neglected this area or treated it with half contempt for they thereby neglected an imperative craving of human nature. She described the outreach of human nature for happiness in both lyrical and psychological terms.

When the latter is yet in its young, unbroken strength, it not only seeks for happiness as for any of the indispensable means of existence, but expects it as its birthright. And when its strength has broken down under the burden of life; when, often deceived, we first refuse to listen to Hope, and then grieve that the voice of the charmer haunts our day-dream no more; when we know how vain it were to expect the twilight to bring the brightness noontide failed to pour, or

"From the dregs of life think to receive
What the first sprightly runnings could not give;"

—even in that season of disenchantment, we would rather believe that it is our own individual fate that has been hard, and that we have been singled out to be exiled from our inheritance, than admit the dreary belief that no inheritance of happiness is destined for man. And we only give it up on earth to cling more earnestly to the hopes of heaven.[40]

Possessed of such vitality, Emily asked, how could the drive for happiness be overlooked or ignored in the educational process, and how could it be reasoned away in the name of theology or philosophy? She said that God gave a craving but did not frame the world so as to ensure its gratification. Furthermore, she asserted that education assisted the human spirit in that quest. She felt that cultivation of a cheerful spirit which sought means to gratify a female's intellectual and spiritual nature was paramount, and necessary in its achievement a philosophy of life which artfully and consistently cultivated the feelings and mind rather than focused on material gratification or created artificial wants. She requested that guidelines for students be geared to self-exertion and as far as possible away from temporary circumstances. And one of the key ingredients in that process she characterized as "the unselfish spirit of activity which seeks out means of usefulness." She defined it as a sense of communion with fellow creatures; social *solidarité* had to be impressed upon learners. "They must feel that no human being can venture to believe himself isolated; that consciously or unconsciously, actively or negatively, we still affect and influence those around us, as we are influenced and affected by them."[41] Thus the Shirreff sisters defined happiness as development of constructive human relationships, spiritual resources, opportunities for service, and intellectual enlargement.

Emily Shirreff thought that influence was at the core of the dynamics of education, and she discussed cogently one of its most telling facets: often parents failed to have impact on their children because they did not unveil their innermost feelings and deep convictions to their own offspring.

> They talk to them, perhaps, a good deal, on matters which they think suited to their capacity but they do not talk freely enough before them, so as to let the full influence of their feelings and knowledge, and of their compound of both, the whole tone of thought and opinion, tell upon those young minds thirsting as they are for impressions. Where this is done, and when children are accustomed to express freely their own feelings, and doubts, and difficulties, there is little need for set discources by which the stronger minds are to sway the weaker.[42]

She concluded that the principles and patterns of one's mature lifestyle had to be outlined by the education of adolescence. She explained that some of the most socially damaging follies and vices prevalent in the upper realms of society could be eliminated if the value of time and sense of accountability for its use were earnestly felt and in a practical way shaped conduct.

In the last stage of secondary education for girls, from sixteen to eighteen years, Emily Shirreff made a considerable departure from the previous stage in regard to curriculum content. In the second stage science and mathematics had taken up two-thirds of the students' time and composition and cultivation of literary style the other third. In the last stage she concentrated upon social science, in particular history which had been temporarily laid aside. She directed students' attention to history in order to counteract the tendency at sixteen to form opinions hurriedly and assist the young student to know the nature of sound opinions and the method of forming them. She considered that to produce a disciplined mind required a combination of intellectual and moral qualities, not simply knowledge, sound judgment, and accurate reasoning, but also freedom from prejudice and an earnest desire to know the truth. The latter she viewed as the crown of education. In regard to methodology to be used by the student who sought a fulfilled intellectual life, Emily stressed a sure grasp of the nature and value of evidence, the care necessary in drawing inferences, and degrees of knowledge necessary to form opinions. She warned against attributing moral merit or demerit to opinions.

The person holding or rejecting them may deserve praise or blame, but this will be for the purity or corruption of their motives, for their diligence in seeking, their indolence in neglecting to seek evidence of truth; these are grounds on which to pass a moral judgment, though we rarely have that knowledge of another heart which entitles us to do so; but the opinion itself, a conclusion of the understanding, never can come under that judgment.[43]

She sponsored the study of logic because it was based on the art of strict reasoning. Geometry earlier in the curriculum had communicated reasoning by means of the relations of figures and space.[44] The mature examination of history she directed to defined goals due to the short period which the students could devote to it, specifically methodology, acquaintance with allied subjects which were essential to a mature comprehension of it, and a brief examination of major periods to glean the interpretive areas to which a young woman could return at a later stage in her life for further analysis. Emily valued highly the study of history for women because so many of them at one time or another during their lives engaged in education of some sort within the family circle. Accordingly Emily contended that a grasp of ethical and metaphysical questions which arose as an integral part of any serious study of history had special relevance for women who gave shape to ideals, goals, and evaluations of the young generation in so many ways.

Debarred from major political experience and knowledge of the world, it is, as I have had occasion to notice before, by this yet wider survey of human action that women must study the application of philosophical truths, and from the consideration of the principles which have led on a large scale to happiness or misery, to success or failure, to the discovery of truth or the cherishing of error, that they must learn what are the principles, the aims, the convictions and motives which the educator should nourish or condemn.

She described political economy as a necessary adjunct to the study of history: the subject gave a needed dimension to the social relations of women.[45]

During the last stage of the young women's education Emily judged of extreme importance the exchange of ideas between female students and males, for the latter had experienced a social life which was so different from women and were shaped by forces with which women had no contact. She advised males of a family, especially the father, to display a sustained interest in his daughter's pursuits and amusements and in conversation lead her to express thought and opinion freely, help her give definiteness and rigor to the conceptions in the process of formation, and encourage her to seek and pursue diligently intellectual interests.[46]

The Shirreff plan of study was similar to the program put forth later by the Oxford and Cambridge Joint Board for the final examination in schools which were to be regarded either as a *terminus ad quem* relative to the public school course or a *terminus a quo* relative to the university and served either for a leaving certificate or for matriculation. The board arranged studies in four groups:

    I. (1) Latin, (2) Greek, (3) French and German
    II. (1) Scripture knowledge, (2) English, (3) History
   III. (1) Mathematics (elementary), (2) Mathematics (Additional)
   IV. (1) Natural Philosophy, (2) Heat and Chemistry, (3) Botany, (4) Physical Geography and Elementary Geology

It required candidates to pass acceptably in at least four subjects taken from not less than three different categories.

Emily Shirreff considered that her educational program was appropriate for a girl of average ability. However, she made clear that modifications of all sorts should be made, dictated by the abilities of the student. For those possessed of limited intellects she urged resort to all means to appeal to the imagination, stimulate curiosity, and excite intellectual activity; it little mattered in what direction.

Major periodicals reviewed Emily Shirreff's *Intellectual Education and Its Influence on the Character and Happiness of Women* in which she had set forth her grand design for girls' education. The study received unqualified endorsement from the *Athenaeum* not only for its wise counsel on the education of women but for the element of genial good sense which "pervades it like sunshine." The reviewer said Emily Shirreff treated women as rational beings; she had not ventured into the excesses of equality and emancipation. "She knows that Nature may be trusted to adjust her own balance in such matters."[47] The reviewer concluded that Emily Shirreff aimed to make women more strong and true to lead their own lives and carry out the duties of the state of life where they found themselves. The *Spectator* called the study a good book on an important subject containing valuable thought, the result of experience and meditation but "too elongated."[48] The *Saturday Review* in its assessment said that young women could benefit from reading it, and Miss Shirreff avoided the error of claiming that the educational scheme was universally applicable. However, the reviewer decided that the extensive character of her system was preposterous, both undesirable and impossible of fulfillment. "It carried the rage for over-education to a point which we could not have believed possible."[49] The reviewer considered that Emily's suggested scheme ran counter to Henry Thomas Buckle's advice on over-education.

While Emily was writing *Intellectual Education*, Buckle said that in examining what others had done in her chosen field and comparing it with what she was able to do, she should feel sanguine. "You know that I make it the business of my life to study what pertains to the intellect, and I may therefore venture to believe that on such a point I am a fair judge; and I do honestly and deliberately say that what you can and will do must be valuable—looking at the amount of careful thought and of natural power you have already expended on the subject of education." Buckle read Emily's manuscript of *Intellectual Education* pior to publication. He reported to her the arrangement was good, clear, and symmetrical. "I am sorry I can't find more fault, it is so pleasant to be spiteful—at least I enjoy it."[50] Chapter one was the only section about which he had reservations. Although he felt that the entire work might be too long judged as "a work of art, I have not the slightest doubt of the success of your work."[51]

Maria Grey as well as her sister Emily gave attention to the traditional women's studies. In the early seventies Maria expressed regret that an enlargement of the scope of studies pursued by girls had resulted in no increase of time allotted to them; the wider curriculum often led to superficiality. She complained that in order to counteract fears about inclusion of so-called male studies in curricula for young women, the older studies were often retained, that is, domestic economy, cookery, and needlework. "We need scarcely say that the young lady subjected to this process learns neither how to cook well nor to reason well, and that her science and domestic economy are about on a par and equally likely to break down on a trial." Maria set forth what she thought should and should not be taught in school or during school-age years and what belonged to a higher stage of education and what to preparation for practical life. The Shirreffs determined that the special skills required of women in the household could be adequately acquired outside the regular curriculum by several means, special classes, lectures, reading, and guidance in the home. Notwithstanding that position, Maria recognized the importance of domestic skills, management of the sickroom and nursery, account keeping and basic business knowledge. She believed that ninety-nine out of one hundred girls who married did not have the faintest inkling about them. Maria Grey advocated that acquisition of these skills be carried on *pari passu* with female higher education. She pointed out that time spent at Girton College and other similar establishments amounted to approximately six months per annum, so that girls had sufficient time to master domestic accomplishments. But all in all the Shirreffs maintained that the substantive features of women's role as guide of domestic and familial affairs had to be acquired in large measure in the home and by apprenticeship.

In 1880 T. H. S. Escott, a journalist, presented an appraisal of English life in his era. Earlier in his career he had been an academician. He served as a lecturer in logic at King's College, London, and then became professor of classical literature from 1868 to 1873. Thereafter he moved into an active journalistic career as lead writer for the *Standard* and successor of John Morley as editor of the *Fortnightly Review*. During the last generation of the century in numerous works he commented on the contemporary scene. Escott observed that female education in England among the upper and middle classes had made considerable progress in the previous generation. As proof of his claim he pointed to the existence of a respectable number of women's colleges throughout the country as well as high schools where many subjects were taught, supplemented by a plethora of organizations to promote lectures for women. The Shirreffs had taken an energetic part in the establishment of that system which is discussed elsewhere in this study. However, Escott catalogued defects which existed. He had no doubts that a substantial number of young ladies who participated in the new educational opportunities gradually developed into intellectual and cultivated women, and yet a sizable amount of the education at finishing school was pretentious and so not sound and carried forward under high pressure. He described their curricula as often devoted to narrow textbook material and manuals and minute and sometimes irrelevant details. As a result he charged that women's intellects were imperfectly trained.

They have been instructed, not educated. No attempt to educate them, save in the particular matter of music and dancing, has been made. They have in other words, been crammed with the letter of textbooks; they have not been taught subjects. So long as parents are satisfied with this, so long as the examinations to which these young people periodically submit—and their success in which is cited by the lady principal of the school as conclusive proof of the excellence of her establishment—proceed upon their present method, are mere tests of book learning, and not of general intelligence, such will continue to be the case. The worst of it is there are few counterbalancing advantages to the system of which the modern schoolgirl is too frequently the victim. Although her mind is not being enriched with philosophical views of history, it is not necessarily turned towards the theory and practice of domestic management.[52]

And a few years later, by means of fiction, George Gissing called attention to the vogue of women gaining superficial knowledge but not true education. In *The Year of Jubilee* he dealt with the middle-class family of Arthur Peachey, who lived in the London suburb of Camberwell in a comfortable home cared for by two servants. His household included his wife and her two unmarried sisters. Gissing wrote about the women. "All declared—and believed—that they 'knew' French; Beatrice had 'done' Political Economy; Fanny had 'been through' Inorganic Chemistry and Botany. The truth was, of course, that their minds, characters and propensities had remained absolutely proof against educational influences as had been brought to bear on them."[53] At another point in the novel Gissing made a direct attack on superficial female secondary education. "Miss Lord represented a type; to study her as a sample of the pretentious half-educated class was interesting; this sort of girl was turned out in thousands, from so called High Schools; if they managed to pass some examination or other, their conceit grew boundless."[54]

The Shirreffs in their several major writings in the fifties and in shorter pieces in the following three decades contributed to developing the educational structure referred to by Escott with schools, colleges, and university as places of a character comparable to those offered males. But the Shirreffs also demanded, as detailed in this chapter, that the necessary educational structures foster independence of mind, analytical skills, and sound moral and philosophical concepts upon which humanistic education rested. The sisters were concerned about the process of education and not simply mechanisms of knowledge acquisition.

In 1876 Emily Shirreff reviewed two critiques of British education which gave her the opportunity to enunciate her own schema because the two pieces affirmed a number of her key concepts. Mountstuart Grant Duff presented curriculum suggestions in the *Fortnightly Review* of August 1876. Grant Duff had served in Parliament and had been undersecretary for India in the Gladstone ministry (1868-1874). He was a perceptive observer of affairs, public spirited, and graceful and elegant in society. Emily used Grant Duff's article as a vehicle to discuss general education as a most suitable curriculum for large numbers of boys and girls, "children of ordinary intelligence." "Those who are *hors ligne* by nature will assert their supremacy whatever the method to which they are subjected; but public education should ever be adapted to make the best of average powers to whom the dry technicalities of ordinary school teaching are utterly wearisome."[55] In effect she propounded as a viable course of study for the mass of the population the curricular ideas she had sought for girls for more than twenty-five years, an emphasis on mastery of English composition and literature, modern languages, basic mathematics, science related to the world in which the student lived, with postponement of the study of classical languages until adolescence. But crucial to the success of such a program was the factor emphasized by Grant Duff which Emily had always put in the forefront, that is, educational guidelines that were flexible and oriented to the aptitude and needs of the individual student. "It pleads for wider culture but sacrifices no accuracy of grounding." Such a curriculum built upon the Froebelian pattern of the early years she judged would give to young men or women "sufficient mental discipline to enable them to pursue profitably any subject they may prefer; sufficient general outline to make them at home with really well-informed persons, and sufficient glimpses of the pleasures of knowledge to make its pursuit in one form or another one of the permanent enjoyments of life."[56]

Emily Shirreff also examined the work of Ludwig Wiese, *German Letters on English Education,* written during an educational tour in 1876. Wiese had been a long-time observer of English education. A generation earlier he had visited England and reported on its educational system. His survey was translated into English in 1854 by W. B. Arnold, son of the headmaster of Rugby.[57] At that juncture Wiese headed one of the oldest royal foundation schools in Berlin. Subsequently he became counselor to the minister of public instruction, and in that post superintended the technical administration of all the higher schools in Prussia, the *Gymnasea* and *Realschulen.* Emily Shirreff rejected his position that girls should not have the same quality of education as boys because their natures were different and they did not have the same intellectual capacity as boys. Yet Wiese made complimentary reference to the efforts of the Girls' Public Day School Company to expand education for girls. Emily found relevant in Wiese's essay his basic confirmation of her own indictment of the philosophical and operational deficiencies of

English education. He referred primarily to boys' education; she felt the situation in girls' education was analogous but simply more intensified, specifically, want of a definite order of schools classified according to their purpose, want of fixed classes according to age, short time for work due to considerable emphasis on games, the custom of giving prizes, much attention to examination, and scarcity of good teaching.[58]

Throughout their long careers devoted to improvement of the lives of women, the Shirreffs conceived of education as a flexible and dynamic force designed to get the best work from the faculties of each individual and make the best of her potential in all circumstances. The best they defined as recognition of the paramount objects in education, the training of the reason to form sound judgments, the will to obey the law of familial and civil duty, the imagination to conceive, the heart to love, and the mind to implement in daily life pure and noble ideals which emanated from God.[59]

Doubtless large numbers of females who participated in the new secondary and university education for their sex in Victorian and Edwardian Britain did not find it satisfying due to its selective focus, scholarly orientation, fastidiousness, and emphasis on personal dignity and the power of self-control. But the new system of education provided a viable pattern to females to create their own intelligentsia comparable to the male intellectual establishment in the areas where males had been unchallenged leaders. Members of the new female intelligentsia looked to academia for careers, a subject discussed from a statistical point of view elsewhere in this study.

Born in 1850, Jane Ellen Harrison attended Cheltenham and Newnham College, Cambridge. In her long life of seventy-eight years she achieved the independence of mind, joyousness of spirit, penetrating scholarship, and career success which had been the blessed hope of the Shirreff sisters and other progressive educators for those who followed the scheme for intellectual enlargement which they so forcefully elucidated. Miss Harrison, one of Britain's devoted classicists, brought to her teaching and writing a vivacity and imagination which broadened the horizons of classical scholarship. She moved from lecturing at the British Museum and boys'

schools in the environs of London to Newnham College, her alma
mater, where she spent more than two decades in research and
teaching. Her work brought her into close rapport with male leaders in the field, A. W. Verrall, S. H. Butcher, D. S. MacColl, and
Gilbert Murray. The latter in a posthumous tribute at Cambridge
in 1928 caught the essence of her contributions. He noted that she
sought facts not for facts' sake but in order to reach for new interpretations, in particular those which illumined varied concepts of
beauty.[60] In the *Prolegomena to Greek Religion* (1903) and *Themis:
A Study of the Social Origins of Greek Religion* (1912) she developed knowledge and interpretations of Greek religion in a framework of universal religious themes. In the quest to arrive at valid
generalizations she aroused controversy. "She was always frowned
upon by a fair number of important persons: she was always in
spirit a little against the government, against orthodoxy."[61] And
Jane Harrison never lost her deep desire for spaciousness for her
sex. "She fought all through life for the freedom of the young,
especially of young women, and she was determined not to spoil
that freedom by trying to dictate what use should be made of it."[62]
She wrestled with the task that the Shirreff sisters considered of
high moment for the mature and cultivated intellect—a search for
the meaning of human existence and an exploration of varied facets
of the human spirit. She started with Platonic and Aristotelian
thought but broadened her perspective to the writings of William
James, Vladimir Solove'ev, Emile Durkheim, Henri Bergson (in
particular *L'Evolution créatrice*), and the psychologists Karl Jung
and Sigmund Freud. She was impressed by the latter's *Totemism
and Taboo*.

Jane Harrison found joy and satisfaction as a single woman. The
Shirreffs had as a priority development of formulas for achievement of happiness in that life-style which they said was possible by
a self-sustaining intellectual life of the type Miss Harrison embraced.

By what miracle I escaped marriage I do not know, for all my life long I fell
in love. But, on the whole, I am glad. I do not doubt that I lost much, but I
am quite sure I gained more. Marriage, for a woman at least, hampers the
two things that made life to me glorious—friendship and learning. In man

it was always the friend, not the husband, that I wanted. Family life has never attracted me. At its best it seems to me rather narrow and selfish; at its worst, a private hell. The role of wife and mother is no easy one; with my head full of other things I might have dismally failed. On the other hand, I have a natural gift for community life. It seems to me sane and civilized and economically right.[63]

But certainly the new intelligentsia was not merely a club of single women. Jane Harrison's circle at Newnham when she was a student included women who found fulfillment in marriage such as Mary Paley (Mrs. Alfred Marshall), Margaret Merrifield (Mrs. A. W. Verrall), Ellen Crofts (Mrs. Francis Darwin), and Alice Lloyd (Mrs. Dew Smith).

Despite the emergence of a dynamic female intelligentsia in the years immediately prior to World War I, women of accomplishment found it difficult to move to the highest echelon of power and leadership in academia, the professions, and certainly most clearly in the world of publishing, business, and finance that had been opened to them. But even among those committed to the women's cause, enthusiasm about the new opportunities seemed to overshadow somewhat concern about the very real remaining difficulties. Havelock Ellis was an intimate of Olive Schreiner, a women's rightist well aware of the discrimination suffered by her sex. Of course his research and seminal studies of women's sexuality shocked and scandalized British society.[64] In 1912 he wrote in the introduction to *The Woman Movement* by Ellen Key, "At the present time there are very few vocations and professions in civilized lands, even in so conservative and slowly moving a land as England, which women are not entitled to exercise equality with men."[65]

# 7

## The Women's Education Union and the Girls' Public Day School Company

In 1871 Maria Grey launched the National Union for the Improvement of the Education of Women of All Classes, more commonly known as the Women's Education Union, which in turn spawned the Girls' Public Day School Company and the Teachers' Training and Registration Society. These agencies gave basic shape and spirit to secondary education for girls in Britain in the last generation of the nineteenth century, its seminal stage of development. As detailed in previous chapters, the Shirreffs for a generation prior to the establishment of the union had been deeply committed to the creation of viable educational programs for girls.

At least two events stimulated action; doubtless the most important was the revelations about the abysmal state of female education by the Schools Inquiry Commission. Maria Grey felt that the issue had been brought to the public, and a constituency of concerned citizenry had appeared which could be tapped to remedy the situation. Secondly, Maria Grey's participation as a candidate for a place on the London School Board had introduced her to several influential people who encouraged her to carry forward her ideas. She also found great satisfaction in public service which she had experienced only in a peripheral way.

Mrs. Grey recognized that the reformer who sought success without command of sizable funds or wide public recognition had to depend upon alliances with other people of like mind. Other dedicated reformers certainly had read the situation similarly; however, she faced a difficulty not encountered by those who desired change in several other fields. A pattern had emerged in areas in which legislative or administrative action was the means to rectify evils or deficiencies—the spread of information about conditions to the public by speeches and pamphlets, together with organizational activity to arouse the public about conditions and stimulate it to put pressure upon governmental authorities for action. Maria Grey, on the other hand, had to chart a course which was not so clear-cut—achievement of a valid system of female education by private initiative. "Reformers who depend upon voluntary action alone see no such close to their labours; they need, therefore, far more sustained effort, a far wider circulation of right principles and convictions."[1] A number of associations and dedicated men and women had worked for the cause for decades; they had defined problems and offered suggestions to solve them.

Maria and Emily saw the necessity to bring the scattered flock into one fold. Cooperation was needed simply to get a project outlined. Maria Grey listed the forces that had to be contended with: "vested interests of the most powerful kind—the interest of blind custom, time-honored prejudices, of ignorance calling itself common sense, long-standing associations created by false definitions and question-begging appelatives; our modes of fighting all these enemies must be varied, as manifold as the forces marshaled against us."[2] As pointed out previously, the Society of Arts, moved by several of its devoted members, was used as a forum to present the scheme for an educational union for females. A favorable response in that setting led to a major presentation to a public gathering in June 1871. Maria Grey endeavored to reach out at that stage in her plans to provincial areas. A logical ally was the North of England Council for Promoting the Higher Education of Women. A foremost leader in that organization, Josephine Butler, wife of George Butler, educator of Liverpool, had attracted much attention for her zeal for women's rights but also aroused controversy. In 1869 she had edited *Women's Work and Women's Culture* which had explored the problems of Englishwomen, but by 1871 she had undertaken as her primary task the alleviation of the desperate plight of prostitutes and their legal harassment.[3] Her crusade had aroused much ire.[4]

Women educationalists and genteel elements of society were somewhat loathe to ally closely with Josephine Butler. On learning that Maria Grey desired to speak before the North of England Council, she issued an invitation. Her letter casts light upon her feelings but also on the path chosen by Maria Grey to reach her objectives.

My own private feeling about great names is that they do harm to a good cause—not only that they do us no good, as you have probably expressed on other occasions your dissent from my views. I hope you will excuse me for expressing my own convictions; this thing may seem peculiar and even false to you. If, however, you really can utilize these great names (as Moses fleeced the Egyptians of their finery for a good end), I shall be glad, and pleased to find myself in the wrong.... Many of my educational fellow workers in the North remarked to me that you seem to have been careful all this last year to disavow any connection with us.... Personally I have always said to my friends "consider the bad odour in which I am with all persons who are in *good society*; can you expect Mrs. Grey who is obliged to seek the aid of the upper classes in order to give an impulse to her work in London should run the risk of appearing to be in any way associated with a person at present under a cloud." I say this without bitterness; all great moral battles have had their pioneers who must fall, before others can pass over their bodies to victory.[5]

Once the two women had the opportunity to meet and work together, Maria Grey held Josephine Butler in high regard. In her biographical sketch of her sister Emily she commented that Mrs. Butler was an apostle of a cause bearing even more vitally on the interests of women than education. Further, Maria commented that her friendship with Josephine Butler "I have held to be one of the great honors of my life."[6]

Maria Grey throughout her subsequent career in the several ventures that she undertook made skillful use of "good society" referred to by Josephine Butler. Her warm relations with Princess Louise, which included personal advice by Louise on medication for sleep and exchange of small gifts, and friendship with leaders of the aristocracy and clergy she used to further the cause of education. She relied on influential people to keep her name and cause before public leaders. In 1892 Lady Frederick Cavendish wrote to her, "I must just send a line to tell you that I got Mr. Gladstone at a quiet moment this morning and told him of your warm regard for him and how he had your enthusiastic good wishes now, on your sick bed as throughout your life. He was much touched and said 'It is very good of her—God be with her.' "[7] Some of the personal-professional contacts gave the sisters the opportunity to shape views of officials who shaped public policy such as Sir Charles Reed, chairman of the School Board of London, Anthony Mundella, and Henry Bruce, Lord Aberdare.

At the meeting of the North of England Council for Promoting the Higher Education of Women, Maria met a number of men and women concerned about female education who became allies including Dorothea Beale of Cheltenham Ladies College, Professors Sheldon Amos and Henry Sidgwick (the latter helped to found Newnham Hall), Professor James Stuart, and Fanny Metcalfe, headmistress of a boarding school at Hendon, one of the few girls' schools commended by the Assistant Schools Inquiry Commissioners. In the autumn of the same year, 1871, Maria presented a paper on the topic of a women's education union at the annual meeting of the Social Science Congress at Leeds. Lord Frederick Cavendish served as president of the education section that year and endorsed her project.

The Women's Education Union was officially inaugurated at the Royal Society of Arts on November 17, 1871, with Lord Lyttleton in the chair. Maria Grey was elected first chairman but relinquished that post to become the honorary organizing secretary. Emily also became one of the honorary secretaries. The union created a coalition of the sectors of society which for generations had brought success to various reform and public-service-oriented organizations. Queen Victoria's daughter Louise, marchioness of Lorne, accepted the presidency and took a fairly active role in its activities. Vice-presidents included prominent members of the nobility, bishops of the established church, educators, politicians, and public-spirited citizens, the countess of Antrim, the earl and countess of Dufferin, earl and countess of Lichfield, Lord Lyttleton, Lord and Lady Napier and Ettrich, Lord Henry Lennox, Lord Lawrence, the archbishop of Dublin, the bishops of London, Exeter, and Manchester, Sir Alexander Grant, principal of the University of Edinburgh, the provost of Trinity College, Dublin, H. Austin Bruce, MP, J. Stansfeld, MP, and Sir J. Kay Shuttleworth. The central committee of the union, which exercised direct control, had as chairman Joseph Payne of the College of Preceptors, Lady Stanley, J. Kay Shuttleworth, the Reverend Canon Barry, principal of King's College, Professor W. Hughes, King's College, Mrs. Baden-Powell, George C. T. Bartley, James Bryce, Mrs. Albert Dicey, Leslie Stephen, Mrs. Henry Kingsley, Mrs. Charles Malet, Mrs. William Grey, Miss Mary Gurney, and Miss Emily Shirreff. In addition the union gained representation on the central committee from some of the major educational agencies in the nation; Frances Mary Buss represented the London Schoolmistresses Association; the Reverend Dr. Heron represented the Scholastic Registration Association, Edwin Pears, the Social Science Association, and E. C. Tuffnell, the Society of Arts.

The union set forth eight different areas to which it direced efforts. Doubtless its key focus was to promote for the benefit of all classes the establishment of academically sound, low-fee day schools above the elementary level, with boardinghouses in connection with them when necessary for pupils from a distance. The union supported day schools for three reasons: first, a conviction that the best type of education was a combination of home influence and class teaching, secondly, that this type of school kept expenses reasonable and so accessible to large numbers, and thirdly, it encouraged a greater mix of social classes. As a prime object the union sought to raise the status of female teachers by encouraging women to make teaching a profession and qualify themselves for it by a sound and liberal education and thorough training in the art of teaching. It wanted to supplement training colleges by attachment where possible of a class of student teachers to every large school and to secure the efficiency of student teachers by examinations by a recognized authority and subsequent registration. Two key points in this goal were improving the efficiency of teachers and raising their social condition, and to a certain degree the two were indissolubly linked.[8] Emily Shirreff noted that the meager academic attainments of teachers and their low standing in society were reciprocally cause and effect. In fact the union insisted that teaching skill was an art or science or both which had to be acquired by study. Both Maria Grey and Emily Shirreff had developed that thesis in their various writings, and Joseph Payne of the College of Preceptors agreed in *The Importance of the Training of the Teacher* (1872). Emily observed that children of the working classes had been secured an acceptable level of elementary education by government assistance and indeed regulation. In contrast the daughters of the more materially comfortable classes stumbled along wretchedly prepared for adulthood; anyone who simply had the inclination, which was often based solely upon economic need, could teach their daughters. Teaching was the only respectable occupation open to genteel young women.

Women teachers labored under special disabilities which Emily Shirreff detailed in comments about the mission of the union. Practically all the most prestigious teaching posts in institutions attended by girls were held by men, so that women were relegated to the lowest sectors of the one profession open to them. The union endeavored to improve the quality of instruction by females by enlightening public opinion, especially in provincial areas where teachers had less anonymity than in the capital. It asked mothers to refuse to hire governesses or send their daughters to schoolmistresses who could not produce proof of capacity and merit. The total lack of teacher training facilities greatly alarmed the directors of the union. They therefore looked sympathetically on the unofficial teacher training facilities at the reputable schools for girls, the North London Collegiate School and Cheltenham Ladies College, as an immediate remedy to a deplorable condition. Moreover, teacher training projects became an essential activity of the schools formed under the auspices of the Girls' Public Day School Company. Maria Grey in 1876 told Frances Mary Buss that each school should have a class of student teachers. "I think it is the part which has been most universally approved of." She noted that she never dreamed of putting student teachers in full control of a class for any lengthy period.[9]

To meet another temporary but pressing educational need of a different nature, the union offered to supplement "the existent system of itinerant lecturers on special subjects, for all places not of sufficient size to maintain a permanent staff of efficient teachers." It regretted that in small towns it was more difficult to attract competent lecturers for women's classes due to lack of financial support. The union wanted to serve as a coordinating agency which could provide effective lecturers for several towns that wanted to pool their resources and agree upon common lecture topics.

Several objectives of the union related to an extension of programs already in operation, and thereby the union became an organized pressure group. It promised to seek an increase in the number of women and girls who participated in the University Local Examinations, encourage the opening of new centers, and diminish the cost of attending them. The union hoped to prevail upon grammar schools to form classes for girls and utilize their regular teaching staffs for any newly established girls' division. The latter suggestion fell on deaf ears. At the same time the union pursued another path to secure resources for expansion of secondary education for girls but achieved limited success. It sought "to restore" to the use of girls' endownments originally intended for their use and secure a fair share for them of other endowments applied to education.

The eighth and ninth guidelines of the union related to education beyond the regular school years, specifically university and adult education. It endorsed all means of education beyond the ordinary school pattern, adult classes as well as libraries where wanted, and enlargement of instruction by correspondence instituted at Cambridge and elsewhere. It commended the Society for Encouraging Home Studies and special classes for women with diverse educational backgrounds and needs in all parts of the country. Indeed the union promised to initiate classes for women in selected suburban areas of London which were far from adult centers and institutions which provided courses. It offered to guide girls by correspondence in selection of books and areas of knowledge to master which would be needed for the London University and Cambridge University examinations for women.

At the same time, the Education Union advocated for female students who pursued formal higher education a vigorous pattern analogous to that offered to males. Emily Shirreff presented the union's position on the latter issue.

It may be very generally thought that our University curriculum is not the best for young women to follow, that other branches of knowledge might be pursued with better effect; but we need system even more than knowledge. We need to get rid of the dilettante character of female education, and to be able to try it by acknowledged tests. The objection against the curriculum will yearly lessen, as the curriculum itself is extended, and public opinion lifts other subjects to a nearer equality of favour with classics and mathematics; but if this were never to happen, the education would still be of the utmost value to women, in giving method and an authoritative aim which for these years at least must govern studies.[10]

She decided that such a program would result in applying a "fancy standard" to women, and thereafter it would be impossible to subject women to unequal examinations. She felt that thorny social questions would receive more thoughtful consideration and more imaginative solutions would be framed if women gained from education the knowledge to take part in the affairs of the day. The union admitted that its contribution to university-level education had to be limited—to work to eliminate prejudice against higher education for women and offer as a token of the high value it placed on that sector of education a few scholarships to the several new, reputable women's educational institutions. The union gave public commendation to Girton College, one of the new higher education facilities for women in which the Shirreffs had a special interest.

The union made a commitment to education for the mature working woman. It stated that the meager education available to that sector of the female population had to be supplemented by lectures and classes as well as opportunities for cultural pleasure. It chose the Working Men's and Women's College in London as a model. The union accepted as a responsiblity a campaign to stimulate the government, local authorities, and private agencies to broaden opportunities for women to enroll in technical education courses, such as those offered by the Science and Art Department and Queen's Institute, Dublin.

Lastly the union wanted to enlighten the general population on the value of education, "to create a sounder public opinion with regard to education itself, and the national importance of the education of women by means of meetings, of lectures, and of the press, and thus to remove the great hinderance to its improvement—the indifference with which it is regarded by parents or by the public." The union made clear that a basic reason for the failure to establish a thoroughgoing scheme of education for females was prejudice and apathy as well as the fact that large numbers of people saw no monetary reward to women for their education. Leaders of the union wanted their organization to define in a comprehensive manner the multitudinous needs of females in the field of education, open opportunities for them on as many fronts as possible to assist those in need, and at the same time encourage others to participate in the endeavor and frame their own programs. They wanted the union to carry forward its mission until a new generation could assume leadership in Britain and on the foundations which the union helped to set down revise and expand the goals of women. "When some sign shall appear that public opinion is moving in that direction, then, and not till then, will the National Union feel that its work is safe; and trust that new habits fostering new principles, the path will be cleared for another generation to press forward unfettered in the career of progress."[11]

The several missions of the union which have been sketched can be divided into major and minor ones. In the latter category was the work of several committees which gathered information and gave aid to individuals in the education field. The Teacher Education Loan Committee from 1873 to 1877 provided financial aid to ten students. The union awarded each year during the seventies approximately five scholarships of 25 pounds each year; the recipients studied at Newnham Hall, Girton College, the Kindergarten Training College at Luneburg, Alexandra College, Dublin, and the Ladies Collegiate School, Belfast. In late 1875 the union established a teachers' library; it purchased in addition to educational works valuable to teachers volumes recommended by the Syndicate of the Cambridge Higher Local Examinations.

The statistical committee gathered educational information of various sorts which could be valuable to the union in its various activities. By the end of 1874 it made contact with educational institutions and associations in all parts of the country, in that year ninety-four private schools and organizations in such places as Birmingham, Bradford, Bristol, Clifton, Darlington, Dublin, Edinburgh, Hastings, Huddersfield, Ipswich, Leeds, Norwich, Plymouth, Rugby, Wakefield, and York.

The lecture program of the union began modestly in 1873-1874. Miss Macomish, recommended by Huxley, gave a series of lectures in the field of physiology. In 1875, in addition to the lectures of Miss Macomish, Mrs. W. M. Williams offered lectures in social science and Miss Shore on constitutional history. In that same year the union sponsored lectures concerning the teaching of several subjects, the English language, foreign languages, physical geography, geometry, and the Galin-Paris-Cherk method of teaching music. In 1877 the union held evening lectures that dealt with educational materials useful to teachers in various regions of greater London, at schools at Woodlands, Clapham, Warrington Lodge, South West London College, Putney Hill, high schools at Chelsea, Notting Hill, and Hackney and at the Home and Colonial Training College.

At its establishment the union formed a standing committee to watch over the interests of girls in the distribution of endowments and keep members informed of conditions in that field. Yearly the committee told the public of the feeble response of the Endowed Schools Department of the Charity Commission to the needs of girls in education. The annual report usually was introduced by the statement, "very little has been done in the way of establishing or endowing girls' schools by the Charity Commission during the year under review."

The London *Times* criticized the union for its vigorous efforts to gain for girls endowments reserved for boys; indeed it characterized the efforts of the union as "coveting thy neighbor's goods." Maria Grey replied to that charge in the columns of the newspaper. She pointed out that the union did not ask for equality of grants for women, simply rectification of a gross injustice; the census showed that the proportion of women who supported themselves by professional work was to men in the professions as one to seven, but their share of educational endowments was one to ninety-two.

Maria Grey faced many frustrations in the campaign to get women an enlarged share of endowments. In June 1876 a large delegation of prominent public leaders, including Lord Aberdare, James Stansfeld, Lady Stanley, Maria Grey, Emily Shirreff, and

Frances Mary Buss, met with the Charity Commission. The commission had abandoned the policy of the Endowed Schools Commission to allow women on the governing bodies of endowments of which all or any part was intended for girls and indeed in certain cases made it obligatory that a certain number of the governors should be women. The delegation rejected the compromise offered by the commission—a ladies' committee attached to schools. Maria Grey said that such committees had only the power to interfere but not the power to amend or initiate. The commissioners refused to set down a binding principle but promised that they would assign women an influential place in the management of all schools to be established for girls.

At the dissolution of the union Maria Grey decided that the situation in regard to endowments for girls had improved. She believed that the impact of public opinion and the activity of the friends of women's education within the Charity Commission had brought about a more farsighted attitude toward female education. She commended the outlook of Secretary Douglas Richmond. By 1882 fifty-three educational schemes had been approved for applying a part or all of local endowments to secondary schools for girls. In addition, scholarships and exhibitions for girls had been founded where there were no local means to launch a school.

Doubtless the major work initiated by the union was the Girls' Public Day School Company, Ltd. Maria Grey came to the conclusion, based on her fund-raising efforts for the North London Collegiate School and other educational programs, that no scheme to provide new schools for girls could depend for its success on endowments or voluntary subscriptions. She decided that new schools had to be launched as commercial ventures which paid interest on the capital raised. Secondly, she adamantly maintained that any overall scheme had to be flexible and large enough to meet the wants of the entire country. The Girls' Public Day School Company (G.P.D.S.C.) came into existence at a large public meeting in Albert Hall in June 1872. Lord Lyttleton presided, and Maria Grey and the bishop of Manchester gave details of the project. The platform guests included W. Cowper Temple, Joseph Payne, J. Fitch (assistant endowed school commissioner), several leading educators, the Reverend Canon Barry (principal of King's College),

E. A. Abbott (headmaster of the City of London School), the Reverend Dr. Rigg (principal of the Wesleyan Training College), and the American educator, Julia Ward Howe.

The model offered by the day school company was a school to be financially sustained by a private company which sold shares at the rate of 5 pounds each, the capital raised applied to the rental, purchase, or erection and furnishing of a school with a percentage kept as a reserve fund. Any profit from students' tuition would be applied to payment of a dividend. Applications of the children of shareholders would be given preference, providing the girls met the entrance requirements. The suggested fee scale varied from 2 pounds 2 shillings per term in the preparatory department to 8 pounds 8 shillings per term in the senior department. The company proposed large schools with three departments, preparatory, junior and senior. The powers granted the headmistress were analogous to those of the headmaster of a public school. The company pledged that member schools would insist upon trained teachers of ability insured by a regular system of inspection by qualified examiners.

The company set forth as a valid goal of the schools the preparation of pupils for the Oxford and Cambridge Local and other university examinations and those of the College of Preceptors. The proferred curriculum included reading, writing, arithmetic, bookkeeping, English grammar and literature, history, geography, French, German, logic, elements of science with emphasis on physiology related to health, and social and domestic economy. Special provision was suggested for separate denominational religious instruction for students who desired it. The company proposed a class of student teachers attached to the schools with special instruction for them in the theory and practice of teaching. Instrumental music, solo singing, and dancing it designated as extra subjects which required additional fees. The company described the curriculum, the faculty, and the methodology which it advocated as a way to remedy the evils of existing girls' education so tellingly outlined by the Schools Inquiry Commission, specifically "want of thoroughness and foundation; want of system, slovenliness and showy superficiality; inattention to rudiments; and these not taught intelligently or in any scientific manner." The company saw the function of its schools to train pupils for the practical business and duties of life.[12]

The union turned to a commercial venture to spread women's education not because it rejected endowments on principle or pride. Emily Shirreff said it was unrealistic to struggle for resources which had been largely allocated. "Like Schiller's poet, they bring their claim when all rich and more gifts have been divided long ago among the more ambitious or the more covetous sons of earth."[13] Yet the needs of women were great. It was estimated that more than a quarter of a million girls were without adequate education beyond the elementary level. The company defended the extensive curriculum it sponsored as endeavoring to meet the wants of various ages and conditions. It expected that not all students would go through the entire course of study in the curriculum, but it selected its basic subjects with much care in order to give sound mental training. The company rejected technical instruction and called for humanistic learning which gave habits of accurate observation, clear reasoning, and patient, resolute work under difficulties. "The school educates, the technical school instructs; the task of the latter is easy in proportion as the work of the former has been complete." The company insisted that schools formed under its auspices adhere to a number of principles, including firstly, a public character which admitted no class or denominational distinctions. It sponsored religious but nonsectarian teaching. Secondly, the union and the Girls' School Company, its progeny, demanded that the quality of education provided should equal that at the best boys' schools.[14]

Influential sectors of the press which represented diverse political constituencies greeted with real enthusiasm the foundation of the union and the Girls' Public Day School Company. The *Times* observed that enthusiasts for female education had long been active, but they had lacked an organization which the paper felt the union could provide. "Such an association as the National Union will in a few years, do more to obtain women a fair and full hearing before the world than could result from a century of the random agitation of philosophic whims." The paper rejoiced in the fact that adequate female education could be obtained without heavy emphasis on philosophical foundations and explorations of theories because education was more a matter of prose than poetry and more fact than fancy. All in all it judged that the union was an important association which put forth clear programs and stood as a responsible body. The *Times* pointed out that for the first time in English society the framework of a complete system for girls had been established, public girls' schools, the university examinations for girls and women, and women's colleges.

The *Spectator* gave unqualified support to the Girls' Public Day School Company and used the occasion of its launching to attack the plethora of ladies' seminaries scattered throughout London and the provinces which enrolled from fifteen to thirty female students and used a domestic dwelling as a schoolhouse. The periodical charged that they were often poorly ventilated and lighted and possessed meager equipment. But the most serious indictment centered on the poor education given, namely, the low caliber of instruction and severe curricular limitations. It pointed out that girls of all ages and abilities in such institutions were usually guided by one or two poorly trained teachers. "No one who has not examined them for himself can form any conception of the listlessness, the waste of time, and the mental stagnation which characterise the ordinary ladies' seminary." The journal, however, did not condemn instructors in such schools for idleness or indifference.

The *Spectator* favored large public schools for girls because they had proven successful in Germany, the United States of America, and Scotland specifically the upper Girls' School of the Merchant Company in Edinburgh. The periodical urged the Girls' Public Day School Company to undertake as its first task the elimination of public prejudice against large public schools for girls. The weekly listed the benefits of large schools—adequate facilities and equipment, qualified teachers, fair distribution of work among faculty members, broad and suitable curricula, and lastly, control of the institutions by a public and responsible body which carefully supervised the enterprise, hired and fired teachers, instituted examinations, and brought about change when necessary. "It is hardly too much to say that this project undertaken by the National Union, though not claiming the dignity of great political movement, has in it the seeds of great social consequences and that if it succeeds, it will confer unspeakable advantages on the entire community."[15]

The strategy of the Shirreffs not to become deeply involved in the controversy about intellectual equality of male and female was shown in the operation of the union. A number of its major male supporters, upon whom some of the success of the venture depended because they gave it respectability, publicity, and financial support, expressed in unmistakable terms their belief in male superiority. At the June 1873 meeting of the union at Willis's Rooms the message came loud and clear. The marquis of Lorne, who presided, commended the growth of the Girls' School Company during the first year of its existence. Sir Stafford Northcote, who in February 1874 became chancellor of the exchequer in the Disraeli ministry, proposed the following resolution—"That this meeting, recognizing the great deficiency of good schools at a moderate cost, approves of the scheme of the Girls' Public Day School Company and recommends it to the support of the public." In his subsequent address Northcote said that women's nature readily lent itself to education. In some areas he maintained that they had an advantage over the opposite sex in their greater quickness of observation and greater grace of application to certain classes of studies in which the latter quality was paramount. At the same time in other branches of study, he stated that they were inferior in power and ability to men, and it was useless to point to a few who were the exceptional cases. "Women, in general, it must be admitted are not equal in power of reasoning and severe study to men." F. G. Talbot, MP, seconded the resolution and presented a few ideas on the topic. He observed that no one in the late nineteenth century denied that women possessed a large share of intelligence, though it was an undeniable fact that they were not qualified by nature to compete with men in all branches of human intelligence. Further, Talbot wished to make clear that he did not sponsor a new female educational system because he believed that in future it would produce great female poets, painters, writers, and politicians who would be equal to men.[16]

Maria Grey in the early seventies as organizing secretary traveled to all parts of the country to speak to local affiliates of the union and at special meetings which launched day schools. In January 1872 the union was introduced to Ireland. Miss Tod invited Mrs. Grey to Belfast, and Mrs. Jellicoe, lady superior of Alexandra

College, asked her to come to Dublin. On the trip to Ireland she visited Jane, countess of Antrim, a kinswoman, at Glenarm Castle in order to attend the celebration of the coming of age of her son, the future earl of Antrim and met there Lord and Lady Dufferin. She induced Lord Dufferin to chair the Belfast meeting. The public meeting was held on August 25 under the auspices of the Women's Education Union and the Ladies Belfast Institute in the lecture hall of the Ladies Collegiate School. Those in attendance included Sir Thomas McClure, mayor of Belfast, four members of Parliament, a host of academicians, and clergy. Mrs. Grey's address set forth a key principle of the Union. "I must mention that the cardinal principle of our schools—that they should be open to all without distinction of class or creed—has worked thoroughly well." A Belfast branch of the union had been thus successfully launched. At Dublin she carried forward a similar pattern; she conferred with several people of importance to the women's education movement: Miss Heerwart, headmistress of a model kindergarten who later became affiliated with Stockwell College, South London, Archbishop Trench, and Dr. Lloyd, provost of Trinity College. The latter two gentlemen became vice-presidents of the union. The exertions in Ireland so exhausted Mrs. Grey that she took to her bed on return to London.[17]

In September 1873 Maria Grey and Emily Shirreff launched a branch of the union in Norwich while they attended the Social Science Congress there. In February 1875 Dr. Bradley of Oxford, later dean of Westminster, invited Maria to be his guest at University College and represent the G.P.D.S.C. at the meeting to launch a girls' high school at Oxford. The mayor chaired a meeting there, and a corps of clerical and academic luminaries attended including Mark Pattison, rector of Lincoln, Dr. Acland, Professor Max Muller, the Reverend G. W. Kitchen, later dean of Durham, Professor Bonamy Price, and Professor Harry Smith. Citizens quickly supported the proposal for the school and took up the requisite shares so that a school opened with thirty-three students in the following November. In 1875 Maria also spoke to a Birmingham educational gathering on "Religious Teaching in Undenominational Schools." In the latter half of the year she visited girls' high schools at Nottingham and Norwich as well as Girton College and the newly opened high school at Oxford. In the winter of 1876-1877 the Shirreffs were abroad, but in 1877 Maria traveled to Sheffield to a meeting at Cutlers Hall and gave an address on girls' high schools to aid the project to launch a girls' school by a limited liability company there.

In the mid-seventies the Shirreffs kept abreast of continental developments in their fields of educational interest. They visited training institutes for teachers in Germany at Karlsruhe and conferred with the grand duchess of Baden at Darmstadt. During the time they spent in Britain the sisters attended the innumerable meetings of the union, the G.P.D.S.C., the Froebel Society, the Charity Organisation Society, and the Friends of the Medical School for Women.

Within two years of its foundation the union had as affiliates Ladies Educational Associations in Plymouth, Hampshire, Birmingham, Falmouth, Guernsey, Belfast, Windsor and Eton, Bristol and Clifton, East London, North London, West London, Wakefield, and Cheltenham. In addition the Cambridge Classes for Women, the Ladies Council of the Yorkshire Board of Education, the Norwich Committee, the Rugby Council for Promoting the Education of Women, Huddersfield Branch Committee, Committee of York, and the Governesses' Association, Dublin, became allied organizations. In greater London, the union had a number of branches, at Clapham, Ealing, and St. John's Wood.

The first school of the Girls' Public Day School Company opened in January 1873 at Durham House, Norland Square, Chelsea, with twenty pupils in attendance. Miss Mary Porter, a well-known educator, became its headmistress; she had been recommended for a similar post, headship of the first endowed school for girls at Keighley, by the Endowed Schools Inquiry Commissioners. Early in 1873 the G.P.D.S.C. began an effort to establish a second girls' school in the greater London area at Notting Hill. A prime piece of property, suited for a school, came on the market, and the financial assistance of Emily Shirreff made possible the purchase of a lease and therefore the opening of a school there in October 1873. Miss Harriet Jones became headmistress with about twenty students.

In the autumn of 1874 the third school of the company opened at Croydon under the headship of Miss Nelligen. It was designated the first provincial school which adhered to the principles laid down by the company; the area had proven in a *bona fide* way the widespread desire for a school there by formation of a local committee which took a percentage of the shares sufficient to cover the initial cost of the venture. The launching of the schools were cause for local celebrations. On July 12, 1879, the archbishop of Canterbury laid the memorial stone of Croydon High School at the site on Wellesley Road almost midway between the East and West Croydon Railway Stations. A religious ceremony followed the public meeting in the Whitgift School. Lord Reah and Lord Cavendish attended the gathering. The archbishop gave the G.P.D.S.C. high praise. However, he said that it was somewhat discreditable to a great country that no determined effort to provide females with a thorough education had been undertaken except by a private company. But he maintained that the success of the company in performing such an important task deserved the deep gratitude of the community. He deprecated the vogue of fearing strong-minded women; he said the nation had more to fear from weak-minded ones. Although Maria Grey was absent due to illness, several speakers praised her farsightedness in launching the company and her deep commitment to its concepts.[18]

By 1880 schools under the auspices of the Girls' Public Day School Company, in addition to those already discussed, operated at Clapham, Hackney, Bath, Brighton, Norwich, Nottingham, Oxford, St. John's Wood, Ipswich, Sheffield, Gateshead, and Highbury and Islington. Between 1870 and 1880 schools were established on the same principles as those enunciated by the company in a number of regions; they were independent of the company but had close and friendly ties with the leaders of the union. The Manchester Association for Promoting the Education of Women established a girls' high school; the Devon and Cornwall Girls' School Company had a school at Plymouth; the Hastings and St. Leonard Collegiate School opened in January 1874; and the Southampton Girls' College Company started one just a year later.

The growth of the Girls' Public Day School Company was impressive during the seventies. In 1873 it had two schools with a combined enrollment of 85, in 1874 it had five schools with 314 students, in 1875 nine schools with 1,000 pupils, in 1876 twelve schools with 1,600; in 1877 the number of schools remained stationary but enrollment increased to 1,966, and in 1879, seventeen schools had 2,804 students.

In April 1883 at the formation of the Boys' Public Day School Company the *Spectator* assessed the work of the G.P.D.S.C. which at that juncture had existed for more than a decade. The periodical called the G.P.D.S.C. a major success.[19] At its foundation it had a modest goal of 12,000 pounds capital which it struggled for some time to gain. In 1883 it had 100,000 pounds in capital, and on the twenty-six schools founded, it paid shareholders an annual dividend of 5 percent. Most of the schools were self-supporting; the few that were not were sustained by the profits of the others. The G.P.D.S.C. continued after the dissolution of its parent, the union, in 1883. At the time of Maria Grey's death in the opening decade of the twentieth century the company was converted into a trust, and at that juncture it had thirty-three schools with approximately seven thousand students.[20]

The success of the G.P.D.S.C. stimulated an imitator in 1883. The established church with considerable fanfare in July 1883 launched the Church School Company. Within six months it had subscribed capital of 35,865 pounds. It opened its first high school for girls in Surbiton, and others followed at Sunderland and Durham. Dorothea Beale and Helen Gladstone served on the guiding council of the organization. By 1890 the Church School Company had twenty-four schools with an enrollment of 1,834 students and subscribed capital of 45,000 pounds.

The Girls' Public Day School Company had as its president until 1881 the earl of Arlie, the son-in-law of Lady Stanley. He was succeeded by the dear friend of the Shirreffs, Lord Aberdare, who supported them in all their ventures. The council of the company, on which both sisters sat, kept power firmly in its hands despite some suggestions from shareholders that they should have a greater voice in conduct of affairs. A few local committees called for representation on the council. Both sisters served on the education committee of the council, Maria until 1890 and Emily into the 1890s.[21]

During the eighties several matters concerning company policy came to public notice. Maria Grey took part in one of them. In December 1888 an anonymous letter appeared in the *Pall Mall*

*Gazette* which raised the issue of teachers' salaries; it claimed that the company adopted an inadequate salary schedule. Maria answered the charge in the columns of the same paper. She said that the salaries were competitive with the national average. She noted that company schools paid inexperienced teachers 70 to 90 pounds and senior assistants 135 to 200 pounds, and the schools had scores of applicants for each vacant post.[22] Maria wished that the compensation could have been greater, but the restricted financial resources of the company schools made higher pay impossible at that time.

The company schools developed solid but diversified curricula which included the classics but emphasized the wide range of subjects which educational innovators had advocated: a variety of sciences, literature, foreign languages, art, and theater. The schools gained a reputation for academic excellence.[23] Indeed some criticism arose that their academic demands on their students were too heavy. The impact of rigorous academic life on the health of young women, which was a much-discussed matter throughout the century, came before the council of the company in the form of a memorial. In 1890 the company published excerpts from the Oxford and Cambridge Schools Examination Report of that year which commended in an almost unreserved way the academic performance of its students. In botany examiners called attention to the "general excellence" of the work and made a similar assessment of mathematical examinations. "I feel bound to say that the excellence of the work is of a very high order." But doubtless the examiner's evaluation of what the school offered to students in the field of English literature was the most fulsome. "The results have only confirmed the Examiner in the high opinion which he formed two years ago of the general excellence of the Literature works of the schools. It is still distinctly Literature work and not merely linguistics; it is even more intelligent and quite as full of genuine appreciation as it was in 1887. They have proved what a short time ago seemed doubtful to many, that English literature can be taught; and so be taught as to afford a generous and most valuable education."[24]

In the quest to demonstrate the equality of the sexes the company schools prepared girls for the same school examinations and university courses as young men were pursuing. Accordingly, their curricula in major ways mirrored that adopted by progressive boys' educational establishments. However, the new girls' schools did not simply imitate; they did not become exclusively scientific or classical. Moreover, company schools gave considerable attention to art, music, and modern literature. The company schools pioneered the concept of day institutions; they brought school and home into a closer relationship than had been possible in previous generations and encouraged a tone of camaraderie between teacher and students and receptivity on the part of the faculty to educational innovation. Schoolmistresses were encouraged to seek new approaches to subject matter in order to make it appealing and relevant and break through the crust of convention and make contact with the humane and aesthetic interests of students. The schools in organization and educational methodology were somewhat experimental. Although discipline was strict, it was often secured by respect established between faculty and student body and acceptance by the latter of the validity of institutional standards. Teacher training programs found warm advocates in company schools, and they oriented the institutions to concern for effective classroom presentation. The schools recognized the needs of the average students and the desirability, if not necessity, to create a commodious and attractive learning environment.

The company schools made physical education and hygiene an integral part of their programs. Dr. Mathias Roth, who won acceptance from the Froebel Society and warm support from the Shirreff sisters, worked energetically to make physical education a reputable part of the regimen of students in company schools. He advocated that they become knowledgeable about the natural growth and development of the human body by means of proper food, clothing, and physical environment together with exercises of the free system of Pehr Henrik Ling (1776-1839), Swedish educator who had headed the Gymnastic Central Institute, Stockholm.

An examination of the outlook and spirit of Mrs. Woodhouse, headmistress of Sheffield High School (1878-1898) and Clapham High School (1898-1912) provides more light on the previously mentioned strengths of company schools in their formative years. She was much interested in teacher training patterns integrated with the life of the high schools that she headed in order to create a faculty responsive to the needs of the student body. Moreover, she gave much attention to the type of curricula appropriate for the average student who formed the majority in high schools. To that end she evolved alternative curricula open to girls at the age of sixteen after they had mastered basic material in mathematics, science, or the classics; they proceeded to courses in history, English literature, art, and music. "I would plead too...for more lectures on subjects of living and dominating interest." Yet Mrs. Woodhouse insisted upon a serious and deep approach to learning. "We require more intensiveness in the pursuit of studies once undertaken."[25] She honored physical activity for her students and carefully monitored their physical well-being by regular medical check-ups.

In the opening decade of the century Mrs. Woodhouse in addresses to the Association of Headmistresses, which she led, presented the basic stance of the leadership of the public day schools in the first generation.

Our plea for the completest possible development of the child—whether the process is called primary or secondary education—cannot stop short of the recognition that both the *raison d'être* and the means of personal culture, or self-realization in the true sense, lies in the service to others. . . . Society has come to the adult stage of self-government and self-control. In view of all this, one of the greatest needs of our day is to find some way of training our girls for the increased responsibilities and duties of citizenship that more and more come within the sphere of practice and actual life for women as well as men.[26]

Professor Edith Morley in 1913 under the auspices of the Fabian Women's Group studied the position and impact of women in seven professions, including teaching. She contended that the Girls' Public Day Schools due to their number and prestige had been able to establish a tradition of innovation and flexibility in girls' secondary education. She saw as valid Miss Woodhouse's contention that freedom granted by the company to headmistresses encouraged an individual spirit within institutions that led to healthy differentiation of type and character. Moreover, Miss Woodhouse had seen that this quality allowed faculties and administrators to engage in educational experimentation. Professor Morley feared that as the twentieth century progressed, control of schools under the Board of Education would become "too much office-managed and state-regulated, thus loosing life in routines." She placed the burden to resist such a tendency on "capable women of the highest power and academic standing."[27]

Mrs. Humphrey Ward in reflections about late Victorian and Edwardian society called attention to a deep commitment that was evident among faculties of female secondary schools. "They [the schools] are almost entirely taught by women, and women with whom, in many cases, education—the shaping of the immature human creature to noble ends—is the sincerest of passions; who find indeed, in the task that same creative joy which belongs to literature or art or philanthropic experiment."[28]

Professor R. L. Archer in 1921 in a professional assessment supported Mrs. Ward's judgment. He noted that a working spirit had existed between faculties and students, indeed a great friendliness between teachers and their students.

The average schoolmistress thinks more about methods than the average schoolmaster. She is less conservative and more aware of new ideas. She knows more of other types of education beside that in which she is herself occupied. Literature, art and other cultural subjects are taught with more genuine enthusiasm and welcomed with less regard to their examination value. The school is a more civilising influence. There is no tradition from the ages of barbarism to wear down. Headmistresses looked to what girls naturally were; headmasters have looked to what boys after a hundred years' tradition of idleness, bullying, housing in hovels, and worship of physical strength, had become.[29]

Professor Archer also pointed out that Girls' Public Day Schools threw the weight of social prestige on the side of day schools; all towns could develop a truly fine school if they desired without crushing competition from a fashionable boarding school that drew away the best academic students. Parents of moderate means had access to excellent education for their daughters which had a major significance to society.[30]

Professor Archer noted that if the new female education had borrowed curricular ideas from progressive boys' schools, it had also contributed to reassessment of male secondary education. It had given dimension to the teaching of literature, art, and music in boys schools and moved it away from a mechanical drill in technique. Further it emphasized that the discipline and influence in the home and schools were not diametrically different. And finally female education endorsed the value of formal teacher education.[31]

The headmistresses of the Girls' Public Day Schools regarded themselves as professionals and their schools somewhat as model societies that etched as a professional ideal an authoritative but reserved and unostentatious demeanor. By the last decade of the century only teachers with university degrees could expect preferment and advancement in company schools. Doubtless the social background of teachers as well as the prevalent ideology in women's colleges in the universities and in company schools explain the sense of social responsibility and Victorian middle-class virtues propagated by faculties. Prior to 1894, 64 percent of the student body at the four women's colleges at Cambridge and Oxford universities were daughters of businessmen and tradesmen.[32] The leadership in company schools developed the Arnold themes—a mindfulness of individual, familial and societal needs, a corporate spirit, that is, the public virtue of loyally working with others for the common good, a development and respect for powers of organization, and the importance of games to personal, institutional, and societal health and vigor.[33]

The Girls' Public Day Schools, as well as institutions of a similar character, placed in a female context the spirit of godliness and learning which had been a motivating force in the revitalized boys' public schools in the early Victorian years. That spirit drew strength from evangelical morality, primarily the heritage of philanthropy, missionary zeal, and enthusiasm. "If the scholarship of Evangelicalism had become barren, and its attitude of mind narrow and unbending, the tradition of piety and good works was active throughout the Victorian age: most particularly it set the pattern of Victorian family life and the ethical training, perhaps the most important formative power behind the eminence of the eminent Victorians."[34] Despite different doctrinal positions and systems of philosophy a singular class ethic arose—a combination of intellectual toughness, moral earnestness, and deep spiritual convictions.

Edith Patin, who entered Blackheath School in 1881 and after graduation continued her education at Newnham College, commented in retrospect on the liberal spirit of the Blackheath institution. "As I try to sum up the impression of our school years, I asked myself what made those years so enlightening and quickening, so full of happy energy.... I think our greatest gain was a sense of freedom from some of the mid-Victorian restraints."[35]

It would be much too simple to view the company schools as beacons of light and progress. In truth they reflected the confusion and uncertainties of middle-class Britain in the last generation of the century. An examination of the Blackheath School attended by Miss Patin shows some of the crosscurrents. In 1880, the year the school opened, Blackheath had the character of a separate suburb of London; professional people and city merchants provided leadership to the area. It had a small literary club, an arts club, and a concert hall. The meeting which launched the school was held in the drawing room of the Reverend S. Wiltin South, headmaster of Blackheath Preparatory School. His wife, Frances Julia, who had attended Newnham, spearheaded the campaign for the new school. Maria Grey, Emily Shirreff, Helen Taylor, and about one hundred residents of the area attended the meeting. Subsequently seven hundred men and women subscribed for shares. A new school building was erected to the design of E. A. Robson, a celebrated architect of a number of public buildings in the London area. Robson, who lived in Blackheath, was an active member of the coalition of citizens of the region who made possible the new educational venture.

Several factors shaped the ideological approach to education in Blackheath. Many parents had a vague and ill-defined educational goal; they desired training of character and wanted their daughters fitted to occupy successfully whatever position fate decreed for them. Educators at the institution did not have a unitary educational ideology. One group sought training of character through the mental nutriment of ideas acquired by vigorous discipline of the intellectual process; a second group favored a more flexible regime based on self-direction they said nature had intended. One student at Blackheath felt that these viewpoints were mirrored in the attitudes of students who had absorbed them from "the atmosphere in varying proportions."

Class day orators of national repute at the Blackheath School in 1891 and 1892 justified from several points of view the pursuit of a liberal education. In 1891 Dr. Butler, former headmaster of Harrow and then principal of Trinity College, Cambridge University, set before the student body as the desired motivation purusit of knowledge for its own sake. Classicist Arthur Sidgwick the following year called for pursuit of knowledge to provide the necessary training to equip the character for work in the world. Miss Gadesden, principal of the school who subsequently served as president of the Headmistresses Association, pointed out that the object of the education offered at the institution was training, especially in the habits which made for good character, and "last but not least that they [the students] should learn the duty of service to others." Messages given in company schools were heavily threaded with advice directed to self-control and self-discipline, appropriate areas of intellectual satisfaction and contributions to society. An alumna reflected about what appeared to the student body as a multiplicity of foci which led to some confusion.

I have a distant recollection of the value set on ideas—as originating in the minds of the students by more than one of the staff. Another reminiscence is an address given to the school by the Head just before holidays in which the main theme, as I recollect it, was home duty, especially the duty of an obliging and unobtrusive demeanor. The force of conflicting ideas in our minds made us sometimes "thorny" young persons, I fancy.[36]

A logical exploration of educational goals and development of a clear-cut educational philosophy did not have priority in middle-class schools, and often students became confused. The company schools accepted the several existing educational ideals which became a permanent part of female education in the new century.

Jane Ellen Harrison, famed classicist of Newnham College, after university study and before her collegiate appointment worked for a short time on the council of the Girls' Public Day School. She attended regularly the prize-awarding ceremonies at various schools. "The sentiments of these speeches were on well-established lines, and always, always at the end came the inevitable

A perfect woman, noble planned
to warn, to comfort and command."[37]

Girls who attended the newly founded day schools of the last third of the century participated regularly in the ceremonials of education which had been earlier developed as a vital facet of male educational institutions. Mary Vivian Hughes recalled the annual Prize Days and Foundation Days at the North London Collegiate School with mixed feelings, nostalgia, awe, and humor. She remembered the hall filled with interested spectators, eminent guests, and speakers who were usually people of accomplishment in a myriad of fields, members of the royal family, aristocrats, and renowned clerics, displays of students' work, and finally the presentation of awards.

The broad homely accents of Bishop Temple warmed our hearts....He assured us that girls were far cleverer than boys. "Now my wife," said he, looking round at Mrs. Temple as she sat nervously brooding over the piles of books she was to distribute, "always says the right thing at the right moment. As for me, my efforts at speech making consist of what the French call staircase wit, or what you wish you had said as you go downstairs afterwards." Everyone must have rejoiced when this most human of bishops went to Canterbury.[38]

But of chief significance were the formal and informal learning experiences that nurtured the resolute spirit of a corps of independent and innovative young women who appeared on the English social scene at the end of the century. Miss Hughes saw such an attitude in her fellow classmate Mary Wood, who attended Girton. "She certainly typified the 'modern girl' of that time, tame though it may seem to one of today. She had been long before this one of the first women to ride a bicycle, to go on the top of a bus, and to indulge in mixed bathing. But her companions in those excesses were always of the kind that would be called today highbrow."[39]

But the schools also reflected the ambiguous position of so many middle-class young women who by 1890 had been freed from many trammels on their efforts to gain knowledge and engage in careers and yet were still tied firmly to the social conventions of their class which in some areas were as restrictive as in the early decades of the nineteenth century. Middle- and upper-class women were enslaved by the heavy, formal patterns of home and family obligations, buttressed by the formulas of entertainment detailed in the novels of George Gissing and the American expatriates Henry James and Harold Frederic.[40]

In the late years of the nineteenth century and in the opening years of the twentieth company schools were unofficial training centers for the teaching profession; graduates and faculty of company schools staffed a large number of educational institutions for young women. In the first fifty years after foundation twenty-two of the staff of the Blackheath High School became headmistresses, including Alice Ottley who gave her name to the high school at Worcester, Lilian Faithfull, principal of Cheltenham, and Margaret Bishop, president of Holloway College. The company schools served by and large the middle class of Britain and of course only a minority of that segment of society, but they had a far wider impact than their enrollment would suggest because they set patterns and guidelines for the many girls' high schools that were founded throughout the nation. In 1900 there were in Britain approximately 3,137 girls' schools and 1,078 mixed schools which enrolled 133,042 girls. About 36,000 girls, less than one-third of the total, attended the 243 public secondary schools, and thus almost seventy of every hundred female students went to private schools.

Sir Joshua Fitch was one of the few professional educators who participated in a wide range of educational developments for almost two generations. At his death the *Temps* observed that his life had been spent in the reorganization of public education in England. He started his career as principal of the Borough Road College for training teachers, conducted by the British and Foreign School Society. In 1866 he became examiner of English literature and history at the University of London, then inspector of schools in Yorkshire, assistant commissioner of the Schools Inquiry Commission, special commissioner to report on educational conditions at Manchester, Birmingham, Liverpool, and Leeds, assistant commissioner appointed under the Endowed Schools Act, and inspector of training colleges for schoolmistresses in England and Wales. In order to gain greater knowledge of effective educational patterns he visited and studied educational institutions in the United States, Germany, and France.[41]

Fitch claimed that the establishment of the Girls' Public Day School Company had a larger influence on the improvement of female education than any single measure. He said it had familiarized parents with a dynamic pattern of administration, particularly responsible governing bodies which selected and guided faculty and shaped the destiny of the institution for which they were responsible. Moreover, company schools were of sufficient size to admit proper classification and had educational goals that were "high and generous." The institutions, he concluded, had achieved remarkable success and established a viable formula. "For in numerous places independent bodies of local governors have been formed for the establishment of girls' high schools of the same character though not actually incorporated with the Company; and at present there is hardly an important town in England which has not its Public Day School for Girls."[42] And those public schools scattered throughout the nation provided young women not simply the means to cultivate the intellect which had been previously available to men but also their faculties and administrations, as pointed out, called women to active participation in public life. The girls' public schools were part of a system for the creation of a new female elite which came to maturity in the twentieth century.[43]

# 8

# The Teachers' Training and Registration Society and the Fate of the Union

In 1875 Maria Grey presented an acute problem to the men and women gathered for the annual meeting of the Women's Education Union in the rooms of the Society of Arts. She pointed out that the success of the Girls' Public Day School Company had brought into sharp relief a major deficiency in female education— lack of adequately trained teachers to staff schools above the elementary level. She noted that the government demanded that every instructor at the elementary level possess definite qualifications, but no such regulation existed in the higher or middle-class schools. She estimated that forty-nine of fifty female teachers were unqualified both by lack of "the higher class of culture and the skill to impart the knowledge possessed." Yet she believed deeply in women's future role in the profession. In 1872 she said, "I believe that in a few years a great career will be opened to women as teachers.... I feel confident that we shall at no distant day see schoolmistresses holding as honored and honorable position as the schoolmaster." Maria Grey observed that the preparation of skilled teachers was an expensive project; she estimated that to establish a training college in London for only a hundred students would cost approximately 2,600 pounds annually. As an expedient the Chelsea School of G.P.D.S.C. had established a student teacher class under the guidance of Miss Porter.

On May 29, 1876, the central committee of the Women's Union, which had thirty members, half of whom were women, approved

Maria Grey's draft of a proposal for a training college for women.[1] Since the union was not a corporate body, and therefore could not hold or purchase property, a new society was to be formed, the Teachers' Training and Registration Society, incorporated under act of Parliament. In order to make the new project known to the public-spirited sectors of the British intelligentsia, Maria Grey attended the Liverpool meeting of the Social Science Congress and presented a paper "On the Training of Teachers" written by Emily who was unable to be at the meeting. Emily had made a study of teacher training and believed that Germany offered the best pattern to guide Britain. But she noted that the designs there were not fully applicable to Britain because Germany had a tightly controlled state system. Since the British government had not acted to create a registration and certification system, Emily Shirreff and Maria Grey urged the men and women attending the Social Science Congress to make representation to the universities to step into the breach.

Following the sessions of the educational section of the Social Science Congress the Women's Education Union held an open meeting on October 16 in the lecture hall of the Free Library, Liverpool, concerning the proposed society. The Reverend Mark Pattison presided, and Maria Grey gave the major address. She insisted that even though the initial focus of the proposed organization was on women and the establishment of a model teacher training college for women teachers, it intended to benefit instruction provided for both sexes. She revealed that a special committee of the union had studied the methods of training and testing higher-grade teachers in Germany, France, Italy, and Sweden. In all the countries examined three fundamental principles governed educational programs for teachers: first, a lengthy period of study after graduation from school to form and strengthen character and gain additional knowledge, secondly, familiarity with the principles of education as science and its methods as an art together with actual practice teaching, and thirdly, a system of testing the efficiency of the training by competent examiners who issued certificates that were a guarantee of efficiency. In all these countries the government appointed the examiners and made obligatory the examination for all teachers in public schools.[2] Three years earlier Emily

Shirreff in the *Journal of the Womens' Education Union* announced that in France instruction in the principles and method of education had been totally neglected and the certificate was merely a warrant against ignorance.[3]

The new Teachers' Registration Society incorporated the three principles in its schema. Since men at least could gain higher education but not instruction in the science of education at universities, it seemed imperative to meet the needs of women who lacked adequate facilities in both areas. In regard to the science of education Maria observed that the society planned not merely to give theoretical instruction but to place students in the classroom for practice teaching under the guidance of skilled teachers in neighborhood schools. In order to gain the third objective—testing the efficiency of training by competent examiners whose certificates to recipients were guarantees of their ability to teach—Maria Grey repeated her earlier advice and urged appeals to the universities for action on the matter. She suggested that universities be induced to form a joint board to pass on the competence of prospective teachers. Maria asked that examinations conducted by such a board be open to all males and females over twenty-one and that candidates be examined in principles and methods of education. She admitted that examinations were not always effective in determining tact and the ability to read character and deal with different minds, skills essential to good teaching. Therefore, she suggested that prospective teachers as a part of the accrediting process be judged as student teachers in the classroom. She hoped that any examination would be conducted in a manner that would give the greatest possible weight to intelligence and the least possible weight to memory.

A part of the Endowed Schools Act provided for a registration scheme, but that section was not passed by Parliament. In France by 1870 certification was required only in the matter of opening schools, while in Germany no one could teach any subject without a certificate of fitness. Emily Shirreff considered the certificate of fitness vital for the integrity of girls' schools in Britain in the last third of the nineteenth century. She knew full well that masters and teachers at first-class boys' schools often failed to be systematic educators but were not ignorant men, and publicity often made known the evils of the poor instruction. "But when we turn to the education of girls we have a totally different state of things. There nothing is known, nothing is publicly tested, nothing is even cared for enough to be seriously inquired into." She observed that Girton College was the only women's institution of the period which issued a certificate of competence.

In early 1873 a deputation met with W. E. Forster, lord president of the council and a personal friend of the Shirreffs, and urged the government to sponsor a bill for registration and certification.[4] Maria, a member of the deputation, represented the Women's Education Union and made a spirited plea that examination of teachers be made identical on the same subject for both sexes and the same principle adhered to in regard to inspection and examination of schools for males and females. "There must be no lowering of the standard to meet the lower work of the girls; let them fail again and again if need be, and have their failures exposed until they learn to put forth their strength and exercise it in the right direction; thus alone will they improve." She wanted enforcement of the male standard because it had been directed in education to work, accuracy, and thoroughness in contrast to women's standard which had emphasized show, quickness, and superficiality. In 1879 the close allies of the Shirreffs, Dr. Lyon Playfair, Arthur Mills, Sir John Lubbock, and Lord Francis Harvey, sponsored "A Bill for the Organization and Registration of Teachers engaged in Intermediate Education in England and Wales, printed March 13, 1879." The bill was abortive.

In 1879 the senate of the University of Cambridge, in compliance with memorials from headmasters as well as women's groups, appointed a Teacher Training Syndicate which established an examination schedule in the history, theory, and practice of education.[5] The syndicate also sponsored lecture courses in the academic year 1879-1880. The Reverend R. H. Quick offered a course on the history of education in the Michaelmas term, James Ward in Easter term gave a course on mental science in relation to teaching, and J. G. Fitch a second offering in that term on the practical aspects of the teacher's work. He had a class of about one hundred, sixty men and forty women. These classes were the first in the field of education offered at an English university.

J. G. Fitch, who had taken a deep interest in and participated in the plans and projects of the Shirreff sisters, held similar views about female education. He felt that the traditional subjects for women which had been so heavily stressed in curricula, that is, music and art, should be taught to every girl but carried only to the point at which each student could determine whether she was likely to excel in those fields. If no special aptitude existed, he saw no reason to pursue them in any greater depth. He sought for girls equality with boys in regard to curriculum. "Experience has not yet justified us in saying of any form of culture or useful knowledge that it is beyond the capacity of women to attain it, or that it is unsuited to her intellectual needs. Meanwhile the best course of instruction which we can devise ought to be put freely within the reach of men and women alike."[6]

Fitch's definition of liberal education was in accord with that of the Shirreffs. He sought to educate the person and not create the effective mechanic, tradesman, or physician. The largest proportion of work in primary school he called acquisition of the essential elements of education: power to read, write, and do certain things while the formative elements came into focus in the higher grades. Nevertheless, he insisted that the latter should not be absent from a child's school regimen which ended at eleven or twelve years of age. The formative elements he characterized as those which sought to give power and capacity—language, logic, and science. In accord with the Shirreffs he disliked the designation classical or science schools because they implied that all intellectual training was to be one kind or another.

The first examination in theory, practice, and history of education occurred in late June 1880 at both Cambridge and London. The subjects examined were the best methods of teaching and the reasons advanced for one method rather than another, the best modes of training the memory, the use and abuse of emulation as a stimulus to learning, the sanitary conditions of school life, and the visual and tangible apparatus for illustrating such subjects as arithmetic and geometry. The *Spectator* published a truism on the operation of the new examination. "Doubtless after everything is said, it will remain true that many a man is an excellent teacher who knows little of the theory of teaching and that many who know the whole history of their subject remain bad teachers; but that is equally true of medical men and yet no one has ever advanced it as a reason for not testing the theoretical knowledge of medical men."[7] At the institution of the examination by Cambridge University Maria Grey wrote to the *Times*, "The proposed examination of teachers at once constitutes teaching into a regular profession and opens its doors to women on the same terms as men." London University followed Cambridge in the establishment of education examinations. The examinations by Cambridge and London universities treated men and women equally in regard to admission to the examination, standard, and certificate.

In 1874 Maria presented a lecture "On the Study of Education as a Science" which showed her feelings about the primacy of that area of knowledge in the creation of a successful teacher and its wide-ranging character. She described the low opinion about the need to master educational principles which was current in British society.

There is no conception of education as the direction given to the development of the whole human being, by the external influence brought to bear upon him, aiding, arresting or distorting his growth; no clear sense of the vital importance to the individual and society, that education should be conducted in accordance with the laws, or to use a less ambiguous word, with the order of nature, physical, mental and social. . . . We unhesitatingly trust our children during the years when every faculty is most sensitive to external influences, first to servants ignorant of everything but the routine prescribed by the social position of their masters, and then, at the later but no less critical age to tutors and governesses who may know Greek and Latin, French and German, but have never even thought of learning anything of the nature of their pupils and of the complex conditions of every kind which must influence them for good or evil. Every mother is credited with an intuitive knowledge of infant management, as simple and as easily supplied by instinctive affection as those of the chick or the lamb, and it is deduced as the principle reason for denying to women any higher training than that of the average schoolroom, that they are intended to be mothers, and therefore can not want it! The whole process of education is of the happy-go-lucky kind, governed by practical necessities, by customs, fashions, class habits and prejudice by anything but a well-defined purpose, and a scientific method of attaining it.[8]

Mrs. Grey asked Could the application of scientific method to education bring about the desired objective, that is, human beings developed to the full extent of their natural capacity and trained to understand their work in the world and to do it? She answered that factors were too numerous and their interaction too complicated to answer in the affirmative with certainty, but the mission should be to equip the voyager of life with all the known equipment so that he or she could have the best opportunities for success.

Maria observed that the human being possessed a three-fold nature, physical, intellectual, and emotional, blended into an indivisible unity yet subject to different and often conflicting sets of laws together with the power of volition. She said some elements of a person's constitution were common to the whole human race, others to his division of the human race, others to his immediate line of descent and still others peculiar to himself; the latter formed a person's individuality. The study of the latter, she said, should form the most important task of the practical educator. Thus the science of education had to impart knowledge of the factors common to all, and at the same time make the teacher aware of and focus upon the particular individual under her charge. First, Maria stressed the need for the science of education to utilize the principles of physiology which she conceived to be not simply cultivation of the health and strength of the body but also qualities of the spirit which imparted grace and vitality. Secondly, she listed as a basic need of the science of education integration with psychology; she placed under that rubric determination of the subjects to be taught and varying methodology in relation to the growth and maturation of the human being. She considered that exploration of the various facets of physiology by educators would provide the final answer to "that external *cui bono* which is the bane and the torment of every educational reformer—what should and should not be taught in schools for girls and boys and for different classes of society."[9]

A crucial ingredient of the master power of education she defined as how to form habits, the creation of a sort of second nature which acted instinctively as the original one. "How little this is generally understood may be seen by the common case of education acting by contraries, the son of a miser turning out a spendthrift; the son of a pious clergyman becoming profligate."[10] But the study of education she defined as more than utilization of physiology and psychology which gave what she called the statistics of human nature; the other dimension was the study of the dynamics of human nature or human nature in action. The latter she saw manifested in the history of human societies, and human development through religion, literature, art, science, and legislation, a sort of living spring of human activity which could not be assayed by the psychologist. She maintained that nations had a character and the educator had to come to grips with the questions of what conditions favored the grace and checked the evil in them, how far they were modifiable at all by direct action of any sort, how legislative enactments affected the character of a people, and what defects in legislation produced the very evils intended to be checked. She made a plea for the inclusion of sociology as a crucial ingredient in the science of education; she called it the psychology of society. And Maria included in the purview of the science of education in its various configurations analysis of the overriding social and human issues of the era in which the person lived.

One of the vital areas which she said cried out for attention and to which the psychology of society gave insight was the relationship of social class to existing and projected educational patterns. In the evolution of a national educational system to which Britain had reluctantly turned its attention, a vital dimension, to her, was a study of the national educational systems in Scotland, Germany, Switzerland, and the United States of America into which no class distinctions had been built. In contrast Britain had maintained in its various educational arrangements the class distinctions which prevailed in the country. Impartial study of the several national systems in regard to moral and social as well as educational results, she judged, would assist Britain in the gradual extension and remodeling of its educational system.

Maria Grey raised a second issue which she felt the science of education had to confront—appropriate education for the two sexes. She set forth the areas to be pursued—whether the differences between males and females were of a kind, degree, or only of proportion in regard to various mental and moral faculties, how the differences should be dealt with in education, and whether the best training for both sexes could be achieved by the same methods under similar school arrangements, by a mixed system, or establishment of female education within well-defined channels, whether regular and sustained mental effort under hygienic conditions carried out from girlhood to womanhood was in any way injurious to the perfect development of women's physical constitution or possibly calmed and steadied their nervous system and established a healthy balance between the intellectual and emotional nature which was essential to perfect womanhood. Finally what was perfect womanhood?

The third issue to which she directed the science of education was an operational concern and yet transcended that mission—the function of examinations. She asserted in a straightforward manner that examinations were in danger of becoming the sole end and aim of learning. Instead of following the lead of teaching, it seemed to her that teaching worked up to examinations. Hence, she said that a determination had to be made on the scientific principles by which examinations were constructed—whether they tested the acquisition and retention of knowledge or the power of using knowledge acquired, whether the knowledge dealt with words and rules or the ideas and principles that undergirded the rules, whether the power they valued was accurate retention of facts or accurate reasoning from the facts remembered. She prophetically noted that since examination had become the inevitable portal through which every professional career was entered, "I venture to say that as is our system of examination, so will be our system of education."[11]

Similar criticisms of the examination pattern in the country had been voiced by educational progressives F. D. Maurice and Professor De Morgan. And within a generation a growing number of the most perceptive leaders in the professions as well as public-spirited citizens became concerned about the character and preeminent place of examinations in the national educational system. In 1889 Auberon Herbert published a study which contained a collection of criticisms and an official petition to the Queen which had first appeared in the *Nineteenth Century* in November of the previous year.[12] More than four hundred prominent politicians, public leaders, and educators, male and female, petitioned the Queen for a royal commission to investigate the quality, purpose and scope of examinations conducted in schools, in universities, by professional organizations, and indeed for entrance to government service. The signatories included academicians who held prestigious posts such as Arthur Napier, professor of English Language, Oxford; Professor E. A. Freeman; the Reverend B. F. Westcott, professor of divinity, King's College, Cambridge; Sir Frederick Pollock, the Reverend T. Fowler, president of Corpus Christi College, Oxford; T. A. Walker, dean of Peterhouse; Miss E. Wordsworth, principal of Lady Margaret College, Oxford; Dorothea Beale, Alice Woods, and Annie Besant.[13]

Maria noted that she had depicted the science of education as a discipline which seemed impossible for the average person to master. She thought that many people would smile in derision and ask whether she expected every teacher, governess, or mother to master the range of knowledge which she had detailed or give solutions to the problems raised.

My answer is, that I no more expect it than we expect the captain of a ship to construct the chart he sails by, and still less create the science of navigation. I want to see our schoolmasters and mistresses and all concerned in practical education placed in the same position as our navigators, furnished with the principles of a science they have not had to discover for themselves and with charts to guide their general course, while leaving to their individual judgment and acumen the modifications and adaptations required by special circumstances.[14]

She asked whether society wanted any tyro to try experiments willy nilly, not *in corpore vili* but with the most delicate and precious of materials, the human body and mind, and the most powerful forces, human passions and human will, upon whose success or failure depended virtue or vice and happiness or misery.[15] For substantiation of her charge that large numbers of students received miserably defective moral and mental preparation she referred to materials presented by the Public Schools Commission and the Schools Inquiry Commission, evaluations of vast numbers of school inspectors, the reports of various medical examining bodies, the Civil Service Commission, the Local University Examinations, and opinions of the most skilled school teachers. Lastly, she asked citizens to examine social life as they saw it and determine whether it indicated a general diffusion of sound moral and mental culture or the reverse.

In short, during the seventies, when the study of education came into the respectable higher realms of academia, Maria tried earnestly to cast it as a discipline which transcended techniques of imparting the principles of specific studies. She defined it as an area of knowledge which incorporated several disciplines that probed the multifaceted nature of man, woman, and society and had as one of the chief goals the achievement of an equitable community which cultivated the potential of all its constituent members. She maintained that much had been done; yet, the valuable information had not been coordinated into a body of science which took its legitimate place in the hierarchy of the sciences. In a dramatic way she linked her own secondary position as a woman with the secondary place that the science of education had achieved in the academic constellation.

It has for its advocate only a woman,—a woman, and therefore weak; a woman, and therefore debarred in youth from aiding her weakness by the higher training reserved for the stronger sex alone—even here, and such as I am, I dare boldly aver that this science, so little thought of, so contemptuously ignored, is the crowning science of all, for it is the application of all other sciences to the production of the highest of all results, the perfect man.[16]

Miss I. M. Drummond, president of the Incorporated Association of Assistant Mistresses, in a lecture in 1912 entitled "The Life of a Teacher" presented what was *de rigueur* for teachers in secondary schools. In effect she affirmed what Maria Grey had advocated in her teacher training program.

In a lesson in a good school there is most often a happy give and take between the teacher and the class. The teacher guides, but every girl is called upon to take her part and put forward individual effort. The homework is no longer mere memorizing from some dry little manual but requires thought and scope for originality. The whole result is a rigorous mental discipline, real stimulus to original thought, eager enthusiasm in learning. . . . It means an enormously increased demand upon the teacher.[17]

Miss Drummond said it was essential that teachers not become jaded; they had to get relaxation, exchange ideas, mix with diverse peoples, and be involved in satisfying personal activities. She demanded professional growth, every teacher abreast of new developments in her field as well as innovative educational methodology. Miss Drummond saw the work of the teacher and the institution of which she was a part to nurture independence and self-reliance in each student together with a public spirit which led to an active life in the community. She considered "the most interesting and important work of the teacher, and also the most exacting the encouragement and guidance of extra curricular activities."[18]

Maria Grey persevered in her plans to launch a teacher training college in spite of failures by others and adverse opinions. In March 1876 the Reverend R. H. Quick of the College of Preceptors had a discouraging message.

> The fates seem against the training of teachers. Our committee today was too large; when so many have to discuss a document they never agree; an astute person at Harrow used to say that something should be given to a large committee for them to object to and the real thing kept till the first had been disposed of. I trust this temporary discouragement will not deter you from going on with the most important work. I would gladly join in bearing the expense of circulating your prospectus.[19]

Dr. Abbott, headmaster of the City of London School, wrote in a somewhat similar vein. "I sympathize, of course, with your desires. . . . People are very dull and lethargic in recognizing the necessity of training teachers. But a year or two ago some of us attempted in conjunction with Lord Lyttleton and Sir J. Kay Shuttleworth to agitate for a training college for teachers above the elementary. I gave up a great deal of time to attending meetings of this committee but the thing collapsed."[20] In September of that same year Sir J. Kay Shuttleworth informed her that he had hoped to launch a college but did not have the strength or health. T. Phillips-Jodrell made known to her that he also had been involved in an unsuccessful scheme to set up a training college.

Maria Grey, who had recruited a circle of sympathetic men and women in her successful campaign to launch the Women's Education Union, turned to them for aid in the Teachers' Training and Registration Society and its first offspring, a teacher training college. Joshua Fitch endorsed the project and noted that he had become interested in a proposal to found a college for teachers at Bristol by means of endowments. Other public leaders who responded to Maria Grey's preliminary solicitation in a positive manner included Sir John Lubbock, C. Kegan Paul, Princess Louise, her husband the marquis of Lorne, and James Stuart. They promised aid; still others gave her sympathy and approval but for personal or career reasons did not wish to stand in the forefront. Matthew Arnold was one of the latter. "I had rather that Government or the Universities should do what you want than a private society, but they will not, and I am glad to see that you do not merely propose to examine but also to teach. My connexion with the Education Department obliges me to be very shy of joining conferences and societies, for my official superiors would not like it." He noted that as they allowed him freedom in literary efforts, he strove not to engage in public and platform activity to which they might have objections. He desired to join the society as a regular member but not serve on the council or hold office.[21]

In its official prospectus the Teachers' Training and Registration Society offered advanced instruction in all subjects which fell within the chart of a liberal education plus necessary basic educational methodology and philosophy. It promised to work for an independent examining board empowered to grant certificates of competency. At the first annual meeting of the society at the Westminster Palace Hotel under the chairmanship of the Reverend William Rogers, Oscar Browning, secretary to the Cambridge Syndicate, who had been appointed to inquire into the teacher question, gave an address. He informed the gathering that the syndicate had come to the conclusion that examinations should be held and certificates of proficiency issued. He hoped to present a scheme for carrying out the project to the senate before the conclusion of Michaelmas term.[22]

The society set forth regulations for institutions which it intended to establish—that they be for day students only, that no person be admitted to them under seventeen years of age, and that entrance examinations be required which could be waived upon presentation of a certificate of having passed an examination deemed of sufficient weight by the council. Schools or colleges formed under its auspices would have three divisions, upper, middle, and higher, and within the upper and middle two departments, one literary and the other scientific. Students would be allowed to choose which department they wished to enter and subjects they wished to take within it, but instruction in principles and methods of education was obligatory for all students. In addition, students would be placed in practice schools. Examinations for certification would cover knowledge in the latter area.[23] Lord Aberdare accepted the presidency of the society and the vice-presidents included members of the coalition upon which depended the success of a service-oriented organization in the nineteenth century, as well as two headmasters of prestigious boys public schools, the Reverend G. C. Bell, headmaster of Marlborough College, and the Reverend Montagu Butler, headmaster of Harrow. The Shirreffs formed a close personal friendship with both men; they had known Bell since 1871 and paid short visits to the homes of both men in July 1877. Other vice-presidents included Sir Henry Cole, at that time secretary of the Science and Art Department, W. E. Cowper-Temple, MP, W. E. Forster, MP, Sir John Lubbock, MP, Samuel Morley, MP, Sir Francis Goldsmid, MP, and Lady Stanley. Members of the council of the society included women of the era strongly identified with better education for their sex, Miss Buss, Miss Chessar of the school board for London, Mary Gurney, Maria Grey, and Emily Shirreff as well as clerics who also championed female education, the Reverend E. A. Abbott, the Reverend Mark Pattison, rector of Lincoln College, Oxford, the Reverend R. H. Quick, the Reverend J. H. Rigg, principal of the Wesleyan Training College, Westminster, the Reverend W. Jowitt, formerly headmaster of the Middle-Class Corporation School, London, and C. Kegan Paul, J. P. D. Meiklejohn, professor of Education at St. Andrews, R. N. Shore, and James Stuart of Trinity College, Cambridge.

The society launched a training college, which was later named in honor of Mrs. Grey, on a modest scale. Maria noted the difficulties it faced. "They began that dreary work of begging for funds, the most wearing and deadening I know, and of which I had a taste in begging for Miss Buss's noble work, the North London Collegiate School, and Emily for Girton College."[24] It took two years to get the doors of the college opened, and even its modest beginnings were made possible largely through the efforts of the Reverend

William Rogers, rector of Bishopsgate, who had raised 20,000 pounds for a middle-class boys' school. He gave to the new Women's Training College his rectory on Skinner Street near the Great Eastern Railway and gained permission to send the students for their practice teaching to the Bishopsgate Middle-Class Girls' School.

To enter the college without examinations, students had to produce a certificate from the Senior Local Examination from any university or a leaving certificate from the Joint University Board or an equivalent certificate signed by the examiner or principal of a public or preparatory school or a certificate of any Higher University Examination. The students were classified and placed in one of the three levels on the results of the examination. The Lower Division consisted of students who obtained a third class at the entrance examination or the minimal certificate for exemption from an examination. The course for students in the latter category lasted three years or nine terms. The course of study in the first year emphasized general academic work to build a foundation in the liberal arts with no instruction in educational methodology. In 1900 the college was able to eliminate the preparatory division because the increase in institutions which prepared students adequately made it unnecessary. The Middle Division consisted of those promoted from the Lower, those who obtained a second class on the entrance examination, or those who produced a certificate for the Examination of Women of the University of London, of the Cambridge Higher Local Examination, or the Pass Examination of the Oxford Scheme for Women. The course in the Middle Division spanned two years or six terms. The Upper Division enrolled students promoted from the Middle Division or those who obtained a first class on the entrance examination, or produced a certificate of having passed an examination equivalent to the BA of Oxford or Cambridge or a certificate from a public institution of higher learning which attested to three years of successful study.

The course of study in the Upper Division consisted of theories of education which embraced characteristics of childhood, mental, moral, and physical, practice of education, including methodology appropriate for various subjects, model lessons given by master teachers, uses of educational materials, the history of education with prime attention to the innovators of the era such as Pestalozzi, Froebel, Stowe, and Jacotot, and for advanced students systems which dealt with instruction in music and art. In addition to the professional course students of the Upper Division had required work in human physiology, hygiene, and logic. The college emphasized practice teaching.[25] Students visited various types of schools and observed, then engaged in practice teaching in neighboring schools. Once a week two students gave a lesson in the presence of the staff and fellow students; the latter observed the techniques used and gave critiques. The following day faculty, student teachers, and student observers engaged in a general discussion. The two sessions aimed to develop self-control, encourage free discussion, and prepare the student for the required presentation before the official examiner.[26] The college issued its own certificates until 1880. In the latter year a major step occurred in the campaign to get some sort of official registration and certification of teachers. Maria Grey had been a leader in the effort to give examinations and issue certificates of competency.

The Maria Grey Training College in the first few decades of its existence had able leadership. Agnes Ward had a message of significance to the participants of the Headmasters Conference of 1881 at Wellington College. The Headmasters Conference had been launched in 1869; it grew out of a special meeting to consider the Educational Bill of 1869. Dr. Thring took the lead in making it an annual gathering. On the whole it was a conservative body. Its major contribution was the establishment of the Oxford and Cambridge Joint Board to examine first-grade schools, and girls were admitted to the examinations in 1878. Miss Ward urged the educators to endorse teacher training. J. M. Wilson of Clifton noted that the conference had been "coquetting with the subject for ten years," and the system in operation was to put a man into a form and bid him to find out how to teach. Miss Ward had made a survey of thirty-five headmistresses of leading high schools. She reported that thirty-three expressed strong support of teacher training, one took a neutral position, and one rejected it. She presented the teacher training system in operation at the Maria Grey Training College in modest terms.

We do not aim at training specialists in the few months each student has to give. We hope rather to develop at as small cost as possible to the children, teachers who, by experience of teaching all the ordinary school subjects, may be in a position to choose out those for which they are specially apt, and who above all may know something of the place of each subject in an ordinary curriculum.

She urged the assembled headmasters to support the Cambridge certification program which had been instituted in 1879 for a three-year period and was coming to an end in 1881. In addition she asked them to get other universities involved. "I trust we may look forward to a day when for higher grade schools, and indeed for all schools, the necessity of duly trained teachers will be acknowledged, and when the preliminary test of some such course as ours may discourage the unfit from entering, and further qualify the fit to enter the profession."[27]

Miss Ward was an articulate but subdued spokesperson for one of the vital educational campaigns of the late years of the nineteenth century and the early decades of the twentieth—adequate professional preparation of teachers at all levels of education. Female educators had pioneered that concept, and Miss Ward spoke for the progressives who wished to make it acceptable to the mainstream of male education.

Alice Woods assumed the post of principal of the Maria Grey Training College in 1892 at the resignation of Miss Ward. During her tenure of more than a generation, she maintained the progressive thrust of the institution. It remained, therefore, in the mold which was the desiderata of the Shirreffs. Miss Woods set forth major areas that needed to be explored in a serious and imaginative fashion. The chief goal of education in initial contact with the student she defined as giving freedom to the child's highest self to come to the fore. To accomplish this goal she marked out cooperation between the generations and the sexes—the latter entailed free access to all occupations, trades, and professions as well as government appointments for women and differences between the sexes recognized as not a matter of superiority or inferiority.

Another cardinal area of cooperation in education she considered to be positive relationships between parents and teachers and a prime agency to further that goal the coeducational day school. Miss Woods edited a collection of essays by various educational leaders on the desirability and practicality of coeducation. She saw it as a necessary means to bring about true equality of the sexes. In the spirit of Maria Grey she discussed the topic in a judicious manner; she wanted gradual growth of coeducation rather than an attempt to launch it as a universal pattern due to adverse public opinion and division within the profession on the issue. She saw the spread of coeducation in board schools in large towns as a hopeful sign. But she recognized that realistically different types of schools would continue to exist in Britain, and to forge amicable and fruitful relationships among them and indeed create international links to evolve new and relevant educational methods and ideas appropriate for the entire school population were mandatory steps.

Miss Woods considered of extreme importance changes in the spirit of education—that factor she judged to be more important than acquisition of knowledge. Previous eras, she said, had made a fetish of knowledge; she wished to bring into the learning regimen as a reputable focus arts and crafts. "The creative impulse and its use in education lead us to look forward hopefully to an education that means a more complete living." For the teacher of the future she wanted a general education until the age of nineteen or twenty, the professional course which followed constructed to allow time for independent thought and a widening of viewpoints through social experience, both sexes educated together in the professional sequence, and every type of educational experiment encouraged.[28]

Miss Woods' years of confident leadership were in contrast to the first two years of life of the Maria Grey Training College. At that juncture it was in difficult financial straits; indeed it had to draw upon 200 of the 500 pounds in its bank account for survival. Despite financial problems the college took pride in the fact that in 1880 twenty-four of its students passed the examination of Cambridge University. Maria Grey, due to illness, was unable to work actively for the college in the founding years. In 1879 she wrote from Rome and expressed appreciation to Frances Mary Buss. "How kind it is of you and Miss Chessar to work for it as you do, and Dr. Abbott deserves more thanks than I can express."[29] Miss Buss wished to associate the college with the North London Collegiate School, but the council of Maria Grey College decided against the linkage. The student body remained small in its first decade, eighteen in 1881 and only thirty-two a decade later. It did not organize its Lower Division until 1881 and then opened a special kindergarten section in 1883. In 1885 the institution moved to a tall, gloomy building of somewhat forbidding aspect in Fitzroy Square and assumed the name Maria Grey Training College. The practice school had been in the square since 1881.

In 1887 the college launched a campaign for funds to construct a new, adequate building. A canvas took place, but a few large donors made the effort a success by gifts of 1,000 pounds each, and the Emily Pfeiffer Fund made a grant of 4,000 pounds. The college marshaled support and gained public attention. In July 1887 a meeting at Draper's Hall, Throgmorton Street, London, to raise funds drew a number of public men and women; Queen Victoria's daughter, the crown princess of Germany, attended as did Earl Granville, the marquis of Ripon, Sir Lyon Playfair, and A. J. Mundella. Two years later the empress Frederick again showed her interest in the venture and made a formal visit to the college. A new building, which cost 13,000 pounds, was constructed at Brondesbury; it housed a day school for girls and a kindergarten. In Gothic design, it contained classrooms, studio, music rooms, laboratory, library, and a refectory.

The Maria Grey Training College was the first training college under university inspection in which full training was offered for teachers in secondary schools. In fact the college opened the field, and other institutions of a similar sort followed, a residential training college at Cambridge in 1884, and nonresidential St. George College, Edinburgh, Bedford College, and Mary Datchelor and training departments at Cheltenham Ladies College, and the University College at Aberystwyth.

The Maria Grey Training College had a considerable impact on the educational system of the nation, since its graduates assumed leadership of various institutions within a generation of its foundation including principal of St. George Training College, Edinburgh, principal of the West Cornwall College, Penzance, head of the Training College, Stockwell, head of the Saffron Walden College, and headmistresses of high schools at Portsmouth, Brighouse,

Yorkshire, Brondesbury, Kilburn, and the Royal School for Officers' Daughters, Bath. In addition the Maria Grey Training College placed graduates in key posts in overseas possessions and foreign countries: principal of the General Female Training College, Jamaica, headmistress of Queens College, Barbados, and high schools at Kingston, the Cape, Bangkok, and in Japan. In India one graduate became inspectress general of the girls' schools in the Punjab and another principal of the Normal School, Madras.[30]

Although Maria Grey was not directly involved in the operation of the college which bore her name, she was the symbol of the spirit of the institution. Margaret Hodge, a woman who made major contributions to early childhood education in Australia, wrote to her in 1897.

Fifteen years ago I was trained for a teacher at the Maria Grey Training College and during that time I have been a lecturer at the College. I gained much of my training and have always considered that it was to it that I owe my delight in teaching. I am now starting a new scheme with my friend and co-worker at the Maria Grey Training College, Miss Newcomb, to extend the system of training teachers . . . such as you and the Council instituted in England at Bishopsgate in 1878 to Sydney. I did not like to go forth on this new work without telling you how much we both feel we owe to you.[31]

The two young women traveled to Australia and shaped the kindergarten movement there. Harriet Newcomb reported on their activities in 1890 in *Child Life*. A rather extensive pattern of training and certification of kindergarten teachers had been developed. In 1897 Miss Hodge and Miss Newcomb supervised the educational preparation of teachers in that field. The training course extended over a two-year period. An examination was given by the Teachers' Association and a certificate of competence issued. In 1900 twenty-six students were enrolled in the program conducted in the Sydney region. "The students have also formed a Local Research Society, so named after the Society formed nearly ten years ago by the old students of the Maria Grey Training College, London—the college which the Sydney students regarded as their parent college."[32]

Female secondary school teachers in the two generations prior to World War I established professional organizations and somewhat tentatively probed a number of concerns which related to their achievement of a respected and influential status in British national life which the Shirreff sisters had earnestly sought in the seventies and eighties. The Headmistresses Association and the Association of Assistant Mistresses in public schools gave attention to general educational as well as purely professional problems. Both had representation on the Registration Council, and the Board of Education sought their opinions. Secondary school teachers also had access to the Teachers Guild of Great Britain and Ireland, the College of Preceptors, and the National Union of Teachers. In the latter two their colleagues included elementary school teachers and in the first two private teachers. Often secondary school teachers also belonged to specialized organizations: the Ling Association (physical education) as well as historical, geographical, and various scientific groups. Membership in the latter type was not confined to teachers and so brought them into dialogue with diverse men and women of intellect.

Tenure was indeed a hazy area. Usually the headmistress of an institution had the preponderant voice in the selection of her faculty. The Girls' Public Day School Company gave to each headmistress the right to nominate and dismiss during the probationary period subject to a veto by the board of governors, which was rarely exercised. Permanent teachers often had the right of appeal of dismissal to the appointing body, that is, a board of governors or a local authority. By the opening of World War I teachers had not developed any comprehensive pension scheme. Poorly paid members of the profession came under the National Health Insurance Act and were provided for by the University, Secondary and Technical Teachers Insurance Society which had eleven thousand members by 1913; its dividend section offered voluntary health insurance to those who were not compulsorily insured. Clearly the desire for health protection encouraged the associational movement among secondary-level teachers.

Several vital concerns to teachers surfaced in the opening years of the twentieth century, including the impact upon students and the profession of excluding married women and the use of organizational power to achieve equitable pay scales. The president of the Association of Assistant Mistresses in 1913 said that "there would be a strong feeling against definite organization for the purpose of

forcing up rates of renumeration"; yet, the association investigated
pay scales set by local authorities and protested when posts were
advertised at low rates.[33]

To many teachers pay scales were not adequate in light of the
time, expense, and education required for entrance to the profession; in addition to a degree from a university attendance at educational training programs was required by school administrators.
Indeed, by the Conditions of Registration issued in late 1913, one
year's professional training was demanded for all who joined the
teaching profession after 1918.

The Assistant Mistresses Association in 1912 suggested 120
pounds per annum as the minimum salary for those who entered
the field with a degree and professional training, rising to 220
pounds in ten years and 250 for those with special responsibilities;
it established the range 100 to 180 pounds for those without a
degree. The Girls' Public Day Schools and local education authorities with the exception of the London County Council did not meet
the desired scale. Women teachers' salaries were lower than males':
The scale set by the London County Council in 1913 was:

| MEN | - Assistants | - | 150-300 |
|-----|--------------|---|---------|
|     | Heads        | - | 400-600 |
| WOMEN | - Assistants | - | 120-220 |
|     | Heads        | - | 300-450[34] |

Teaching became the chief profession for female university graduates in the last twenty-five years of the century. Teaching also
meant spinsterhood in that, as already noted, married women were
not welcomed in the profession. Newnham College between 1871
and 1893 had 720 students. In that period 374 of them entered the
teaching profession and 128 married. Girton College from its foundation until 1893 had 467 students of whom 355 received certificates; 123 became teachers, and 46 chose matrimony. Somerville
Hall, Oxford, enrolled 173 students between 1879 and 1892; 73
became teachers, and 29 married. Holloway College had been in
existence less than a decade by the latter date. It had 197 alumnae;
69 taught, and 7 married. From 1871 to 1893 Girton, Newnham,
Somerville, Holloway and Alexandra colleges matriculated 1,486

students; 680 became teachers, 208 married, and 11 entered the medical field.[35]

Certainly at a propitious time, in January 1873, the Women's Education Union launched its own periodical, the *Journal of the Women's Education Union*. Emily Shirreff and G.C.T. Bartley edited the monthly. The *Journal* gave foremost attention to the several objectives of the union and recorded information about the projects which it undertook. It gave publicity to the G.P.D.S.C. and the Teachers' Registration Society. However, it also took a bird's-eye view on a regular schedule of the whole range of educational opportunities for women in England, Scotland, and Ireland; it reported on education for females from kindergarten to university level. The *Journal* vigorously propounded educational reform; it informed the public what was needed in female education, detailed the efforts of various organizations, listed the difficulties and prejudices encountered, and cited the reasons for failures. Clearly it sought to arouse public-spirited citizens and create a coalition to bring about programs of all sorts. "Here it must suffice to remind our readers that where the aim is to influence public opinion, isolated action is feeble action; that scattered efforts, however valuable, possess little weight compared with what they acquire when combined as portions of a systematic movement."[36] The periodical regularly contained articles on educational methodology and philosophy written by educational reformers of the era. It had a missionary flavor to its tone of urgency. Emily Shirreff wrote in the premier issue, "To want of education for women may be traced most of the evil, the loss, and suffering that blot and canker our apparent prosperity, and all that clogs the path of women and lower their influence."

The union in 1878 reached out to working women but in that year its financial condition limited action. It established an Evening College for Women, taking as its model the Evening College for Men and Women in Bloomsbury. Mrs. Grey had devotedly supported the Bloomsbury venture; indeed in the autumn of 1875 she chaired a general meeting of friends of the college at St. George's Hall. The union launched the Brompton Evening College for Women at 1 Queen Street, Brompton, in March 1878. The college served women in Chelsea, Brompton, and Kensington. W. F.

Cowper-Temple presided at the opening session attended by its other supporters, Sydney Burton of the London School Board, Sir George Young, R. N. Shore, the Reverend J. M. Hoare, the Reverend Gerald Blunt, and Rowland Hamilton. Cowper-Temple emphasized the value of the institution as a social center. Indeed he saw its prime function as serving the female community as a club; he regretted that women had not established a center where they could gather for relaxation. The college contained a library and a comfortable sitting room, and light refreshments were available to students. The college offered basic courses in reading, writing, spelling, elementary arithmetic, and geography. Cost varied from 2 shillings and 6 pence for two nights of academic work per week to four shillings and 6 pence for four nights per week. In addition it offered courses in grammar, composition, English literature, history, natural science, and mathematics.[37] The executive committee of the college included R. H. Shore, chairman, Mr. and Mrs. C. S. Roundell, Mrs. Lecky, Mrs. Stair Douglas, Miss Westmacott, Mrs. W. E. Hall, and Miss Frances Martin. It rented the college building for five years for 120 pounds. It enrolled forty-five students in the first session. Shop girls, nurses, upper servants, and teachers attended the college. Friends of the college donated many of its fittings, easy chairs, a piano, and other equipment. The college sponsored travel lectures, literary readings, and musical evenings.[38] The union in 1879 in its annual report noted that the college was a heavy financial burden. The union expended 250 pounds on the project; the return was 64 pounds in donations and subscriptions and 21 pounds in fees.[39]

In 1880 the Women's Education Union endeavored in a limited way to fulfill a stated goal which it had ignored up to that point, aid to a sector of the educational profession quite at the mercy of society, the unorganized sisterhood of governesses. The union revealed that hardly a week passed without governesses soliciting it for posts as well as families seeking governesses. In the autumn of 1880 the union launched a governesses registry. Although private agencies abounded, the union believed that a sound reason existed for its entrance into the field. Some governesses did not want to go to a commercial agency because of a number of factors, the most important probably being the high cost of the service, often 25 percent of the first year's salary. The union promised to establish full files on governesses who became affiliated with the registry in contrast to the vague information available in many commercial agencies. The union also promised minimal fees for its services.[40]

The Women's Education Union existed eleven years; it dissolved in July 1882. Maria Grey urged that step throughout the spring of 1882 because the organization had completed its mission. "The Union and its promoters could sing their Nunc Dimittis with clear conscience and they did."[41] The union had labored diligently to keep out of debt. The Girls' Public Day School Company had been a financial success, but the *Journal* and the other projects of the union had not achieved a firm financial footing. It is quite obvious from a letter written by Maria Grey in 1880 that she had urged the dissolution of the organization as early as 1878. At that point the *Journal* had been reduced to a mere four pages. "Neither my sister nor I had any voice in the matter, and I cannot help feeling mortified and grieved that the Union founded with so much care and labour should be allowed to die of starvation instead of, as I urged two years ago dissolving itself, having done its work, and retiring in a dignified manner from the field in which the battle had been won."[42]

The various projects of the union drained the meager resources of the organization. In 1877 Maria Grey made a public appeal by letters to the *Times* and the *Daily News* for donations. In spite of the depressed economic condition she was able to raise sufficient funds to carry the organization through the year. The total expenditures of the union and the Teachers' Training and Registration Society in the year 1877 amounted approximately to 1,467 pounds. The major expenses are listed in Table 1.

The Teachers' Training and Registration Society had made a herculean effort to get the Maria Grey Training College launched and developed into a viable institution, and it did not seem feasible to found other institutions because the society could not command the sizable financial resources needed. The union had fulfilled major goals; it had been the parent of the organization which established a system of secondary schools for girls, and secondly, another offshoot opened a model teacher training institution. It had undertaken valuable publicity missions; it explored with other educa-

| Table 1 | | |
|---|---|---|
| | *POUNDS* | *SHILLINGS* |
| *Union* | | |
| Rent | 90 | 9 |
| Salaries | 193 | 7 |
| Printing and Salaries | 37 | 18 |
| Advertisements | 11 | 17 |
| Postage | 33 | 3 |
| Expense of meetings | 1 | 5 |
| Journal publications | 154 | 5 |
| Scholarships | 225 | 0 |
| *Teachers' Fund* | | |
| Teachers' library | 10 | 5 |
| Lectures | 45 | 2 |
| Teachers' loans | 50 | 0 |
| *Teachers' Training and Registration Society* | | |
| Registration fees | 67 | 15 |
| Lecture fees | 45 | 0 |
| Secretary's salaries | 48 | 0 |
| Sundry expenses | 12 | 16 |

tional agencies as well as government authorities the issue of an enforceable system of professional preparation and standards for teachers; it made known to women a variety of educational opportunities which were available to them; it brought to public notice progressive educational methodology and relevant areas of educational development on the Continent and in the United States. Finally the union had been a prime instrument for the creation of a women's educational movement. Despite Maria Grey's feeling that the work of the union had been accomplished, the *Daily News* discussed an area where it believed the union could fulfill a need, and that need was not met in subsequent years.[43] It considered that some of the union's peripheral missions actually were most necessary. It saw the union as an ideal agency to organize the process of female education on some rational and coordinated method—to be a center of communication and information, a Bureau of National Education for Women.[44]

Certainly at the launching of the union Maria Grey had evoked for it an animating spirit which would have been applicable to such a mission. In the first volume of the *Journal* she observed that the union was designed to be a framework of sufficient scope to include all partial and local organizations multiplying their power by combination and cooperation. She commented that although the women's educational movement had spawned organizations of magnitude and dedication, none had been large enough to cover the entire ground.[45] But a decade later Maria did not see the necessity for the union to lead the women's educational movement into a second stage, for she had been impressed with many educational triumphs for her sex in institutional development. Women's educational leaders in the twentieth century saw the situation as more complex than that envisaged by their predecessors.

In the main the Shirreffs wished to bring women's education into the large picture of which they saw it as an integral part.

Below the question we have specially set ourselves to answer: How should women be educated?—lies a broader and deeper one, What is education, and why is it wanted for men or women?, and the answer to the former can never be satisfactory, it can never rest on principle as distinguished from the expediency of time or place, or social degree, till we have the answer to the latter. Hence we have to deal with principles, bearing not on one sex only, but on human nature and human life.[46]

In 1897, the year that Emily died and Maria entered the secluded last decade of her life, Dorothea Beale of Cheltenham discussed the work that needed to be done in education, registration and certification of teachers which was not universal, enlarged and refined teacher training programs, and methodological experimentation. She also issued a special plea for greater work in kindergarten and infant education. She observed that children were often injured and distorted in the nursery. "We need others who will take charge of little children from still earlier years...and treat them from the beginning with such wisdom and gentleness and firmness that Mind and Emotions and Will will be harmoniously developed and the first seven years most precious for the foundation of character may not be wasted."[47]

The Shirreffs had been pioneers in all the areas of education that Miss Beale mentioned. But given the outlook of the Shirreffs, the exclusive control of those areas by organizations totally committed to the women's cause would doubtless in their opinion have been limiting. Miss Buss wrote to Maria Grey earlier that the real struggle which still had to be fought "I fear is the one as old as education itself, How is the child of either sex to be trained to measure of the perfect human being?"[48]

# 9

# Early Childhood Education: The Need and the Response

In 1874 Emily Shirreff embarked upon an area of educational work which became her primary professional focus until ill health and advancing age forced her into inactivity.[1] Miss Beata Doreck, who had founded one of the first kindergartens in England, and Fräulein Eleonore Heerwart invited Emily and Maria to a meeting on November 2, 1874, at the Doreck home to consider launching an organization concerned with the education of the young child on Froebelian principles.[2] In February 1875 at Miss Doreck's home the Froebel Society for promoting the kindergarten came into existence with Miss Doreck as president. A few months later she died at the comparatively early age of forty-two. She had been born in Mannheim, the daughter of a jeweler. She attended normal school at Ribonville, Alsace. For a number of years she worked as a governess in England and then opened a school in Kildare Terrace which she moved in 1868 to Kensington Square Gardens. In December 1875 the society elected Emily Shirreff president, and she undertook her duties with dedication and vigor.

The committee which assisted Emily included Maria Grey, vice-president, the Reverend H. Bourne, Frances Mary Buss, Eleonore Heerwart of the Stockwell Kindergarten Training College, Mary Gurney, Miss Emilie Michaelis, director of a kindergarten at Croydon who formed teacher training classes there, Miss E. A. Manning, Mr. Sonnenschein, secretary, and Dr. M. Roth. In December 1876 Maria Grey sketched out the grand design of the new organization. It disseminated information about Froebelian principles and in the process counteracted the prevalent view that kindergartens were organized play centers which destroyed the individuality of the child. Secondly, the society sought in several ways to provide trained teachers for kindergarten. Mrs. Grey insisted that teachers who entered the field should be well educated.

How indeed can a teacher herself untrained to accurate perceptions, observation, comparison and correct drawing of inferences from facts observed and compared, who knows nothing of mental processes by which elementary facts of geometry and arithmetic became the basis of science, nor of the learning of all these things on the formation of association and habits, use them as Froebel intended as means toward an ulterior and to her an uncomprehended and unthought of end.... The world of action is divided unfortunately very unequally between two classes of people, those who can follow a rule and those who can apply a principle. The former will never make good kindergarten teachers.[3]

Maria Grey recounted the steps the society took during its first year of operation to fulfill that objective: examinations to test the knowledge of teachers and certificates of qualification. Candidates who sought the society's approval had to produce evidence of sound basic knowledge, a certificate from a recognized examining body which attested to the candidate's competency in English, arithmetic, physical geography, and English history. The society's examination focused on special kindergarten subjects to be taught, theories of education, elementary drawing and geometry, and several of the natural sciences as well as evidence of successful practice teaching. Madame de Portugall examined students in professional areas, Dr. Francis Hoggan in scientific subjects, laws of physiology, and hygiene, and Miss Chessar in basic preliminary general knowledge.

Emily Shirreff, and to a lesser degree Maria Shirreff Grey, shaped the Froebelian movement during its second and enlarged stage of activity in Britain. Doubtless Madam Bertha Ronge, who came to London at mid-century with her husband Johannes, a refugee from Germany, was the pioneer Froebelian leader.[4] She belonged to the public-spirited Meyer family of Hamburg. Its male members, wealthy Jewish businessmen, gave generously to various educational agencies and causes there. Her father, Henry Adolph Meyer, gave to Hamburg a zoological garden and aquarium and supported the Froebelian cause in North Germany. Bertha Meyer had been a pupil of Froebel and married, against her family's wishes, Johannes Ronge, a radical who had abandoned the Catholic priesthood. Her sister Margarethe, who came to London to assist her, met and married there Carl Schurz, a German refugee. Margarethe Schurz, who migrated to the United States, became a foremost proponent of the kindergarten in her new homeland. Her husband, of course, became a major political leader in the United States of America. Madame Ronge established a small kindergarten in Hampstead in 1851 but moved to a more central location in Tavistock Square in 1854. Members of the Hill family, who had established their experimental educational center at Hazelwood, aided her venture. Madame Ronge also organized a kindergarten in Manchester and lectured on Froebelian principles there. She recruited a number of able assistants, in particular Mr. Borschetzky, a musician who imaginatively employed music, songs, and gymnastics in the educational regimen, and Maria Boelte Krauss who had studied with Froebel's widow in the latter's home and after migration to the United States become a devoted and respected early childhood educator there. In 1858 the Ronges noted that they had given Froebelian instruction to about fifty teachers, mothers, and nurses, and they estimated that thirty kindergartens operated in various parts of the country on Froebelian principles.

Informal and personal contact spread the new educational ideology among influential circles. Maria Boelte gave some details. While she served at the Ronge kindergarden, she met a diversified group of people including Charles Dickens, Arnold Ruge, Carl Blind, G. Kinkel, Angelike von Lagerström, Joseph Mazzini, and Charles Kean. At the closing of the Ronge venture she served as a teacher in the family of the daughter of Chief Justice Lord Denman, who was the sister-in-law of Lord Macaulay. Lord Brougham's grandchildren were her pupils, and James Nasmyth, engineer and inventor, became a zealot for the cause. Leaders of the Jewish community in Britain, the Goldsmids, the Waleys, the Rothschilds, Moses Montefiore, and Sir David Soloman, sympathized with the innovative Froebelian methodology.[5]

In 1854 at the International Exhibition of Educational Systems and Materials at St. Martin's Hall, London, Charles Hoffman of Hamburg presented Froebel's ideas, and half a dozen years later at the International Exhibition (1862) in London, Froebelian concepts were developed for interested citizens by Heinrich Hoffman, Maria Boelte, and the Misses Praetorius. Baroness Marenholtz-Bülow came to Britain in the late fifties to meet the public and spread the Froebelian message. But it took another generation for the first tentative official action to occur. In 1874 the London School Board appointed Caroline Bishop to lecture on the methods and principles of the kindergarten to teachers in infant schools, and in the same year Eleonore Heerwart was hired by the British and Foreign School Society.

Victorian writers and artists shaped the ideas of educated men and women about the qualities of childhood and the needs of the child. The work of creative men and women in art and literature often contained messages that supported Froebelian thought, particularly the non-simplistic character of childhood and its importance in the total structure of each person's existence as well as in societal life. Of course any analysis of the multifaceted nature of childhood depicted by artists and writers would be a major research project. In this study the field is merely opened for consideration.

Popular novelists of the era made children central characters in their works. Charles Dickens imparted individuality to his child characters and treated them in a sensitive way, creating Oliver Twist, Pip, and Little Nell. Indeed, in such novels as *Nicholas Nickleby, David Copperfield,* and *Hard Times,* he probed the effect of education, family relationships, and contemporary social problems which grew out of industrialization on child life. In *Little Dorrit* he said, "The tragedy of Little Dorrit, then, is the tragedy of childhood, distorted, betrayed, forgotten, buried so far down that it no longer seems to exist."[6] Yet he characterized the attributes of childhood as redemptive. "All levels of society are so imprisoned in their selfish delusions that only the mystery of divine goodness incarnate in the childlike form of Little Dorrit can be a liberating force."[7] Writers of fiction often used childhood as a symbol of the earnestness and virtue so venerated by the age.

George Eliot, in *The Mill on the Floss,* drew vivid contrasts between the personalities and interests of Maggie and Tom, the two major child characters; in the novel Eliot discussed education, memory, and the nature of childhood. In *Silas Marner* Eppie was Silas' link to life. "There was love between him and the child that blent them into one, and there was love between the child and the world—from men and women with parental looks and tones, to the red lady-birds and the round peebles."[8] The epigraph of the book was from Wordsworth's "Michael."

> A child more than all other gifts
> That earth can offer to declining man,
> Brings hope with it and forward looking thoughts.

Novelists showed the complexity of childhood, depicting the child's mind, emotions, and relationships, as well as his resilience and optimism, his vulnerability and dependence on others, and above all, the primacy of his moral nature.

And from the opening of the century the child was a recurring focus in the flood of ephemeral sweet and bittersweet verses which appealed to genteel families. Felicia Hemans (1793-1835), whose popularity in retrospect seems difficult to grasp, wrote "The Adopted Child," "The Child's Last Dream," "The Child and the Dove," "Casabianca," and "The Child's First Grief." Several of her poems were set to music, increasing their circulation. George Eliot wrote to Miss Lewis: "I am reading eclectically Mrs. Hemans' poems, and venture to recommend to your perusal, if unknown to you, one of the longest ones—The Forest Sanctuary. I can give it my pet adjective—exquisite."[9] Mrs. Hemans also wrote verses for children; her *Hymns for Childhood* dealt with the young person's affinity for the beauties of nature. The poetry of the age showed a widespread fascination for the lost land of childhood. Typical was "To a Sleeping Child," by John Wilson, professor of moral philosophy at the University of Edinburgh, who wrote under the pseudonym Christopher North in *Blackwood's Magazine.*

> Oh! vision fair! that I could be
> Again, as young, as pure as thee!

Vain wish! the rainbow's radiant form
May view, but cannot brave the storm;
Years can bedim the gorgeous dyes
That paint the bird of paradise,
And years, so fate hath ordered, roll
Clouds o'er the summer of the soul.
Yet sometimes, sudden sights of grace,
Such as the gladness of thy face,
O sinless babe! by God are given
To charm the wanderer back to Heaven.[10]

The almost forgotten Martin Farquhar Tupper, a poetic voice of middle-class England, won fame and adulation for several decades in the mid-nineteenth century. He missed a knighthood by a hairsbreadth, which was doubtless beneficial for the reputation of English letters. In "Of Education" from *Proverbial Philosophy* Tupper sketched both the progressive elements and the limitations of the new middle-class concern over child development. The poem was in accord with the Froebel injunction "Come, let us live with our children."

When his reason yieldeth fruit, make thy child thy friend,
For a filial friend is a double gain, a diamond set in gold.
As an infant, thy mandate was enough, but now let him
    see thy reasons;
Confide in him, but with discretion: and bend a willing
    ear to his questions.
More to thee than all beside, let him owe good counsel
    and good guidance;
Let him feel his pursuits have an interest, more to thee
    than to all beside.
Watch his native capacities; nourish that which suiteth
    him the readiest;
And cultivate early those good inclinations wherein thou
    fearest he is most lacking:
Is he phlegmatic and desponding? let small successes com-
    fort his hope:

Is he obstinate and sanguine? let petty crosses accustom
him to life:

Showeth he a sordid spirit? be quick, and teach him
generosity;

Inclineth he to liberal excess? prove to him how hard it is
to earn.

Gather to thy hearth such friends as are worthy of honour and attention;

For the company a man chooseth is a visible index of his
heart:

But let not the pastor whom thou hearest be too much a
familiar in thy house,

For thy children may see his infirmities, and learn to cavil
at his teaching.

It is well to take hold on occasions, and render indirect instruction:

It is better to teach upon a system, and reap the wisdom
of books:

The history of nations yieldeth grand outlines: of persons,
minute details;

Poetry is polish to the mind, and high abstractions cleanse
it.

Consider the station of thy son, and breed him to his fortune with judgment:

The rich may profit in much which would bring small advantage to the poor.

But with all thy care for thy son, with all thy strivings for
his welfare,

Expect disappointment, and look for pain: for he is of an
evil stock, and will grieve thee.[11]

In the closing stark sentiment Tupper brought middle-class hopes
and detailed plans for individual improvement under the dark veil
of original sin.

The frequency with which children appear in literary surroundings which
discuss man's fallen nature (and the surprising tendency of these discus-

sions to support the orthodox position of the Church) suggests at least the premise that the child figure in English literature generally appears in thematic surroundings which discuss the Fall of Man, and that the norm against which we have become accustomed to measure these discussions is the Christian doctrine of Original Sin.[12]

The Shirreff sisters sponsored a theology that was comprehensive. Their religion was largely non-doctrinal and stressed the joyful application of general principles found in the New Testament. "Where fear is the ruling motive, we shall find only so much of integrity, purity, and obedience as may secure safety from punishment instead of the unconstrained and joyful obedience of the heart, 'whose service is perfect freedom.' "[13] They rejected what they called Christian extremists—on one side, those who considered only religious emotions and sentiments as worthy and rejected reason as impious, and on the other side, those who relied totally on dogma, obedience to the church, and outward conformity. "Bigotry and intolerance has ever been common to both."[14] The sisters felt that both groups often feared and mistrusted science and literature. They claimed that although buildings consecrated to the worship of God were needed, the wide universe was God's true temple and every spot was equally consecrated by His all-pervading presence. Quite clearly Maria and Emily sought a flexible approach to religion. "To be consistent with our own principles, we must admit that sincere and earnest conviction is the only test we have a right to require of the religious feelings of another."[15] Such attitudes were compatible with Froebel's religious emphasis. The Shirreffs wanted to bring to the child Christian principles and ethics and have him apply them daily. They deplored the separation of religious and secular life and the failure to relate one to the other. "The child feels this discrepancy long before he understands it. It widens with every succeeding year...and ends at last, but too often, in open irreligion,or in that formal profession which is almost worse."[16]

In the mid-Victorian period the popular reading material which adults directed to children often depicted the young person as an eager learner. Froebelians agreed with that assessment of child nature but not with the way in which traditional education had fostered learning. At the end of the seventies Lilian Faithful wrote about the young generation's changed outlook. "We inherited these lesson books, but a new era was approaching, and we resented what our elders had accepted meekly enough, and scorned the priggish children who were introduced as asking intelligent questions, and who appeared genuinely anxious to learn."[17] Many of the children's stories in the late decades of Victoria's reign were in accord with the key themes favored by Froebelians. Charles Kingsley in *Water Babies* touched the child's imaginative powers and presented information about natural history. "I have tried in all sorts of queer ways to make children and grown folks understand that there is a quite miraculous and divine element underlying all physical nature."[18]

Leading artists also made portrait studies of the child. Of course artists had given considerable attention to young people in the late eighteenth century, but there was a new focus on the special qualities of childhood which enhanced or gave dimension to the accepted standards of the era—truth, sentiment, and health. "But the constant refrain in all the writing of the period and the touchstone of every judgment was whether the work attained 'truth' generally to nature and therefore, by implication, to God's creation, whether it was morally healthy and therefore fit for consumption."[19] John Millais, in *A Child's World*, showed a blond, bright-eyed, young boy blowing bubbles with an expression of enchantment on his face. Pears, a soap company, in the spirit of enterprising industrialism purchased the right to reproduce the painting and used it as a commercial symbol. In *Cherry Ripe* Millais presented a sweet-faced girl, the essence of female innocence, and in 1881 the *Illustrated London News* reproduced six hundred thousand copies of the portrait. In the same category was James Sant's *Little Red Riding Hood* which achieved phenomenal popularity when it was reproduced for a mass audience. That fictional character was portrayed by several artists, including Landseer, Millais, Watts, Mostyn, William Oliver, and Sophia Anderson. Artists showed children in a variety of moods—joyous, recalcitrant (Landseer's *The Naughty Child*), pampered, cherubic, maltreated and forlorn—and as beings of intense feeling, capable of a wide range of emotions, but above all as God's creatures waiting to be brought to full potential.

Sentiment led easily to sentimentality in art, and this tendency appeared at times within the Froebelian league.

Children also appeared as central characters in historical, allegorical, and other genre paintings. These paintings were popular with Victorians, and artists produced them in a seemingly endless stream.[20] G. K. Chesterton noted that it was a world in which painters were trying to be novelists.[21] Artists depicted children as an integral part of human civilization; the problems and joys of society were theirs, as well as adults', and shaped their lives in crucial areas. Alexander Farmer focused on the sickness of children in *An Anxious Hour*; Charles Leslie, in *A Garden Scene*, on the exuberance of children at play. W. F. Witherington selected a similar theme, a romanticized scene of working-class children on a holiday, in *The Hop Garden*, as did William Collins in *Rustic Civility*. George Mulready explored the vivacity of childhood in a number of paintings; in *Giving a Bite* and *The Sailing Match* he drew children in a playful mood, while in *The Fight Interrupted* he emphasized their aggressiveness. In a different mood Thomas Faed disclosed, in *The Mitherless Bairn*, the sorrow of the orphan.[22]

Members of the Cranbrook Colony of Kent were especially interested in children. In *Rocking the Cradle* Thomas Webster showed a child facing a conflict between the duty of caring for an infant and his desire to join playmates. In *Sickness and Health*, he contrasted the healthy child with the ill one. J. C. Horsley explored the qualities of youth and adulthood in *Youth and Age*, and F. D. Hardy gave attention to the child's imitation of the adult in *Playing at Doctors*. These visual stimuli led middle-class and upper-class English families to reflect on the child and his involvement in society.

While these artists examined the attributes of childhood with an eye to the social gospel and moral guidelines of the age, Thomas C. Gotch, who achieved recognition at the turn of the century, was child-oriented in a post-Froebelian sense. He studied at Heatherly's School in London, the School of Fine Arts in Antwerp, and worked at the Slade School as well as the studio of John Laurens in Paris. In such works as *The Child Enthroned* and *A Pageant of Childhood*, he cast the child as the incarnation of a revitalized society.

It goes beyond the idea that the child has a claim upon the state for education; it recognizes the previous duty of the state to insure as far as possible that the child shall be so born and nurtured as to derive from education the utmost benefit.... In a new sense, therefore, and a higher one, it believes in the sanctity of childhood, and as a necessary corollary, in the sanctity of motherhood.[23]

Charles Caffin, author of this evaluation of Gotch's ideology, pointed out that it looked to a future reign of reason, when the sanctity of childhood would not be tainted by inherited disease or evil environment.

The annual exhibitions at the Royal Academy in the mid- and late-Victorian era often drew more than two hundred thousand people. In 1892 about three hundred journalists and reviewers attended its annual press day and reported on the exhibition to the general public. On a regular schedule the various art societies and private galleries in London and provincial cities held exhibitions which also drew large numbers of Englishmen and women. The Manchester exhibitions of 1857 and 1887 and the Jubilee Exhibition of 1887, organized by Agnew, were national events. Periodicals in the art field, such as the *Art Journal* and the *Magazine of Art*, discussed the social and moral ideology of nineteenth-century British art, and the *Illustrated London News*, the *Studio*, and in the last decade of the century, the *Graphic* reproduced popular paintings, as did a variety of publishers. Thus millions received the message of nineteenth-century art.

Maria Grey, although not as prominent in the field of early childhood education as her sister, became an active member of the Froebel Society. She noted that an adequate kindergarten was an expensive institution; it required small classes of no more than fifteen, a playground, adequate equipment of all sorts, a museum containing a variety of materials, and a library. She maintained firmly that the Froebel Society advocate instruction of females in principles of early childhood education, not merely those who intended to become teachers but all females because the majority had close contact with and indeed guided children sometime during their lives. "The spontaneous movements of the infant, and the order in which they occur in the first years of his existence will convey a world of knowledge to the observer who has learnt to connect the facts, and to draw from them a sound inference. But they will convey to the untrained observer nothing more than a sense of pleasure as indications of a healthy life."[24] Maria sought for nurses and governesses special education because in her estimation the numbers of children turned over each year to vulgar, ignorant, and prejudiced maids was a national scandal.

By the opening of 1876 the Froebel Society had about one hundred fifty members; in that year it held monthly lectures on a wide range of professional subjects including physical education of young children by Dr. Roth, kindergarten games and music by Madame Michaelis, kindergartens in Germany and Italy as well as the history of kindergartens by Fräulein Heerwart, vocal gymnastics by Alexander Ellis, and the kindergarten as a basis for reform in education by W. H. Herford. Debates and questions followed lectures. Although the society candidly pointed out that many qualifications of kindergarten teachers could not be fully ascertained by examinations, it maintained that the process provided a means to indicate indispensable areas for study, set forth standards in those areas, and brought to public notice the need for adequate preparation in the field of early childhood education. The society published a syllabus of examination subjects in November 1875 and held an examination the following July 18 to 22. Thirteen women passed the examination; six had studied at Stockwell Training College, three at the Girls' College, Southampton, and four had engaged in private study, supplemented by practice teaching in the classroom.[25]

In 1876 the society sponsored classes in physiology, kindergarten songs and games, the art of relating stories, and kindergarten occupations at the College for Men and Women, Queen Square. Between thirty and forty people attended the classes; the majority were assistant teachers and mothers. Another class operated at 24 Chilworth Street, Hyde Park. In the autumn of 1877 the College of Preceptors launched kindergarten classes at its center. The society formed alliances with the several kindergarten education centers in the country, perhaps most closely with the Kindergarten College and Practice School, 21 Stockwell Road, conducted by Fräulein Heerwart under the auspices of the British and Foreign School

Society. It had approximately sixteen students in 1877. Madame Emilie Michaelis had a training program in conjunction with her Croydon kindergarten. Miss Sherwood and Miss Sim had a program for prospective kindergarten teachers at the Girls' College, Southampton, and the Manchester Kindergarten Association held classes regularly. In 1878 the Froebel Society instituted the London College for Kinder Garten Teachers under the supervision of Miss Bishop; all students there took examinations prepared by the society.

In 1883 the Maria Grey Training College absorbed the Froebel Society's Training College. The former training college remained oriented toward the education of women for work with young children. The college employed Professor James Sully as a lecturer on the theory of education from 1879 to 1892. Sully and his more famous compatriot Dr. Ward, who gave his brilliant and forward-looking lectures on education and children at Cambridge University in 1880, were the major English psychologists concerned with children.[26] Alice Woods, principal of the Maria Grey Training College (1892-1913), subscribed to the flexible reading of Froebel's writings which had been the stance of the Shirreffs. She noted that modern Froebelian thought considered of first importance that the child gain ideas and learn to express them through varied contact with his environment. "It is through self-consciousness and self-determination that his instincts and impulses are, through desire and feeling, to develop into a perfect will. To attain this object he must live in surroundings which will offer every opportunity for action and experiment.... The material he is to use is to be whatever will most closely link him with real life around him." Moreover, she believed, Froebelian thought encouraged the integration of education and psychology. She commented that only slowly and imperfectly had the two areas come together. "The majority of us steadily refused to follow the advice of Froebel and learn directly from the child. We have never left the child free enough to show us what his needs are. We adults have decided from the outset what is good for the child.... We have a profound distrust in the higher and deeper human tendencies."[27] Agnes Ward and Alice Woods, both principals of the college, followed Miss Lushington on the council of examiners of the Froebel Society.

The Girls' Public Day School Company, also due to the guidance of the Shirreffs, sought to improve early childhood education—a large number of its schools developed kindergarten departments. In a letter to the tenth annual meeting of the company Maria Grey repeated her earlier strong endorsement of Froebelian ideology.

No part of our work is more important, for the principle of the Kindergarten, as laid down by its great founder, Froebel, than are the fundamental principles of all scientific method in education; and the value of their application to the sound and natural training of infancy, in preparing and facilitating all later cultivation, is so immense that, if it could be fully grasped by the public mind, it would be felt that training in Kindergarten teaching ought to form a part of the education of every woman having any natural call or capacity for the care of children, whether for love or bread winning.[28]

Emily Shirreff wrote a number of pamphlets for the society, including *A Short Sketch of the Life of Fröbel* (1876), *Kindergarten Principles of Fröbel's System and Their Bearing on Education of Women* (1876), *The Kindergarten at Home* (1884), *Home Education in Relation to the Kinder Garten* (1884), and several of her speeches on Froebelian topics were published. In the late seventies on visits to the European continent she conferred with the leading disciples of Froebelian thought, including Mlle. Proegler and Madame de Portugall, who had been in London earlier but had become inspector of infant schools in the canton of Geneva and later headed the training college of Mrs. Salis Schwabe at Naples. The sisters also advised the grand duchess of Baden on educational matters; she had established a school at her palace.[29]

Emily also conferred on Froebelian teaching with Princess Alice, daughter of Queen Victoria, who resided at Darmstadt. Mary Gladstone gave charming view of Princess Alice's family when she visited the German city in 1878. "At 3 we stalked off to the Palace and paid our respects. As nice a sight as ever I saw—Princess Alice and her 7 children, all ages from 5 to 14, particularly good-looking, bright eager faces, only one boy in the middle. Uncle B talked to H.R.H. and the children gathered round me and made the best of friends."[30]

In the early eighties Emily, freed from editing the *Journal of the Women's Education Union* which had become an increasing burden due to her weakened eyesight and migraine headaches, turned with dedication to the cause of early childhood education. In 1885 the Shirreffs attended an educational conference in Manchester presided over by Lord Aberdare. At the conference they forged a close alliance with Froebel workers in that area; W. H. Herford, a schoolmaster in the city and a zealot for the kindergarten movement gained the adherence of the Manchester Froebel Committee to a union with the Froebel Society of London for the purpose of examination of students and establishment of common standards. The Froebel Union thereby came into being.[31] In 1885 the Froebel Society listed twenty-seven kindergartens in the London area and thirty-eight in the provinces.

Continued deterioration of Emily's health in the late eighties forced her to limit activities; yet, she continued to make the Froebel Society the central focus of her public life. She wrote a number of pieces for the society, including *Culture of the Imagination*. Sir Thomas Acland made possible the publication of her address to the Froebel Society, *Moral Training, Froebel and Spencer*. In *Knowledge, Duty and Faith* Acland wrote, "On this subject a remarkable address which deals with the principles of Mr. Spencer's book was delivered before the Froebel Society by the venerable Miss Shirreff who has done so much to promote kindergarten work in schools. It was my privilege to bring about the publication of this address, entitled Moral Training."[32]

Emily Shirreff's enthusiasm to redesign or, more accurately, create a viable early childhood educational program in Britain was based on her study of the educational needs of the individual from the cradle to maturity. She worked to gain acceptance of the principle that, education of the individual was an intricate process which to a large degree gained its whole direction in the first few years of life. She saw early childhood education not as an insignificant period of learning which was legitimately largely undirected, but of the first order that required careful planning and execution by skilled instructors. She focused on three existing educational and social considerations in her evaluation of the early years of education. The utmost endeavors of elementary schools only imparted the first and simplest notions of necessary knowledge with more or less use of the instruments for acquiring more, together with general benefits that came from the order and discipline of school life. The religious and moral precepts presented in the schools, she said, children found at variance with life beyond the schoolroom. She observed that if people were to benefit by education, they had to learn how to think more clearly, judge more correctly, act according to more fixed principles, have more common sense and relevant notions of duty, and finally have perception enough to take advantage of the opportunities that life presented to add to their stock of attainments. Emily questioned whether these goals could be expected to follow from reading and writing and other small achievements of the elementary school. Yet she decided that such achievements were all that could be expected from that institution even if better methods were introduced. The imperative necessities of life limited the number of years which could be devoted to school, and the work that could be accomplished there was limited by the neglect of those that had gone before.

Emily Shirreff pointed out that the large number of children dealt with in a haphazard manner in infant schools thwarted many of their educational efforts; at an age which required individual attention children were dealt with in masses. She agreed that the influence on character of order, regularity, obedience, and enforced cleanliness were of inestimable value, but in regard to strictly intellectual developments the system of education had not been designed on a scientific plan, and its effect seemed incidental rather than the direct outcome of a clear methodology. The direct teaching, she noted, was supposed to prepare for later school work, but in truth it prepared by a foundation of reading and writing rather than the foundation of "quickened faculties, exercised heads, and habits of comparing and judging, of speaking and moving accurately." Moreover, she added that a vast number of students did not even come under the imperfect guidance of infant schools.

In such a situation, Emily said, the schoolteacher dealt with students who were not only ignorant but already warped in their moral and intellectual growth. And so secondly, she charged that the rapid expansion of children's faculties which progressed from birth in most cases went forward unwatched and undirected, and so a great amount of what they had learned by themselves had been inaccurately absorbed and thus hindered rather than aided the instruction they received in school. Therefore, Emily said that the early period of life, when mental and physical growth were so important, was treated in a slipshod fashion, which caused a failure of education in later life. She insisted that education was not just the absorption of knowledge but a disciplining of the faculties in order to observe, draw inferences, and make judgments. "The child inevitably uses his faculties as he uses his limbs. The only question is whether he shall grope with the former or learn to use them rightly and with a purpose as he learns to walk or throw a ball."

Emily Shirreff insisted that female education was inevitably bound up with infant education and the latter the basis for societal progress. "We may fearlessly lay down the axiom that education in its true sense, as a real civilizing power, will remain in abeyance till women are recognized as the natural educator, and till then we shall continue to make vain efforts to supplement with instruction the absence of the wider influence of education."[33] She saw the process of education appropriately launched at the earliest dawn of life and the mother the natural educator. She drew upon the analysis of Pestalozzi and Rousseau but more particularly Froebel and advocated a definite, far-reaching, conscious infant education in place of desultory bringing up, and women were the crucial element in its success.

Emily Shirreff agreed that some women had an instinctive gift for child rearing; it was a natural ability which could be found in human beings in several other roles. But she insisted that the mass of women were not endowed with a special talent. If that analysis was true, she came to her third point: that a system had to be devised which could be used by vast numbers of women who were engaged in child rearing. She felt that, by and large, maternal affection was widespread and so could be assumed to be innate or, more accurately, natural but not the ability to provide knowledge, whether of human nature in which principles of education had their root or the branches of instruction which furnished the subject matter of education. Although it was not indispensable for women to be teachers, she maintained that they should know what constituted good teaching and the results to be sought for their offspring. All school education, she stated, required the foundation, support, and complement of home education.

Emily characterized the home as the crucial factor in this process. She claimed that a child of ten years or more distinguished between the formal teaching situation and the general influence of home. The child could determine, she added, where he was stimulated to expand his faculties, behave constructively, and seek the praise which meant most to him. Young children, on the other hand, could not make such distinctions and suffered from the shock produced by differences of treatment they could not understand and cope with. Home education, therefore, she judged to be the pivot on which all ultimately turned.

Emily explained that the disappointment which followed the high hopes of those who had looked to universal education as the regenerator of the nation could be ascribed to the lack of attention to areas discussed. She placed wasted forces in three categories, (1) the waste of money and labor in giving instruction which was mainly expected to produce the fruits of education, (2) waste of the immense potential for development of the child's faculties during the years that were put to no acount, and (3) waste of women's educational power and position. The latter she maintained had a direct impact on the other two and so on every count claimed the most serious attention. For that reason she asked women to observe the child's nature and growth and eliminate adverse influences which warped development. She reasoned that early childhood education had not received enough serious study because it did not produce visible results of a traditional sort.[34] If reading and writing were cultivated at that stage, she said, public enthusiasm would be evoked. Manual dexterity, a facet of early childhood education, she felt won approval from the general public mainly by its visibly impressive character.

However, Emily designated as the prime focus of the early years the cultivation of the faculties upon which future work and self-development depended. She pointed out that vast numbers of people were ignorant about the character of the various mental faculties and the reasons why one or another mode of bringing them into action produced good or evil results. To such people, she noted, seeing was much the same as observing, and they perceived little difference between knowing a thing by rote and truly understanding it, and reasoning they believed was the province of the learned. They did not grasp the fact that the same process was vital to avoid blunders in common judgment which at first glance seemed so simple. In reality Emily Shirreff called upon women to recognize how much had to be done to prepare the child to see, to think, to act, and to learn with correctness and precision.

In order to gain the desired objectives, Emily announced that a multifaceted program had to be instituted; organizational activity was vital, but the goal also had to be furthered by parent and teacher relationships. She suggested frequent visits to classes by mothers of pupils and discussion meetings on a regular basis. "All minor difficulties will vanish if mothers learn enough to feel the value of what their children are learning." But involvement of parents, in particular mothers, in the educational process, Emily believed, would also solve some of the most serious and far-reaching controversies in the field. The battle which raged about academic pressure put upon children by modern educational systems, she concluded, would fade away if mothers became seriously involved in the education of their children. She reminded parents of day school pupils that time in school amounted only to 20 hours per week, and they controlled 148 hours of their children's lives. If parents came to terms with their children's needs and desires as well as responsibilities to society, she claimed, mothers would be able to consult intelligently with teachers and set up a program of home life and study which enriched and supplemented rather than frustrated the school regimen. "Naturally mistakes would still occur on both sides, but we should never see the misconception, the antagonism, the divided, often contrary influence, the early neglect and the impatient ambitions that thwart the work of the best schools now."

Miss Shirreff made it clear that her strictures on parents, primarily mothers, were actually strictures on society and the national heritage. "Their neglect was that of the nation at large." Reflecting some of the attitudes basic to her era, she expressed deep faith in the efficacy of educational programs but at the same time the expectation that education was a slow and, indeed, painful process at times. "Very slowly can those who have inherited this burden come to the full consciousness of what it is now encumbent upon them to do; and very slowly will the great number grope their way towards doing it. It is well to remember this when we seem to blame persons and are rather blaming the conditions under which they have grown up and lived."

Nevertheless, Emily Shirreff called "thrilling" Froebel's call to women to be no longer satisfied with simply the lower cares of motherhood.[35] She set forth as a prime mission for women the education of the child, first in the cradle and then the nursery; she asked them not to wait until the education of their children was taken in hand in the schoolroom in a formal fashion. She urged, as did her sister, the inclusion of educational courses, both practical and philosophical, as required subject matter in curricula for girls, even those who planned careers in the professions and business. The advantages to any female she described as development of a clear and cultivated understanding, careful habits of observation and reasoning, basic knowledge of the first principles of biological sciences, an attention to the personality and character of others, a sense of duty and recognition of order and progression to human existence. She explained why such a position was compatible with her basic philosophy of the absolute mental freedom of women, their indefeasible right as human beings to study any subject which attracted them and spend their energies in any direction that promised the most enjoyment or advantage. However, she believed, nature had placed special claims upon men and likewise special claims upon women; the former had to defend their homeland, the latter care for children and cultivate their humanity. She characterized women's commitment to knowledge about children and education as a profession; she used the term profession because in Britain it connoted a role and vocation which enjoyed great respect.

Emily Shirreff rejoiced that the various classes formed for women in the sixties and seventies had contributed to a serious assault upon the popular but shortsighted view that the close of school life was the close of study. However, she recognized that there was no universal acceptance of the ongoing character of learning for women, or what was equally important, curriculum schemes that allowed women to carry forward learning patterns that were relevant to their style of living, their needs and interests. The desultory and piecemeal character of women's education disturbed Emily; a clear line had not been drawn between what was essential and what could be left to individual choice. She wanted to establish a guiding thread, a link of purpose in studies for women that gave coherence and stability. She divided the learning structure into three stages, first, a proper foundation for intellectual enlargement and cultivation of the capacity for work, second, acquisition of what was essential for each person's distinctive duties in life, and third, free choice to gratify love of knowledge which had been developed in the earlier periods. In girls' education Emily stated that such a sequence had been lacking; in efforts to shake off the past it was easy, she thought, to overlook method and purpose in favor of varied acquirements.

Basic knowledge in three subjects, she said, was essential for women to fulfill their role as mother or guide of children—human physiology, mental and moral philosophy, and social economy.[36] She considered these subjects beyond the scope of ordinary school curricula. Indeed she claimed the same subjects were equally desirable for men. It was absolutely imperative, she asserted, for women to know the physical structure and developmental growth pattern of children; hygiene had to be treated as a part of applied physiology or else it was merely a set of rules. She emphasized that students needed demonstrations and lectures as well as texts on the subject. Moreover, she advocated attachment of girls for weeks or months to hospitals.

Emily Shirreff defined mental philosophy as the science that dealt with the particularities of mental organization, that systemized the observations founded on consciousness and showed their connection and tendencies. The study, she said, allowed women to discover qualities of the mental processes and as a result detect in the child symptoms of physical disturbances and counteract them as well as cultivate the will and give it direction. Emily did not feel that love and common sense were sufficient for women to depend upon to shape the growth of the child. She observed that mental philosophy like physiology had to be applied by women.

It is not enough to one who may have the whole welfare of the helpless child cast into her hands to read about the intellectual and moral faculties of man. She must learn to watch the early manifestation of some faculties, and to use each resource that the mental nature affords, to direct and control, to plant and to weed out, to form links for future action, to preserve freedom in the midst of protecting care. Infinite pains, infinite patience, minute observation and careful regard for the future in the midst of the difficulties of the present, all these are wanted.[37]

And so Emily Shirreff suggested study of basic principles of child psychology for women and application of it to their duty of child rearing.

Emily set down as essential for young women a familiarity with and understanding of social economy. The latter she defined in broad terms; in effect it combined the fields of sociology, political science, and consumer economics.[38] Women had the duty, according to Emily, to shape the outlook of the child about these areas of human concern. Firstly, the mother by means of household expenses should bring before the child issues of remunerative or unremunerative expenditure, the character of savings, and employment of labor. Secondly, Emily thought the concept of charity, personal and societal, the duty to depressed members of the community and lastly, examination of public issues of the day and formation of opinions about proposed programs for the general commonwealth should be presented in the domestic circle in order to make them an ongoing concern of children.

The age in which we live is essentially one of social reform—reform needing the united action of unselfish feeling and of sound knowledge based on scientific truth, and carried forward on that wave of emotion which transforms conviction into motive; and therefore it is that the subtle and powerful influence of women is much needed as an instrument of national welfare.[39]

Emily endeavored to answer a query about the applicability of her ideas and schema to the masses, that is, the working-class population, because she had given primary attention in her writings in the mid-century decades to regimens of enlightenment for middle- and upper-class females. "It is only too certain that education like all other benefits of human knowledge will ever be relative to the class addressed. Means and leisure must ultimately give the measure of what can be attained, however just and liberal the system under which we live."[40] Yet this assessment did not limit her high expectations of what could be done; she judged that as an expansive view of life grew and spread among those who had the most advantages for intellectual enlargement, there would arise a movement to adopt every viable means to elevate all sectors of society. The Shirreff sisters earnestly sought to implement the biblical injunction—I am my brother's keeper—which had become a guideline for large numbers of public-spirited men and women in the Victorian era. Emily reminded people that steps which were the necessary preliminaries for effective early childhood education had already been taken; adult education classes for working-class women had been launched in cooking, domestic management, and sanitation and hygiene. "Why should not the education of little children be the subject of instruction given in the same manner— given widely and frequently and earnestly by women who themselves had every opportunity of acquiring the knowledge they would impart?" She propounded the thesis that acceptance of an effective system of early childhood education had as a necessary corollary a widespread system of home education.[41]

Emily recognized that kindergarten learning and a revamped elementary school curriculum coordinated with it would be most beneficial to the upper and middle classes because it was supplemented by important informal learning experience within the family circle, primarily a facility with language and use of objects which refined the sense of touch and enlarged perception. However, if a child of these classes did not receive progressive formal education in early years, if a male, she felt, he had opportunities to remedy the deficiency. Often he proceeded to a grammar or public school and university where he had sufficient time at least to awaken his intellect. "He has time if he learns how to use it to repair the omissions of the past as far as the laws of nature will ever allow the past to be repaired." Further, Emily commented that a young person of comfortable circumstances had a grand life before him if he knew how to use it, that is, leisure, the means to gain knowledge, and stimulants to ambition to rescue him from natural sloth. She claimed also that a youth who progressed through higher education programs and entered the arena of business could find in a life of such labor a remedy to cultural vacuity which followed in many cases the leaving of school. He had opportunities to gain knowledge and establish a life pattern which kept the spirit of inquiry alive amidst "the deadening influence of ceaseless money-making labour."[42]

On the other hand, Emily judged that though the possibilities for intellectual and cultural development were more limited for working-class children who went through the same early childhood educational programs as their more prosperous brothers and sisters, it was no less valuable to them. Indeed she concluded that adequate early education was tenfold more necessary for workers' children. She felt that children of workers in her own era would have only a limited amount of schooling. Therefore, she desired to utilize the short period devoted to formal learning in the most advantageous way to fit them to be not only productive but also happy human beings. So often the poor youth made no use of his school attainments; he learned to read but had no pleasure in knowledge; he learned to write but only in an awkward and laborious fashion; he worked out arithmetic rules but knew nothing of the relations of numbers.

She hoped that in the new system the child of the worker would come to school from kindergarten with eyes and fingers oriented to drawing, with receptive minds for traditional learning skills, reading, writing, and arithmetic, so that time could be devoted to advanced bodily exercises, manual arts, natural history, and imaginative drawing. The practical education acquired from life by poor youths, Emily felt, could scarcely be considered an elevating force. Accordingly she presented the case that school experience in the early years, which was all that society allowed to the poor, had to be designed so that they could learn the lesson of life in the most productive and satisfying pattern that was possible. Emily felt that it was indispensable not simply to give the child keys or skills to acquire basic knowledge but also the desire to use them and accept the injunction that one could not merely live on a breadwinning level, even if the vast portion of life was directed to that end. In a trenchant observation she noted that

Intellectual life is a barren desert to the child who leaves school with such knowledge as an elementary school can have taught under the given conditions, and whose intelligence has received no other training than such teaching can afford. There is barely time for what is imperatively laid down; how can the schoolmaster mould the dull, ill-trained children that come to him full of false ideas and wrong habits into thinking, observing human beings, able to work and to think intelligently and accurately? And yet if he has not done that, what have these schools done for the nation that pays for them?[43]

Emily urged the public to recognize that the rudiments of knowledge were no talisman for making good citizens, and unless mental discipline concerning the uses of knowledge accompanied the acquisition of skills, there was no real education. She made clear that she did not mean the desire to use knowledge to rise in the world, which was so often discussed in her era but that by which life was made more satisfying and nobler, surroundings more comfortable, and the feelings and spirit oriented to a search for the beautiful in fellow human beings and pattern of life to be followed.

Emily made somewhat grandiose assumptions about what was possible because she had adopted essentially optimistic concepts about human development regulated by an effective learning regimen.

It is easy to forget reading and writing through years of disuse; it is not easy to forget the use of our eyes when we have learned to take pleasure in the exercise. It must be remembered that the development of moral and intellectual faculties is as natural as physical development, the only difference being that it carries with it conscious action, and therefore the possibility of being mentally influenced for good or evil; thus the degree of such development that the child has attained under our guidance at a certain age has a far more permanent character than the degree of his knowledge. The latter is given from without; the former is his own growth, an intrinsic part henceforth of his being.[44]

Emily Shirreff in actuality asserted that society had the duty to provide citizens, male and female, what nature had designed for them, the unfolding of their capacities for productive, moral, and culturally satisfying lives.

Despite Emily's plea for the special need of kindergartens for poor children, the idea languished. Not until 1900 did a free kindergarten open. In that year Adelaide Wragge of Woolwich made an appeal in *Child Life*, the journal of the Froebel Society, for financial aid to open such an institution.[45] The kindergarten opened shortly thereafter; a second formed in Edinburgh in 1903, and one in Birmingham the following year. Lileen Hardy, director of one of the early free kindergartens in the slums of Edinburgh, S. Saviour's Child-Garden founded in 1906, assigned the institution a reformation mission that had been envisioned by the Shirreff sisters for economically and socially deprived children. Miss Hardy after a dozen years of work with her students commented on the experience.

It has borne in on me more and more how bad the destroying influences of the slum environment for children are. We have to see our training continually counteracted and our work undone. They came into the world full of good instincts. At three and four we find them brimming over with love of helping, and at five they are eager and alive with desire for the mysterious and spiritual . . . and yet without someone to help them, "the trailing clouds of glory" must go. The evil effects of the streets are appalling. . . . There is deplorable waste of vitality going on in the slums.

By the opening of the twentieth century educational work with poor and disadvantaged children often merged with a growing movement to meet their minimal physical needs by medical and dental inspection, milk depots, and lunches and soup kitchens. It was recognized that learning did not occur where hunger and deprivation reigned.[46]

Emily Shirreff examined her society and decided that workers in maturity were led to focus almost exclusively on bodily necessities and satisfactions, the latter symbolized by the public house. The only agency which touched large numbers of workers in maturity was the church which reached only a minority of workers, and that for a minimal amount of time. Earlier reformers of the nineteenth century tried to reach workers via cultural entertainment and work-related education, but the mechanics institutes, lyceums, and discussion societies had not involved the number of workers hoped for by their promoters. The Shirreffs propounded the theory that the workers had to be engaged in a significant way in the educational process at the opening of his life and thereby gain the outlook, motivations, and skills which would make viable learning programs at the adult level.

Emily Shirreff called early childhood the crucial base from which a progressive pattern of life could be developed. Modern life forced the work of instruction into grooves that were difficult to abandon. In her opinion the exigencies of university and or professional life governed schools, upper schools governed both the lower and preparatory, and yet the only thing that was not prepared for was life, "making its thousand calls upon will and character which we have allowed chance influence to form; life which calls for all active energies, and of which, as Matthew Arnold so truly says 'Conduct makes up three parts and knowledge only one.' "[47] The opportunity existed, she said, to cultivate at an early age the intellectual qualities that affected conduct, judgment, and accuracy of thought— that power of reasoning promptly and correctly concerning things the individual habitually dealt with which was commonly called common sense, and was the direct consequence not of varied knowledge but of mental discipline. She rejected the demand in her day for knowledge and instruction which overpowered education and would continue to do so unless society could counteract that debilitating influence by artfully and fully utilizing for true educational purposes the early years of a child's life which were free from outer claims. If such a policy were followed, she claimed, the child would enter school amenable to the higher discipline of good teaching.

Emily expressed middle-class faith in education as the means to give the working class the ideals, values, and moral code reverenced by Victorian Christian moralists. She clearly recognized the obvious difficulties faced by working-class youth in achieving a decent standard of living and a stable family life, a topic much discussed in journals and by social commentators. But on the other hand, she was apparently unaware or lacked appreciation of the positive life experiences which came to working-class youth. She demonstrated a somewhat extravagant faith in common sense, in a consensual correct way of reasoning, and in a shared notion of mental discipline as possibly the crucial factors for achievement of a happy and productive life. In effect she placed a major burden upon society to shape moral and social values among sectors of the population where the impact of religion was minimal and the family structure weak. But at the same time she evinced political conservatism in that she said the poor person could not be considered disinherited if not provided with material goods because wealth was not a natural possession or one that could belong to all.[48] Thus she gave society a mission of reform but denied it power to provide adequate material goods to each individual, one of the instruments to build the wholesome and socially productive human being she so earnestly desired. In contrast, as has already been discussed, Maria Shirreff Grey, also a devoted Froebelian, considered economic rights for the working class as imperative to achieving a happy and productive population.

An earlier chapter referred to T.H.S. Escott's appraisal of English education in 1880 in order to place in a socially relevant context the plans of the Shirreff sisters to meet the educational needs of youthful English females. Almost a generation later in 1897, the year Emily Shirreff died, Escott wrote an appraisal of the transformations that had taken place during Victoria's reign, *Social Transformation of the Victorian Age*. He warned that the mass education system which had been created in the long reign that was coming to a close had serious defects.

Those just beings emancipated from the illiteracy or semi-barbarism which have been the traditions of centuries have not yet overcome the agitating strangeness of their new and improved condition. Those above them in the social scale have not yet been able to decide whether to conciliate their educated inferiors as possible friends, or to stand on their guard against them as actual enemies. As the situation becomes more familiar, it will prove less strained. Common sense as a supplement to their zeal, seems the chief want of the educational reformers, official or private, of the day. The tendency is to postpone the development of intelligence to the acquisition of knowledge. The masters whom we are now educating are not in the habit of using their minds for the mere pleasure of intellectual exertion.[49]

The Shirreffs, in their attention to early childhood education in the previous generation (1875-1895), had made a bold effort to contribute to the evolution of a thoughtful and progressive citizenry. Of course, that goal was of supreme concern to the public-spirited members of the intelligentsia who saw the fate of the nation linked to it. But by and large, intellectuals did not focus on a reconstructed early childhood educational system as a basic priority to its accomplishment. In the twentieth century, however, social tensions of various kinds as well as expanded human expectations brought closer attention to the early childhood years by ideologues with various points of view from several disciplines.

# 10

## Froebelian Interpreters and Organizers

Emily Shirreff was one of the first Englishwomen to interpret Froebel for teachers of young children and for the British general public. The goal of Froebel she described as the harmonious unfolding of the child's whole nature with a view to free self-development and action. She noted that freedom and action were more valued by Froebel than by other educators; he had no fear of the vigorous character and sturdy will which troubled old-fashioned educators and child-rearing guides who often displayed a convenient prejudice that feebleness was womanly.[1] With such a stance she said that Froebel strove to have freedom exercised within the moral guidelines of conscience, love, and reverence, and intellectual bounds determined by reason and a sense of harmony. She stressed that Froebel exacted obedience but led the child first to feel and then to know that obedience to a higher wisdom was part of the order of nature in which he lived, so that freedom and law were not opposing forces for the child any more than they were for the adult.

Action and conduct were for Froebel the practical expression at once of the character and intellect for which traditional systems of education of his era did not provide. Emily adhered to the assessment that "thus all Kindergarten teaching ends in work—the pupil must reproduce what he has learnt, he must expose his own thoughts or fancies through the medium of the various exercises."[2] The habit of independent work, she wrote, strengthened the will and steadfastness of purpose which at times could make the child less easy to manage and yet was vital to development of a truly mature person. "In proportion as conduct covers a far larger proportion of human life than abstract thought or knowledge, so does Froebel value the child's work—honest accurate work—beyond his progress in information. Work, which is the breadwinning necessity for the masses of every nation, he considers to be also the right engine of mental and physical development of all mankind." Miss Shirreff admitted that most educational reformers since Pestalozzi had recognized the value of labor as a part of the training of youth, but they kept work and instruction too separated, while Froebel so designed the work that it became the vehicle of instruction.

The assumptions and goals of Friedrich Froebel explored by the Shirreff sisters and other interpreters were compatible with the philosophical idealism of Thomas Hill Green of Balliol College and his followers at Oxford and in the Liberal Party, who had a major impact on public policy in the closing years of the nineteenth century and in the opening decade of the twentieth. Thus Froebelians who sought public support and official regulations to further their educational programs dealt with concepts and assessments about human beings and their legitimate social goals that were agreeable to a dynamic reform school of thought of late Victorian and Edwardian Britain. Both Green and Froebel conceived of education as the great social harmonizer and equalizer; men and women who had been at school together, or more importantly enjoyed the same type of education, hopefully would be free from social animosities and jealousy. Froebel's reverence for order and reliance on the Christian moral code were in accord with Green's concept of citizenship based on justice, equality, middle-class values, and an innate quest of the human being for moral improvement.[3] Green also placed in his spectrum of civic virtues a pattern of education that stretched from childhood to adulthood and was accessible to the general population. His social gospel of idealism was the bridge between classes as well as wealth and poverty, and fellowship the effective link between groups which encouraged self-sacrifice from one segment and self-improvement from the other. "A secularized ascetism thus would be put to work in the one task on which all could agree: the individual character of a kind worth developing."[4]

Green and Froebel believed in progress and the necessity to strive for an ideal which involved human interdependence and the duties imposed by solidarity. But those commitments in no way negated their emphasis on self-help. Green's ethic made improvement one of the vital qualities of morality. Emily Shirreff wrote

The poor man suffers privation from deficient knowledge as from deficient comfort, but he suffers wrong when his education is so defective that he cannot use his human faculties aright, when his senses are blunted, his observation and judgment insecure—his moral sense and activity uncultivated. And it is this disinheriting of our poorer brethren that we may avoid by an early methodological training such as Froebel has taught us.[5]

Self-realization, self-satisfaction, altruism and optimism were ingredients in the chart of Green and Froebel. The Oxford don and the German schoolmaster presented not really an analysis of existing life but rather a vision of what life should be.

In sum, Froebel and his British interpreters provided philosophical and developmental analyses of the human being when he or she was most malleable intellectually, socially, and morally, and the directions Froebel set for the child led comfortably to the life goals of Green.

In effect, what is essential, if we are to be capable of the freedom which on any adequate social theory we need, is a philosophy of education for freedom from the start. That is the great Froebelian revolution...that most searching of moralists Immanuel Kant saw the supreme ethical law in the principle: treat every human being as an end in himself. But most if not all ethics is pivoted on the so called "moral subject," either taken for granted or formally declared to be the responsible adult. We may, I think, account it Froebel's greatest revolution that he extended and deepened and transformed this principle by insisting that we must treat not merely every adult but every child as an end in himself.[6]

And Green placed his credo of personal moral and intellectual growth in a socially relevant setting. "Green adapted idealism to the needs of those who wanted justification for the moral code and values of their parents; he gave conscience a political and social meaning and an outlet to the strong sense of duty and obligation to serve so characteristic of his generation." Moreover, Froebel's respect for the integrity and individuality of each human being and Green's improvement injunction placed responsibility upon each person and also required community regulations and laws that justified the rather sweeping reform program of the first decade of the twentieth century. Their ideas formed a natural link with the women's movement in creation of a commonwealth of citizens concerned about exploring the dimensions of human dignity and fulfillment and social progress compatible with British political ideology and the Christian heritage.

The earliest mental manifestation of the infant was notice of surrounding objects and the desire for activity and then play; therefore, play Emily characterized as one of the major ways that Froebel imaginatively directed the child toward his goals. Secondly, Froebel took advantage of the child's innate curiosity and, Emily felt, presented objects in such a way as to develop that natural instinct into a habit of inquiry—the first step on the road to love of knowledge. Along with curiosity, she said, the faculty of observation was directed by Froebelian methodology; roused by light, color, and motion, the child was led gradually by games to dwell on form and other properties of the objects presented. Froebel accordingly took advantage of the sense of enjoyment and trained the senses to accuracy through games, by work in which the child exercised his ingenuity, and especially by drawing, which he held to be vital in almost every department of active training.[7] Emily considered most important his ordering of games in a manner which imparted a sense of something in common among the children who participated, so that they would feel a loss if disharmony, rudeness, or other more legitimate reasons forced companions apart.

Emily placed in a core area of Froebelian methodology cultivation of the sense of beauty, in color, form, and symmetry, artistic work, harmony of sound and rhythm of movement, the latter manifested in song and dance. In the same category she placed Froebel's interest in the physical world, especially nature as displayed in plant and animal life. He did not bring books into the classroom in kindergarten because he did not want to present anything the child could not clearly understand and verify. The child, therefore, in the Froebelian learning center did not study arithmetic or geometry but discovered facts and truths concerning numbers, lines, and angles basic to the later exploration of formal subjects. Ordinary object lessons used in Pestalozzian training and in infant schools in Britain, she charged, appealed only to vision in order to expand understanding while Froebel had the child handle material and reproduce it by building or drawing it. Emily Shirreff believed that the educational result of the Froebelian scheme was significant: the simultaneous training of the senses and hands in conjunction with the mental faculties. Moreover, the utilization of play she considered to be one of Froebel's major contributions to early childhood education, for it was an ideal socialization process; likewise, observation with emphasis on living nature brought the student into contact with a reality of life. And so Emily felt that a key thrust of Froebel's methodology was to alert the teacher to every natural tendency of the child, to have it unfold in a genial atmosphere of love and care, and to direct it so that habit and association cemented every step of progress made.[8]

Emily Shirreff recognized that the promoters of kindergartens faced a problem—to relate them to the existing school system. Indeed, she saw it as the only serious difficulty in the wide application of the German educator's system. Yet, she concluded that since his system was founded on a valid analysis of human nature, it was simply a matter of adaptation. The games with balls and cubes and sticks were suitable mainly to infant intellects, and yet she pointed out that the principles they furthered—the habit of observing resemblances and differences and testing facts by experiences—were no less valuable for more difficult studies in maturity. The kindergarten of Froebel dealt with concrete and accurate language; the latter Emily designated as the foundation of scientific teaching and accurate thought. Therefore, she considered that one of the major factors which made kindergartens attractive was that the child who attended them had nothing to unlearn as he moved forward in school. Nevertheless, the child faced a problem—to pass from the concrete to the abstract, from object lessons of kindergarten to work by rules and formulas of grammar and arithmetic. "Education according to nature is impossible without harmony between the treatment of the earliest years with that of later periods."

That Emily Shirreff was not a classroom teacher was possibly advantageous to her development of a liberal and flexible interpretation of Friedrich Froebel's ideology. She did not limit her focus to simple formulas which could be used easily with children and often brought a visible response which appealed to the director of a classroom. Of course, Emily advocated the use of Froebel's gifts to initiate the learning patterns he desired, but she did not limit herself to what could and often did become a narrow methodology. She advised the teacher to cultivate children's observational and reasoning powers in a broad fashion by utilizing the everyday features of life that surrounded them. She noted that everyday items could be used by teachers to explore with the children their material composition and method of production as well as substances contained in similar objects in the classroom and the way they had been produced, together with correlated themes.

Emily wanted the teacher to use nature in field and roadway, to examine qualities of soil, movement of water, and other features of the physical world which could establish ideas that would lead naturally to principles in mathematics and science at a later date. Flora and fauna she saw as valuable to develop ideas about color, symmetry, design, and basic structure of plants which related to explorations of botany at a more advanced age.

With geography and history, the same advantage will be felt; the early topographical observations he has been led to make around him—the form of a garden or the pond; the stream always running one way; the wider view obtained by climbing up a hill; the sun sometimes shining on one side of the house, sometimes on the other; the moon occasionally lighting him up to bed, while at other times bright stars shine alone in the darkened heavens; all these things which the child has observed, has thought and asked about again and again, and learned to speak of in accurate language, afford so many links by which the physical geography of wider regions becomes easily knit to his experience and interest. The little stories that he has listened to have never been without a purpose. Where they have not related to facts of natural history, they have touched upon conduct, upon the lives of good men—later on of great men, whose goodness or power had a wider field. The stories are necessarily interrupted because the child's ignorance prevents his understanding more, and each such interruption in a child so trained leads to shake off the ignorance, and to take interest in that wide region he begins dimly to see beyond.[9]

Emily considered that tapping the child's imagination was a crucial element in Froebel's educational program, but she had recognized its importance in her first educational writings at mid-century. Emily wanted fantasy stories of all sorts read to the child and music played with participation in songs. She felt that such activities would allow the teachers to stimulate poetic interest and skill when the child subsequently learned to read and write.

The child could not express in words his sense of pleasure in being thus transported into a different region; but we who have chafed longer within the bounds of what we can see and know, and beat our wings so often against the bars of the prison house...Why then should we deny to children the first feeble efforts of a faculty which will more than any other refresh the flagging spirit through the weariness of later years.[10]

Clearly Emily Shirreff worked to implement the five major child-development themes of Froebel's ideology: (1) self-activity, (2) connectedness and unbroken continuity, (3) creativeness, (4) physical activity, and (5) happy and harmonious surroundings. English Froebelianism to a considerable extent maintained a flexible and innovative quality in the twentieth century.

Emily believed the success of kindergarten depended upon one year in a transition class. During that year she wanted the child to become accustomed to learning from books as well as objects, and therefore introduced to reading and writing, select features of natural history, and objects related to physical science supplemented by basic facts about them which formed a groundwork for later studies in physics and natural history. Also she advised that geography be introduced by acquaintance with features of topography and utilization of drawing and dexterity skills in making models of the features of the earth. She emphasized that in both kindergarten and transition classes language development was a core area of learning. Nevertheless, she deplored the fact that children were expected to learn reading, writing, and arithmetic in infant schools by the age of seven. She adhered firmly to the proposition that the introduction of the child to basic skills of reading and writing foreclosed more vital learning areas for him. "What advantage a child derives from possessing these valuable keys to knowledge before he has learned to care for anything they can unlock for him, it is for the defenders of that system to explain."

The Shirreff sisters' attraction to Froebelian educational theories stemmed from many of its basic assumptions about human beings and their legitimate goals which reinforced the Shirreff ideology of self-development and social progress which had been evolved from the study of many thinkers. They had decided that women occupied a central position in the construction of a humane commonwealth of justice in which every individual had the right to self-development. Emily characterized Froebel as one "who roused women, in the name of the nation and the race to realize what was the power and the duty entrusted to them by heaven." The Shirreffs wanted to make moral considerations prime motivating factors in individual and collective life, and Froebel brought them into a central position in early childhood education. The Shirreffs also valued as crucial in human development a spiritual framework, responsibility for one's own learning as central to an educational program, and finally integration of education to the physical and social growth of the individual based on the principle that the greater the development in each stage of human life the richer and more fulfilling would be the succeeding one. In *Self Culture* the Shirreffs had discussed the necessity to cultivate in the educational process personal qualities which Froebel had seen as the keystone of early childhood education: love of truth and a sense of justice. They marked out self-knowledge and self-control as instruments of moral discipline and insisted that mental training demanded attention, observation, and cultivation of reason which involved the utilization in imaginative ways of linguistics and mathematics.

In effect Emily Shirreff described the main thrust of Froebel's philosophy as supportive of the values venerated by the British national community. His educational scheme she defined as the harmonious development of moral, physical, and intellectual qualities; yet, the moral had a distinction which gave it primacy—to it belonged the direction of conduct, and as conduct was the larger part of life, that which tended to determine it was most important, and the other segments related to it as a means to an end. The latter trained the instruments of action while moral education dealt with motives of action, the will of the person, and made the intellect a power for good or evil. Froebel identified human will with the Divine and venerated moral education in the home; the teacher had to follow at a distance in the tracks established by parents. The formation of character then became his purpose for moral training. These ideas the Shirreffs had elevated to dogma in their polemical works in the mid-century decade.

In contrast to Froebel, Emily stated that Herbert Spencer, a popular prophet of her age who examined education, did not bring religious motives into play in his moral system. He stressed feeling and sympathy but rooted in common sense and the perception of a course of action related to comfort and success. Spencer, she contended, depended not upon parental care and authority but on experience as the prime moral teacher; transgressions of natural law brought the child pain, penalties, and privation. Emily believed that in the Spencerian rationale the child simply gained recognition of what was prudent and imprudent. She argued that punishment did not cultivate either moral power or moral feeling. She maintained that moral relations between parent and child were in fact as much a law of nature as more tangible physical laws or conditions. "It is rarely, indeed, that the little child believes less firmly in his mother's tenderness than in the power of the flame to burn him, and in that faith lies the germ of religious trust in the child's heart and of educational power in the mother." Emily propounded the message that Froebel stood for an inner law of right which grew if shaped properly as the restraints of authority were withdrawn. But clearly also Emily Shirreff saw Froebelian ideology as compatible with scientific analysis of human learning patterns as well as supportive of the morality of the Victorian era. Her thoughts on this topic were evident in a number of speeches and in written material, in particular the lecture *Moral Training: Froebel and Herbert Spencer*.[11] Despite this difference of outlook she also pointed out similarities between the two men in a crucial area of the learning process: both excluded arbitrary and capricious action from education.

In regard to moral force as a wellspring for the individual and society, Henry Buckle contrasted his outlook with Emily's.

We look upon affairs from an opposite point of view, and therefore adopt opposite methods. My habits of mind accustom me to consider actions with regard to their consequences; you are more inclined to consider actions with regard to their motives. You, therefore, are more tender to individuals than I am, particularly if you think them sincere; and you hold that moral principles do hasten the improvement of nations. I hold that they do not.[12]

In a sketch of the life of Froebel read to the Froebel Society and included in a translation of the *Reminiscences of Friedrich Froebel* by Baroness von Marenholtz-Bülow, Emily Shirreff presented reasons why Froebel's proposals could be accurately called new education—recognition of practical activity as an integral part of education and mental growth of the human being as parallel to the development of all other organisms in nature. Froebel conceived of outward training related to an inward correlative; thus he valued manual labor not to make a better workman but form a more complete and fulfilled human being. Emily accepted Hanschmann's analysis of Froebel's key point that education or human development had to start in action; life, action, and knowledge were three notes of a harmonious chord. It therefore followed that a young person had to learn to live, seek to understand outer and visible things, and utilize his own creative faculties before he was brought into serious contact with the world of thought symbols and abstractions and gathered up the accumulations of other men's labor and experience. The unfolding of human powers according to inner or organic laws seemed to Emily the vital dynamic of Froebel's theory, and thus education which sought primarily only outward accretion and poured instruction on an undisciplined mind was ineffective. She said the Froebelian scheme assisted natural growth, exercised and refined the budding faculties, placed mental food within the child's reach, and aided him to grasp it. Therefore, the true educator in her Froebelian profile studied the nascent powers of the child, and so constructed the milieu in which the child operated that he or she used the God-given powers in harmonious work that was a necessity and a pleasure.[13]

In 1887 the Froebel Society offered a prize for the best essay on the ethical teaching of Froebel. One of the prize winners, Mrs. M. J. Lyschinska, superintendent of method in infant schools under the

London School Board, presented succinctly the appeal of Froebel to the Victorian woman desirous of a fulfilled life for her sisters. Froebel analyzed educational needs within an evolutional cultural framework, a perfection of the ethical values and humane goals of western civilization. Thus science—ethics together with the physical and psychological factors of human nature—came into the formula which he urged educators to employ in their learning systems that were crucial in achievement of any commonwealth of a progressive sort.

He sees in man the meeting place of two realms, that of nature and that of self-conscious spirit. The law of nature is the law of egotism; the law of man's spirit is the law of love. Both these realms are manifestations of God; they are not essentially antagonistic. The conflict which arises between the two in human life is due to ignorance, the weakness and the freedom of man; he produces chaos where he ought to have established and upheld harmony. To establish this order, first in his own person, secondly, to promote the same in human affairs according to his measure of insight is his task on earth. In the nursery we lay the foundation of that balance between the sensuous and spiritual part of man's nature.[14]

The reformers who clustered about the Froebel Society in Britain in the manner of their mentor sought a strengthened human will, heightened individual capacity by cultivation of the productive power by means of education and understanding, and full utilization of the unique qualities of childhood in the achievement of these goals. Froebel's evolutionary position was predicated on realistic optimism, the pervasive spirit of a divine purpose and harmony between mankind and nature which appealed to many Victorians.

Emily Shirreff admitted that a number of difficulties had to be overcome to gain wide acceptance of Froebel's ideology in Britain. The immediate problems were want of clear and adequate books on the subject and teachers familiar with the views of the master, but more serious was the widespread opinion that no training or breadth of knowledge was needed by a person who taught children between ages three and seven. She pleaded that teachers of young children should not merely be well prepared in the area of professional skills but also be well-educated women. If the Froebelian educational principles formed a system of thought and not simply a narrow technique as Emily Shirreff insisted, it followed that the wider the culture that any mind gained, the greater the aptitude for recognizing and implementing in specific and imaginative ways any philosophical principles. Central to Emily's grand design were the individual teacher's personal observations and reading that would furnish her with illustrations and knowledge to answer children's questions which could not be answered in a textbook fashion. "The child's nature unfolds spontaneously, and the teacher must be able spontaneously also to meet the requirements of that growth."

Emily suggested a two-year course, one year devoted to the essential methodology of teaching young children basic subject matter and the second devoted to practical work as an assistant in a kindergarten. She denounced the popular view that a few months' training was all that was required to fit a person to work with young children. Emily presented the basic educational foundation which was a prerequisite to the study of methodology for any person who intended to become a teacher of young children. She rated highly, first, linguistic skill, the ability to speak fluently and correctly because oral communication had an overriding importance in the learning patterns of the kindergarten, secondly, arithmetic and geometric knowledge of a sound and basic sort and physical geography, history, and literature in order to provide knowledge of humanity and material for illustration in the classroom. She recommended also for potential teachers the study of physiology, natural history, and elementary physics.[15]

The Froebel Society endeavored to get official sanction for an early childhood educational system based on Froebel's principles. It achieved considerable success in its quest. Anthony Mundella became vice-president of the Committee of Council for Education in 1880. The Manchester Kinder Garten Association and the Froebel Society of London contacted other educational organizations and associations, the Teachers' Association, the London Kinder Garten College, the Stockwell Kinder Garten College, and Doreck College, in order to create a coalition to petition the government for recognition of the kindergarten as a part of the educational system and provision for adequate teaching of its material. The leaders in the field, Emily Shirreff, Miss Manning, Miss Hart of the London Kinder Garten College and its director Alfred Bourne, Fräulein

Heerwart, principal of Stockwell College, Miss Bailey, principal of Doreck College, Dr. Gladstone, Dr. Roth, Mrs. Schwabe of Naples and W. Agnew, MP from Manchester and president of the Manchester Kinder Garten Association, formed a delegation to Mundella. They presented a resolution "that Her Majesty's inspectors of schools be directed to allow as teaching suitable to the age of children under seven that which was known as Kinder Garten training and to employ in the examination of the infants in any properly constituted Kinder Garten a method of ascertaining results approved by capable exponents of the system."[16]

In the discussion with Mundella and Sir Francis Sandford, secretary of the Education Department, Emily maintained that if a fair trial were allowed between traditional infant schools and kindergartens, the latter would prove superior. Cultivation of the general intelligence, the faculties of observation and reasoning, and the power of manual manipulation, she said, accrued to students who progressed through the kindergarten course. Miss Shirreff, however, told Mundella that the kindergarten system had to be fully implemented and not introduced in bits and pieces. Several members of the delegation also spoke, including Dr. Gladstone who represented the London School Board. He observed that the London School Board had tried to introduce the kindergarten scheme wherever possible in its infant schools, but the Education Code hindered the movement. Mundella pledged to encourage every experiment that would improve the quality of education in the country. He revealed that he had observed the kindergarten system in operation in Germany, and also visited Miss Heerwart's classes at Stockwell College and had been mightily impressed by what he had seen. He concluded that if skilled teachers could be produced and the expense borne, the system suggested by the delegation would bring benefits to the participants. However, Mundella raised a contentious point—the expense involved made it mandatory not to move in rapid response to a fad but in a steady growth pattern. He promised to give careful attention to the program outlined by the petitioners.[17]

Advancement of early childhood education in Britain to a considerable degree depended upon the favor and sympathy of officials who occupied several key posts. Emily Shirreff was a skillful advocate not simply of the expansion of early childhood education oriented to Froebelian principles but a viable system for professional and liberal education for teachers involved in it by government encouragement and regulation. As already noted, A. J. Mundella, who had a major responsibility for educational programs in the Gladstone ministry (1880-1885) showed much interest in early childhood education. In 1892 he stated that his interest in and knowledge of Froebel was due almost entirely to Emily. Furthermore, he observed that he could not adequately express the high value he placed on the educational labors of the Shirreff sisters. He believed that no two statesmen in any age had achieved more than the sisters in the cause of education.[18]

The Revised Education Code of 1882 promulgated by Mundella recognized the validity of the Froebelian system for infant schools in regard to methodology and curriculum content. Infant schools received a grant of either 9 or 7 shillings per pupil and were eligible for a merit grant of 2, 4, or 6 shillings. In addition to instruction in traditional elementary subjects, the code sanctioned attention to the phenomona of nature and common life as well as provision for varied and appropriate "occupations" for children. Grants were possible for instruction in singing and needlework. The code contained regulations about the physical setting of classrooms and heat, light, and ventilation.

The London School Board in 1888 took the decisive step and introduced kindergarten instruction into its system. In that year the board asked the Froebel Society to select an examiner for infant schools, and it chose Courthope Bowen who served on the council of the society.[19] Further, every teacher in London's infant schools had to attend lectures on the system during the first two years of employment. A prime mover in the endeavor had been Sir Charles Reed, businessman, philanthropist, and zealot for appropriate education for the population of the capital. He had become chairman of the London School Board in 1873 and formed close relationships with the Froebel Society and the Shirreffs. In 1880 he pointed out that during the previous six years certain schools had offered teachers professional guidance in the art of teaching in kindergartens.[20] In 1893 the education department issued a circular which stated, "The Department is desirous of giving further encouragement to the employment of kindergarten method," and it presented as the guiding principles of early childhood education "the recognition of the child's spontaneous activity and the harmonious and complete development of the whole of a child's faculties." In 1896 the London School Board appointed a special subcommittee to make an exhaustive inquiry into the methods used in infant schools. It reported, "The witnesses who have given evidence before us are unanimous in declaring that the methods and results of infant school work have greatly improved during the last twenty years, and that that improvement is due to the influence of the kindergarten." In 1888, 128 candidates took the National Froebel Union's examination, in 1910, 2,063.

Maria Grey, a devoted student of Italian culture, brought to the English-speaking world in the 1880s the educational philosophy of Antonio Rosmini-Serbati. Thomas Davidson also had given a brief summary of his philosophy in English in 1882.[21] Davidson's Fellowship of the New Life was the circle from which the Fabian Society emerged in 1884. Davidson was, in fact, an interesting intellectual and an adventurer. Born in Aberdeenshire in 1840, he graduated from King's College, Aberdeen, and after teaching at several English schools, migrated to the United States and taught in schools in Boston and Saint Louis. He founded a school of philosophy at his farm at Glenmore on Lake Champlain and also a settlement, the Breadwinners College for Russian Jews, in New York City. William Clarke in the *Spectator* called him one of the twelve most learned men in the world.[22]

Rosmini, a major figure in Italian philosophical and political thought in his own day, was somewhat ignored by people beyond the borders of his native land. In 1955, however, at the centenary of his death, an international congress held at Stresa examined his contributions and impact on European thought. A north Italian of noble lineage born in 1797 in Roverto, a small town in the Trentino, he studied at the University of Padua and then carried on clerical duties in the main in the Piedmont. He took part in public affairs but also engaged in scholarly work of a wide philosophical sort. Many Italians linked him in goals to his close friend Mazzoni; both sought to reconcile Italy to the main themes of European thought and counteract a strong current of provincialism. Rosmini sought to bring traditional Catholic thought into serious response to the views of Spinoza, Leibnitz, Locke, Berkeley, Reid, Hume, Kant, Fichte, Schilling, and Hegel. He explored the problems of the individual in society and in the process dealt with politics, sociology, economics, psychology, aesthetics, religion, and education. His complete works in a projected definitive edition would embrace sixty volumes of four hundred pages each, and his letters, which number over ten thousand, would be contained in thirteen volumes.

Rosmini became a prime mover of the Risorgimento, and his ideas of political liberty more closely approximated those of Pope Leo XIII than his contemporary Pope Pius IX in the post-1848 era. President Giovanni Gronchi of Italy in a statement in 1955 described Rosmini's thought in succinct terms. "Besides being a philosopher and political thinker, he was above all an educator...by a penetrating and enlightened understanding of the human heart."[23] Rosmini founded a progressive religious order, the Institute of the Brethren of Charity, known as the Rosminians. The chief activity urged upon its members was charity, material, moral, and intellectual. Rosminians underwent a two-year novitiate, wore no distinctive garb, and conformed to the laws of the country where they lived.

Rosmini gave considerable attention to England. He had been impressed in his political studies by the stability and balance of the British constitution as well as the political maturity of the British citizenry. Rosmini sent a teaching band to Prior Park in the middle thirties under the guidance of Luigi Gentile which led to the permanent foundation at Radcliffe which opened in 1847. The Rosminians had permanent centers at Newport (1847), Rugby (1850), Kingsland (1854), and Cardiff (1854).

In his educational research Rosmini focused on the science of teaching or the expository method. He defined the latter as the subject matter of the science of correct reasoning which gave the rules by which one's knowledge could be imparted to others. He did not give primary attention to the other facets of education such as the polemical which taught how to defend truth or the critical method which gave the facility to separate truth from falsity. The remaining three methods which he described were the demonstrative which gave exact rules for arriving at exact demonstrations, the inductive which taught how to reach the rules as yet unknown through inductions and conclusions already known, and the perceptive-inductive which was not satisfied with arriving at new cognitions by inductions and conclusions from previously known data but which led to the discovery of wholly new data through the perception of new phenomena skillfully produced and made apparent to the senses. The latter Rosmini called the experimental method.

Rosmini, in the fashion of the Shirreffs, believed that the great need of the age was for many people to become engaged in the exploration of educational methodology at various levels in order to bring forward valid patterns. "It is a fact that . . . the want of a clear and well-grounded method is universally felt in our schools. The principles of such a method are being widely sought, and gradually discerned and gathered up, partly from the meditations of the ablest intellects, partly from the experiences of the best teachers." Rosmini argued that establishment of state-aided education did not in any way guarantee movement toward valid methodology. On one hand, control by the state meant that schools were carried on with more regularity; on the other, he warned that schools placed under uniform and unchangeable rules were often the last to admit improvement or change.

Rosmini's educational ideas were scattered through his major writings; he planned an encompassing educational treatise but completed only a part, *The Ruling Principle of Method Applied to Education*. Among the sciences of application basic to a philosophical system he included pedagogy. He placed it on a foundation of anthropology and psychology which imparted knowledge of the human faculties to be educated and their modes of action. He conceived of education as an ongoing process which extended throughout the entire life span.

Rosmini divided life into periods, computed not primarily on time, but on degrees of cognition. The first period commenced at birth and lasted approximately six weeks, and he said no definite cognitions could be assigned although it possessed the fundamental cognition of being. The second period opened with the first smile and tears of the infant, possibly about the sixth week, and the simple cognitions at that stage consisted of perception of things as subsisting to which corresponded the volitions which Rosmini designated affective and instinctive. That period ended with the child's first articulate word. Speech he considered to be a sign that the child had attained the second order of cognition formed by analyzing the first and abstracting the more interesting sensible qualities of things from the idea of the things in the mind (imaginal ideas); and to those corresponded the affective volitions, having for their object the more interesting, sensible qualities abstracted from the actual things, and from the other qualities to which the appetitive faculty was indifferent. The fourth period, Rosmini said, usually began at about three years of age and manifested itself in the aptitude to learn to read and exercise the faculty of judgment which at that stage connected by synthesis the elements of the previous analysis. The cognition of the fourth order consisted in the comparison of two objects previously analyzed and the judgment of appreciation which gave preference to one over the other. The appreciative volitions and the moral sense which existed in germ in the preceeding period developed to a significant degree during the fourth order of cognition.[24]

Conscience dawned, Rosmini said, or possibly manifested itself in the volitions that resulted from the cognition of the fifth order. The cognition of the latter consisted of a synthesis by which were determined the relations that existed between two things combined into one, and conceived as one, of which conceptions the most important was that of the I and self-identity. The period extended until the child had free use of reason. Rosmini's work on education ended with the fifth period of development. He intended to deal with four additional stages of growth. From the age of seven to fourteen he proposed to treat the work performed by the mind through more depth reflection directed to the attainment of conscious reflective knowledge of moral obligation and law, and he considered that period paramount in shaping the moral character which remained throughout life. Adolescence from puberty to about the age of twenty Rosmini characterized as the stage in which the person, having achieved sufficient reflective power and gained clear concepts of duty, law, and goodness, became master of himself and worked out more fully his self-education.[25]

Rosmini's basic educational assessments and goals were those which the Shirreffs embraced. He insisted that the mother was the born teacher, and essential to a valid scheme for learning was proper understanding and utilization of the mother-child relationship. He called the primary tie between teacher and learner benevolence. He sought "integral education," that is, fusion of learning activity, morality, and religion. Rosmini analyzed closely the child, the relationship of the emotions to the will, and infant development of a preconscious morality based on needs. Rosmini venerated the dignity of the child and censured any educational program which was related completely to a future adult status. He gave much attention to creative activity and objected to learning patterns which required too much of the child, in particular attention for long periods to specific, organized learning tasks. He believed that restlessness in childhood should not be checked. Although he gave motives of action a primary place in each phase of education, he advised that in each stage of growth the child should be nurtured with regard to harmony of mind, emotions, and will.[26] Rosmini demanded that the child be treated as a person and thus accorded the same order of justice that the adult claimed as his right. He disliked use of punishment and in particular public chastisement. He accepted emulation as a legitimate element in the education process because it was part of human nature, but he did not want it employed as a motive. Above all Rosmini sought to mold the spiritual nature of the child and direct his search for truth and intellectual and emotional fulfillment.

The Shirreffs found in Rosmini's writings substantiation for Froebel's ideology which they had embraced earlier, but they also found intriguing Rosmini's unfinished framework for intellectual growth from birth through adulthood. During their lives they had undertaken a similar search. Maria Grey wrote on that point, "It is clear that had life, leisure enough been granted to him, he would have given the world what it never had yet—a complete method and art of education based on the applied science of human nature, and having for its aim and end the full and harmonious development of the latter to the measure of the stature of the perfect men." She concluded that Rosmini's plans concerning the first stages of education contained the fundamental principles of method and practice which remained valid with adaptations for the later stages of life, and primarily the application varied with degrees of individual development. All in all she felt that if the proper regimen came into being in the first stages of education, a regimen would be made easier to formulate for subsequent stages. Almost in a spirit of exultation she announced the accord of Rosmini and Froebel on every major area of childhood education. Although they had very different educational backgrounds, family life, and religious views, Maria found they met on the common ground of a profound study of human nature.[27]

Froebel's educational theories came to Italy from different sources. George P. Marsh, United States minister to the Italian kingdom who became an intimate friend of the Shirreffs when they lived in Italy for lengthy periods in the late seventies, directed the attention of the Italian minister of education to Froebelian thought. In 1871-1872 Baroness Bertha Marenholtz-Bülow, who had been one of the major promoters of Froebel's ideas in Germany, was asked by the Italian minister of education to give lectures at Florence on teacher training in Froebelian methodology. In 1872 Madame Salis Schwabe brought the Froebelian system to Naples and gained a commitment from the municipality to design the first step in public education on Froebel's principles. A successful kindergarten started in the Collegio Medici which became renowned throughout Europe.

A network of Froebel workers emerged between 1850 and 1880; the members of the informal brotherhood and sisterhood traveled extensively, became familiar with the progress of their movement in various countries, and formed valuable professional contacts which at times led to close personal friendships. The Shirreffs were dedicated members of that European Froebelian community which had offshoots in the United States.

The Froebel Society under the presidency of Emily Shirreff linked itself firmly to areas which were crucial to realization of the child's potential for health and happiness: first, attention to the infant years, that is, prekindergarten education, second, concern for proper physical growth and healthful living conditions, and third, parent education, a focus not confined to the first few years. As in the second area, however, the early years were vital in establishment of attitudes and patterns of action. The society placed its imprimatur on the first area and indeed encouraged special training for children's nurses. Madame Emilie Michaelis promoted study of the infant in several messages, and her pupil Emily Lord Walter, who became director of the Norland Place Kindergarten of Notting Hill and later president of the Froebel Society, instituted a facility to train nursery personnel. Mrs. Walter launched a nine-month training course for students, three months in the Norland Institute, three months in hospital work, and three months as a probationer in some sort of institution related to children or family life. The student took courses in hygiene, dietary laws and nutrition, simple medical principles and care of the sick, and psychology. She thus learned about the child, his emotional and practical needs, and means to encourage natural growth patterns.[28] *Child Life*, the major kindergarten periodical which became the official journal of the Froebel Society, reported on the project. "The teacher has had too long to remodel what the home regimen has distorted. Let us hope that the scheme opens up a new vista of hopefulness and that the schoolroom will no longer be the hospital for the character deformed by nursery mismanagement."

The Froebel Society gave recognition to those engaged in research about the physical maturation of the child related to his emotional and intellectual nature. Dr. Warner presented a number of lectures to members of the society. He advised teachers to examine closely the physical condition of pupils and, guided by well-defined rules and valid information, recognize evidence of excess pressure on them and emotional problems. Such awareness was most important in order to meet the needs of the so-called dull child or nervous one.[29] The London School Board in the nineties sponsored some special classes for children with such problems. Miss Shirreff presided at one of the lectures and commented that the area under investigation opened a vast field of research which could be pursued legitimately by kindergarten teachers.[30] Members of the Froebel Society in several cities had similar interests. At Leicester through the efforts of the Froebel Society members of the school board formed a special committee with medical representation to examine children who experienced a number of problems and refer them to special classes.[31]

The Froebel Society showed much interest and included in its educational programs for prospective teachers subject matter related to the health, physical growth, and living patterns of the normal child as well as the environment in which he lived and learned. It featured the ideas of a friend of the Shirreffs, Dr. Mathias Roth, *A Plea for the Compulsory Teaching of the Elements of Physical Education in Our National Elementary Schools* (1870). He urged that prospective teachers in training programs be taught elements of sanitary knowledge and physical education followed by a required examination in those fields. Indeed, in all schools he wanted sanitary knowledge and physical education to be taught and form the standard according to which teachers were paid, just as for imparting the basic skills of reading, writing, and arithmetic. Moreover, Roth linked infant education to the more formal educational system of the later years. He believed that schoolmistresses should be instructed in the care and management of infants and a model nursery attached to all training colleges. He charged that ignorance of the physical nature of the infant was a major cause not only of infant mortality but of lack of understanding of the relationship of health to learning.[32]

During the last generation of the century, when the Froebel Society dominated the field of early childhood education in Britain, the members of the society joined in conferences and meetings which dealt with major social and health issues of the era. In 1884 at the International Exhibition on Health and Education a large display was devoted to kindergarten education. At the Seventh International Congress of Hygiene in August 1891, also at London, nine sections held separate sessions; one dealt with education in the early childhood years.

The Shirreffs in their various writings expressed much concern about the necessity to involve parents in the education process in a variety of ways. They endorsed and encouraged the organizational efforts in that area of two women, Lady Isabel Margesson and Charlotte Mason. The former, who launched a Parents' Society in London, considered Emily Shirreff her mentor. "Instead of being impatient and bored by my entire ignorance of even its first principles, she guided and advised me, and lent me books, and fired me with some of her own love and enthusiasm for the cause of the New

Education."[33] Lady Margesson subsequently joined a national organization, the Parents' National Union founded by Charlotte Mason in Bradford in 1887 with eighty members. Isabel Margesson became secretary of the Belgravia branch of the union, one of the largest branches. The Parents' Union of Charlotte Mason established a three-year correspondence course of study for mothers. It sponsored lectures on such topics as the father's place in education, the education of the only child, and the preservation of the imaginative power in children.[34] The organization published the *Parents Review* which had a circulation of about two thousand in 1900. The union's most ambitious activity was the foundation of the House of Education at Ambelside which offered programs to prepare young women to care for children and also become governesses. Emily Shirreff was present at a special meeting, together with the Reverend R. H. Quick and Frances Mary Buss, when the final design of the Parents' Union was established. She became a vice-president of the union and lectured for it.

The Froebel Society in its first generation of existence broadened the concept of education in the early childhood years or redefined it to include a variety of experiences not limited to formal learning patterns.[35] Sir George Kekewich, permanent secretary of the Education Department, spoke about its work in 1900. At that point he had been concerned with educational affairs for about thirty-five years. He said that most infant schools when he first observed them at the start of his career attempted to make little children think as adults. Of course they failed, but in the process he concluded that they tried to force premature development which led to premature education.

We cannot possible overrate, I think, the work this Society has done. It is not too much to say the Froebelian methods and Froebelian principles have in these later years revolutionized the work of all infant schools; and I think that has been to the very great advantage and the benefit of the children, not only intellectually but also as regards their discipline and as regards their moral advantages, and it has promoted what above all, I wish to see promoted the happiness of little children.[36]

The Shirreffs and other progressive leaders in early childhood education brought to the fore several concepts which had relevance to the entire field of education. They stressed the interlocking character of the essential features of a sound education from the cradle to adulthood and yet the necessity to treat each segment as a distinct entity by relating methodology and areas of curricula to the needs, abilities, and physical and psychological maturation of each student at a particular stage in his life.

# Epilogue

The Shirreff sisters who engaged in the varied educational work described in this study enlarged the patterns of life and perspectives of vast numbers of English females. They and their allies in early childhood, secondary, teacher training, and university education freed females of the middle class from the bleakness of ignorance and intellectual isolation and presented them with the means to enter new occupational fields. In truth they provided females with the tools and mind set to forge an independent public and private life. Maria Grey wrote on the latter topic.

What men would like...that has been the standard openly or secretly adopted for the conduct of women, and I would fain hope that the healthier, higher tone of women's education in these days, their far better position as regards independence of marriage as a provision, will more and more rouse them above making their standard of what women should be and do, follow the passing fashion too, which, like most fashions, is set by the most frivolous and worthless of the sex; and that they will learn to fix their standard for themselves on the dictates of their own reason and conscience, and act up to it in the quiet assurance that the men it displeases are the men whose approbation they need not care for.[1]

But the Shirreff sisters and their educational allies, Frances Mary Buss, Dorothea Beale, Emily Davies, and Anne Jemima Clough, in no sense released women from domestic responsibilities, care of children, parents and brothers and sisters; indeed their care of children was redefined and their role of child developer as parent and teacher raised in importance and widened in scope. The aforementioned women conceived of female liberation as purging their God-given missions of wife, mother, and spinster from narrow concepts which had encumbered them due to male exclusiveness and obscurantism, female bondage, and societal prejudice.

The Shirreffs and the other women who built the early childhood, secondary, and university programs for females perpetuated, perfected, and indeed institutionalized middle-class idealism which centered on a range of learning patterns and attitudes about self, family, and community and the purposes of human existence that have been examined in previous chapters. Middle-class idealists called on their adherents to channel efforts to well-defined goals that related to self-improvement, personal satisfaction that entailed development of the intellect, and enrichment of associational and personal relationships. In the institutionalized setting of the classroom and common room middle-class idealism meant inculcation of positive attitudes toward social service, familial responsibility, and firm adherence to Christian ethics and morality.

The founders and directors of the new secondary schools and women's colleges did not encourage their followers to change areas of personal, family, and societal life that would benefit females in a material way if the corollary was violation of the accepted moral norm. Several studies have shown that the mainstream of the women's movement from the early nineteenth century to its closing decades did not spearhead a campaign for family planning. Reduction of the size of the middle-class family which occurred was due in particular to male middle-class desire to maintain the growing luxury of the family, and women accepted that goal as they became less involved in the day-to-day burdens of family life as mother and supervisor of the household and became genteel ladies of fashion.[2] Dr. Elizabeth Garrett Anderson refused to become involved in the family planning question, which also did not become a field for exploration at the London School of Medicine for Women which was supported by the Shirreffs.[3] Annie Besant and Charles Bradlaugh, who were brought to trial in 1877 for distributing birth control information, received harsh treatment from the press and certainly no support from the female educationalists.[4] Despite that fact, the Malthusian League grew in membership, and the adverse publicity may well have stimulated interest in a topic seldom mentioned publicly and thus accelerated a process already underway.[5]

The leaders of the women's movement in the last third of the century attacked the double moral standard so evident in the Victorian age. They demanded that Christian purity prior to marriage and then marital fidelity be applicable to men as well as women. They did not plead for women to have access to the sexual freedom allowed men but rather that men accommodate to the dictates of Christian morality. Maria Grey wrote on the subject. "If purity and the government of the lower and animal by the higher and reasonable nature of the human being be an essential of that code [Christian], how can it be set aside by men while held binding on women?"[6] Josephine Butler's movement for the repeal of the Contagious Diseases Acts and the subsequent agitation to eliminate the white slave traffic took a similar stance.

But certainly the middle-class women's rights leaders who sought to introduce the reign of morality for both men and women were simply one factor in a national campaign for what a twentieth-century historian has called the "respectable norm." Influential sectors of the medical profession, good society, the literary guild, as well as the male public schools, sought to establish it, explore its varied dimensions, and defend it. "Continence in sex and industry in work were correlative and complimentary virtues. The Respectable Economic man must not be the sensual man who had failed to conquer himself, but the Respectably subliminated sensual man."[7] By the seventies when the women's rightists gathered strength and launched many significant programs, opprobrium fell upon moral laxity, the profligate night life of salons, night houses, casinos, and pleasure gardens. The sexual and economic behavior of the gentleman of birth of the Georgian and Regency periods became less a private matter as the aristocratic social system was slowly eroded in favor of the respectable social system. The Church of England in 1883 formed the White Cross Society to promote male sexual purity. The Lambeth Conference of Bishops of 1888 officially endorsed the duty of clergy and laity to promote male purity. With the foundation of the Social Purity Alliance in the early eighties men and women joined forces and so ended sexual segregation in purity reform.[8]

Sanctions fell upon public men, Sir Charles Dilke and Charles Stewart Parnell, whose violations of morality became public, and likewise approbation came to William Gladstone, the moral lion of the age. H. D. Traill, social commentator and journalist associated with a variety of newspapers and periodicals, the *Pall Mall Gazette, Saint James' Gazette,* the *Daily Telegraph,* and *Observer,* in the *National Review* in 1891 commented on the harshness of the attacks on Parnell and more importantly the one focus of the new morality.

Morality means sexual morality only.... To interweave morality with politics means to insist that no man shall be accepted as a political leader who does not practice the virtue of continence—or, at least, who is caught practicing the vice of incontinence.... The purity, in short, of the modern politician is a quality which has nothing to do with cleanliness of the hands. These may be soiled as much as he pleases, either with the dirt of dishonesty or the stain of blood.[9]

Entrance of significant numbers of middle-class women to careers in academia, the professions, and business was made possible by the systems of education built in large measure from 1860 to 1900, but those patterns of education also encouraged women to support and take leadership in humanitarian schemes, causes of social justice, and child care services of a widening scope which became a marked feature of the British reform movement in the opening decades of the twentieth century. The moderate women's rights brigade in which the Shirreff sisters were ardent members explored some of the vital facets of womanhood in the context of the moral values of the age, and called upon British females to engage in tasks of immense significance for human society.[10] But the reform role for women was most demanding physically and psychologically because it fused revitalized domestic duties to vastly expanded occupational and service ones. In truth it freed women and at the same time presented them with new burdens as well as responsibilities. Bessie Rayner Parkes Belloc captured in verse the spirit of the Shirreff sisters and the other intellectually dynamic, morally committed and hopeful women who established foundations upon which women of the twentieth century developed new goals, amended the older ones, and widened the expectations of their sex.

I know not of myself, my soul
Is stranger to me than the smile
On some beloved face; no lights
In future days these days beguile;
I only know I live to learn,
To love, to struggle, to endure, —
When all my sight is swathed in mist
Thou and my work alone are sure.[11]

# Appendix
## A

## Chronology of Events of the Women's Movement

1866. First petition for women's suffrage signed by 1,500 British women.
First Committee for Women's Suffrage.
Alexandra College, Dublin, founded.

1867. Supplemental Charter granted to London University admitting women to special examinations.
May. Amendment to extend the parliamentary franchise to women introduced by Mr. J. S. Mill.
Nov. National Society for Women's Suffrage founded.

1868. April. First public meeting on women's suffrage held in Manchester.
*La Donna*, first woman's paper in Italy, established.
Sept. Ruling by the revising barrister in Manchester against the claim of 5,750 women to be entered on the register of parliamentary voters.
Nov. Women's suffrage declared illegal by the Court of Common Pleas.
This year medical degrees at the University of Montpelier opened to women.

1869. April. *Le Droit des Femmes*, first women's paper in France, established.
May. National Women's Suffrage Society, U.S.A., founded.
Aug. Municipal Franchise Amendment Act, restoring to women their right to vote in municipal elections.
Oct. Temporary college for women opened at Hitchin.
Nov. American Women's Suffrage Society founded.
This year women's suffrage adopted by legislative enactment in the territory of Wyoming.
The first Women's Congress held in Berlin.

Lectures to women by university professors started in St. Petersburg.

1870. Jan. *Women's Journal*, Boston, U.S.A., established.

Feb. The Bill to Remove the Electoral Disabilities of Women introduced for the first time in the House of Commons.

March. *Women's Suffrage Journal* established.

August. Married Women's Property Act.

Nov. First London School Board elections; women stood as candidates.

In this year examinations for apothecaries opened by state decree to women in Holland.

Medical degrees opened to women in Paris.

1871. Oct. National Education Union established.

College for Working Women, Queen Square, Bloomsbury, opened.

Nov. Vigilance Association formed for the defence of personal rights and the amendment of the laws relating to women.

1872. July. Girton College incorporated.

In this year women admitted to matriculate in the Colleges of Melbourne and Sydney.

1873. Jan. First Girls' Public Day School opened.

*Journal of the Women's Education Union* established.

Feb. Bishop Otter Memorial Training College for Schoolmistresses founded.

April. Act to amend the law as to the custody of infants.

In this year examinations in physics and philosophy passed by women in the University of Groningen for the first time.

1874. Feb. Mrs. Nassau Senior appointed poor law inspector.

July. Women's Protective and Provident League founded.

Married Women's Property Amendment Act passed.

Protection orders given to wives in Scotland.

Oct. London School of Medicine for Women opened.

In this year for the first time degrees in philosophy and law at the University of Leipzig taken by women; the University of Berne opened to women.

1875. Jan. Metropolitan Association for Befriending Young Servants established.

April. First woman elected as guardian of the poor in London.

Oct. Newnham Hall, Cambridge, opened.

Women delegates from women's unions at the Trades Union Congress in Glasgow.

Women admitted to the Pharmaceutical Society, Ireland.

In this year all degrees, except theology, opened to women in Copen-
hagen.

The Medical College, Madras, opened to women.

1876. Jan. Manchester New College opened to women.

June. Women's Printing Society incorporated.

August. Medical Qualification Act passed.

British Women's Temperance Association founded.

Dec. Medical degrees at King and Queen's College of Physicians, Ireland, opened to women.

In this year the fifteen universities of Italy opened to women by a state
decree.

1877. July. BA degree conferred on a woman at Auckland.

Trinity College Musical Examinations opened to women.

St. Andrew's opened degrees in letters to women.

Oct. Women admitted to Royal Free Hospital as students.

In this year women admitted to matriculation in Calcutta.

A statute enabling women to witness civil documents passed the Italian
Parliament.

1878. March. New charter admitting women to London University.

May. Matrimonial Causes Act passed.

Factory and Workshops Act passed.

July. Congrés droit des Femmes held in Paris.

Aug. Intermediate Education Act, Ireland, passed.

In this year the University of Geneva opened to women.

1879. August. Irish University Act passed.

Oct. Somerville Hall, Oxford, opened.

In this year first degrees by women in Finland in medicine, in Gottingen
in arts.

1880. Feb. Demonstration by women in St. James's Hall, London.

Sept. Criminal Law Amendment Act for protection of young persons
passed.

Oct. The franchise voted for women in Oregon state legislature.

Nov. Demonstration by women in Colston Hall, Bristol.

Women's suffrage passed in the House of Keys, Isle of Man.

Demonstration by women in Albert Hall, Nottingham.

# Appendix

# B

## Census Returns of Women Workers in Seven Professions in 1911*

| OCCUPATION | TOTAL | UN-MARRIED | MARRIED | WIDOWED |
|---|---|---|---|---|
| I. Teachers | 187,238 | 171,480 | 11,798 | 4,005 |
| II. Physicians, Surgeons, and Registered Practitioners | 477 | 382 | 76 | 19 |
| III. Midwives, Sick Nurses, Invalid Attendants | 83,662 | 55,288 | 11,867 | 16,507 |
| IV. Poor Law Municipal Officers, etc. | 19,437 | 14,439 | 2,514 | 2,484 |
| V. National Government Employees | 31,538 | 25,843 | 3,410 | 2,285 |
| VI. Commercial or Business Clerks | 117,057 | 114,429 | 1,733 | 895 |
| VIII. Actresses | 9,171 | 5,259 | 3,540 | 372 |

*The figures may have to be inflated somewhat, since some women refused to take part in the census compilation as a protest against their exclusion from the franchise.

# Appendix

# C
___

# Schools of the Girls' Public Day School Trust

The following schools were established in the year given:

| | |
|---|---|
| Bath | 1875 |
| Birkenhead | 1901 |
| Blackheath | 1880 |
| Brighton and Hove | 1876 |
| Bromley | 1883 |
| Croydon | 1874 |
| Ipswich | 1878 |
| Chelsea (later Kensington) | 1873 |
| Liverpool | 1880 |
| Newcastle | 1895 |
| Norwich | 1875 |
| Notting Hill and Bayswater (later Notting Hill and Ealing) | 1873 |
| Oxford | 1875 |
| Portsmouth | 1882 |
| Putney | 1893 |
| Sheffield | 1878 |
| Shrewsbury | 1885 |
| St. John's Wood (later South Hampstead) | 1876 |
| Streatham Hill and Clapham (originally Brixton) | 1887 |
| Sutton | 1884 |
| Sydenham | 1887 |
| Wimbledon | 1880 |

Josephine Kamm, *Indicative Past* (London: George Allen & Unwin, 1971), p. 224.

The following schools transferred, were closed, or merged.

| | |
|---|---|
| Carlisle | 1884-1909 |
| Clapham Middle School | 1875-1898 |
| Clapham (merged with Streatham Hill) | 1882-1938 |
| Clapton (Hackney) | 1875-1899 |
| Dover | 1888-1908 |
| Dulwich | 1878-1913 |
| Gateshead | 1876-1907 |
| Highbury and Islington | 1878-1911 |
| Liverpool East | 1891-1912 |
| Newton Abbot | 1881-1888 |
| Maida Vale and Paddington | 1878-1912 |
| Tunbridge Wells | 1883-1945 |
| Weymouth | 1880-1894 |
| York | 1880-1907 |

Between 1897 and 1970 thirty-seven women served as president of the Association of Head Mistresses; twelve were from Girls' Public Day School Trust institutions and four were former Trust School pupils.

# Notes

CHAPTER 1

1. For the educational work and interests of Bruce and Mundella, see *Letters of the Rt. Hon. Henry Austin Bruce, G.C.B., Lord Aberdare of Duffryn: With Biographical Introduction and Notes* (Oxford: privately printed, 1902); Walter H. G. Armytage, *A. J. Mundella, 1825-1897: The Liberal Background to the Labour Movement* (London: Ernest Benn, 1951).

2. John Stuart Mill, *The Subjection of Women* (Philadelphia: J. B. Lippincott, 1869). For controversy about Harriet Taylor's influence on Mill's thought, see Friederick von Hayek, *John Stuart Mill and Harriet Taylor: Their Correspondence and Subsequent Marriage* (London: Routledge & Kegan Paul, 1951); Helmut O. Pappe, *John Stuart Mill and the Harriet Taylor Myth* (Parkville: University of Melbourne Press, 1960).

3. R. K. Webb, *Harriet Martineau: A Radical Victorian* (New York: Columbia University Press, 1960), p. 361.

4. Maria Grey, *Memorials of Emily Anne Shirreff* (privately printed, 1897), p. 56.

5. Gertrude Himmelfarb, *Victorian Minds* (New York: Alfred A. Knopf, 1968), pp. 384-85.

6. Grey, *Memorials of Emily Anne Shirreff*, p. 6.

7. Ibid., p. 7.

8. Ibid., p. 66.

9. Ibid., p. 9.

10. Grey Papers, Add. Mss. 7218, Cambridge University Library.

11. Grey, *Memorials of Emily Anne Shirreff*, p. 11.

12. Ibid., p. 15.

13. Ibid., p. 13.

14. For Grove's work, see Charles L. Graves, *The Life and Letters of Sir George Grove* (London: Macmillan & Co., 1903).

15. For Somerville's work, see Martha Somerville, *Personal Recollections of Mary Somerville* (Boston: Roberts Brothers, 1874).

16. For Charles Lyell's work, see Leonard G. Wilson, *Charles Lyell: The Years to 1841: The Revolution in Geology* (New Haven: Yale University Press, 1872).

17. For Herschel's work, see Agnes M. Clerke, *The Herschels and Modern Astronomy* (London: Cassell, 1895); Janet Douglas, *The Life and Selections from the Correspondence of William Whewell*; William Whewell, *Of a Liberal Education in General: and with a Particular Reference to the Leading Studies of the University of Cambridge* (London: John W. Parker, 1845-1852).

18. Grey, *Memorials of Emily Anne Shirreff*, pp. 19-20.

19. Grey Papers, Add. Mss. 7218.

20. Ibid.

21. Grey, *Memorials of Emily Anne Shirreff*, p. 17.

22. Mill-Taylor Manuscript Collection, Vol. 15, British Library of Political and Economic Science, London School of Economic and Political Science, University of London.

23. Alfred Henry Huth, *The Life and Writings of Thomas Henry Buckle*, 2 vols. (London: Sampson Low, 1880), 1:89.

24. Ibid., 264-265.

25. Grey, *Memorials of Emily Anne Shirreff*, p. 17.

26. Henry Buckle, *The Influence of Women on the Progress of Knowledge* (London: A. C. Fifield, 1906).

27. Huth, *The Life of Buckle*, 2:11.

28. Giles R. St. Aubyn, *A Victorian Eminence: The Life and Works of Thomas Henry Buckle* (London: Barrie, 1958), p. 24.

29. Emily Shirreff, "Biographical Sketch," *Miscellaneous and Posthumus Works of Thomas Henry Buckle*, 3 vols., ed. Helen Taylor (London: Longmans, 1872), 1:xxxvii.

30. Ibid., xxiii.

31. Emily Shirreff, "Our Modern Youth," *Fraser's Magazine* 68 (1863): 115-29; *The Chivalry of the South*, Ladies London Emancipation Society Tract No. 1 (London, 1864).

32. Grey, *Memorials of Emily Anne Shirreff*, p. 22.

33. Maria Grey, *Love's Sacrifice* (London: Hurst & Blackett, 1868), 3:137-38.

34. Grey, *Memorials of Emily Anne Shirreff*, pp. 36-37.

35. *Clara Novello's Reminiscences Compiled by her Daughter Countess Valeria Gigliucci* (London: Edward Arnold, 1910), p. 175.

36. Averil Grieve, *Clara Novello, 1818-1908* (London: Geoffrey Bles, 1955), p. 301.

37. David Lowenthal, *George Perkins Marsh: Versatile Vermonter* (New York: Columbia University Press, 1958), p. 325.

38. Grey, *Memorials of Emily Anne Shirreff*, p. 39.

39. G. Lilley, *Sir Joshua Fitch: An Account of His Life and Work* (London: Edward Arnold, 1906), pp. 233-34.

40. Grey, *Memorials of Emily Anne Shirreff*, p. 47.
41. Letter of Maria Grey, North London Collegiate School Archives.
42. Letter of Emily Shirreff, North London Collegiate School Archives.
43. Ibid.
44. Ibid.
45. Grey, *Memorials of Emily Anne Shirreff*, p. 51.
46. George Perkins Marsh Papers, George Baily Library, University of Vermont.
47. Letter of Emily Shirreff, North London Collegiate School Archives.
48. Augustus J. C. Hare, *The Story of My Life*, 4 vols. (London: George Allen, 1900), 4: 473.
49. The two photographs are in the North London Collegiate School Archives.
50. Grey, *Memorials of Emily Anne Shirreff*, p. 55.
51. Letter of Emily Shirreff, North London Collegiate School Archives.
52. Letter of Maria Grey, North London Collegiate School Archives.
53. Clara E. Collet, "The Age Limit for Women," *Contemporary Review* 76 (1899): 869.
54. Letter, George Perkins Marsh Papers.

CHAPTER 2

1. [M. Astell], *A Serious Proposal to the Ladies...In Two Parts By a Lover of Her Sex* (1697); Florence Smith, *Mary Astell* (New York: Columbia University Press, 1916).
2. Lucy M. Donnelly, *The Celebrated Mrs. Macaulay...Reprint from the William and Mary Quarterly* [1949]; see Lawrence Stone, *The Family, Sex and Marriage in England, 1500-1800* (New York: Harper & Row, 1977), pp. 352-360.
3. Mary Wollstonecraft, *A Vindication of the Rights of Woman With Strictures on Political and Moral Subjects*, ed. Charles W. Hagelman, Jr. (New York: W. W. Norton, 1967); E. Rauschenbusch-Clough, *A Study of Mary Wollstonecraft and the Rights of Woman* (New York: Longmans, Green, 1898), p. 13.
4. Mary Wollstonecraft, *An Historical and Moral View of the Origin and Progress of the French Revolution: and the Effects It Has Produced in Europe*, Vol. 1 (London, 1794); see also biographies, Eleanor Flexner, *Mary Wollstonecraft: A Biography* (New York: Coward, McCann & Geoghegan, 1972); Edna Nixon, *Mary Wollstonecraft: Her Life and Times* (London: J. M. Dent & Sons, 1971).
5. Clair Tomalin, *The Life and Death of Mary Wollstonecraft* (London: Weidenfeld & Nicolson, 1974), p. 132.
6. Marilyn Butler, *Maria Edgeworth: A Literary Biography* (Oxford: Clarendon Press, 1972); Mark D. Hawthorne, *Doubt and Dogma in Maria Edgeworth* (Gainesville: University of Florida Press, 1967); Isabel Constance Clarke,

*Maria Edgeworth: Her Family and Friends* (London: Hutchinson, 1950); Mary Gladys Jones, *Hannah More* (Cambridge: University Press, 1952); Mary Alden Hopkins, *Hannah More and Her Circle* (New York: Longmans, 1947).

7. Leonore Davidoff, *The Best Circles* (London: Croom Helm, 1973), p. 16.

8. *Punch*, 1868, p. 14.

9. Thomas Henry Lister, "Rights and Conditions of Women," *Edinburgh Review* 73 (1841): 192.

10. Ibid., 198.

11. Lady Sydney Morgan, *Woman and Her Master*, 2 vols. (London: Henry Collum Publishers, 1840), 1: 9.

12. Bessie Rayner Parkes, "Mrs. Jameson," *Vignettes* (London: Alexander Strahan Publisher, 1866), pp. 439-48.

13. *Anna Jameson Letters and Friendships, 1812-1860*, ed. Mrs. Steuart Erskine (London: T. Fisher Unwin, 1915), p. 167.

14. Anna Brownell Jameson, *Communion of Labour: A Second Lecture on the Social Employment of Women* (London: Longman, Brown, Green, Longman & Roberts, 1856), pp. 20-21.

15. "Statements of Bessie Rayner Parkes and Jessie Boucherett," *Transactions of the National Association for the Promotion of Social Science, 1859* (London: John W. Parker & Son, 1860), pp. 724-28.

16. Jo Manton, *Elizabeth Garrett Anderson* (New York: E. P. Dutton, 1965), p. 125.

17. Jessie Boucherett, *Hints on Self Help* (London: S. W. Partridge, 1863), p. 3.

18. Harriet Martineau, "Female Industry," *Edinburgh Review* 109 (1859): 336.

19. Bessie Rayner Parkes, *Essays on Woman's Work* (London: Alexander Strahan Publisher, 1865), p. 163.

20. Ibid., p. 182.

21. Hobson's choice, a case admitting of no alternative between one thing and nothing. From Hobson, a Cambridge horse dealer who would not let any horse out of its turn.

22. Frances Power Cobbe, "What Shall We Do With Our Old Maids?" *Fraser's Magazine* 66 (1862): 597.

23. Ibid., 599.

24. Phillis Brown [Sarah Sharp Hamer], *What Girls Can Do* (London: Cassell, 1886).

25. Frances Power Cobbe, *The Duties of Women: A Course of Lectures* (Boston: George H. Ellis, 1881), pp. 176-77.

26. Ibid., p. 187.

27. Mary Taylor, *Friend of Charlotte Bronte: Letters from New Zealand and Elsewhere*, ed. Joan Stevens (Auckland: Auckland University Press, 1972), p. 142.

28. Helen Dendy, "The Position of Women in Industry," *National Review* 23 (1894): 814.

29. Ibid., 812.

30. Ibid., 813.

31. Mrs. Bernard Bosanquet, *The Standard of Life* (London: Macmillan & Co., 1898), p. 148.

32. Ibid., p. 151.

33. Ibid., p. 152.

34. W. R. Greg, "Why Are Women Redundant?" *Literary and Social Judgments* (London: N. Trübner, 1868), p. 378.

35. Ibid., p. 371.

36. Bosanquet, *The Standard of Life*, p. 154.

37. Clara Collet, "Through Fifty Years: The Economic Progress of Women," *Educated Working Women: Essays on the Economic Position of Women Workers in the Middle Class* (London: P. S. King & Son, 1902), pp. 142-45.

38. Clara Collet, *Women in Industry* (London: Women's Printing Society, [1911]); *Wages of Domestic Servants* (London, 1899); *Report by Miss Collet on Changes in the Employment of Women and Girls in Industrial Centres* (London: for H. M. Stationery Office, Eyre and Spottiswoode, 1898); *Report by Miss Collet on the Statistics of Employment of Women and Girls* (London: for H. M. Stationery Office, Eyre and Spottiswoode, 1894).

39. Charlotte Yonge, *Womankind* (London: Mozley & Smith, 1877).

40. Brian Harrison, "For Church, Queen and Family: The Girls Friendly Society 1874-1920," *Past and Present*, No. 61 (1973): 116.

41. Ibid., 127.

42. Sara Stickney Ellis, *The Women of England: Their Social Duties and Domestic Habits* (London: Fisher, Son & Co., 1838), the ninth edition appeared in 1850; *The Wives of England: Their Relative Duties, Domestic Influences and Social Obligation* (London: Fisher, Son & Co., 1843); *The Mothers of England: Their Influence and Responsibility* (London: Fisher, Son & Co., 1843); *The Daughters of England* (London: Fisher, Son & Co., 1845).

43. Elizabeth Poole Sandford, *Woman, in Her Social and Domestic Character*, 5th ed. (London: Longman, Rees, Orme, Brown, Green & Longman, 1837), p. 12.

44. Sara Stephen, *Passages from the Life of a Daughter at Home* (London: Seeley, Burnside & Seeley, 1851); *Anna: or Passages from a Home-Life* (London: Seeley, Burnside, & Seeley, 1851).

45. E. Lynn Linton, *Modern Women and What Is Said of Them* (New York: J. S. Redfield Publishers, 1868), p. 91.

46. E. Lynn Linton, *The Girl of the Period and Other Social Essays*, 2 vols. (London: Richard Bentley & Son, 1883), 1:viii.

47. Merle Mowbray Bevington, *The Saturday Review, 1855-1868: Representative Educated Opinion in Victorian England* (New York: Columbia University Press, 1941), pp. 114-17.

48. Dina Maria Craik, *A Woman's Thoughts About Women* (London: Hurst & Blackett Publishers, 1858), p. 14.

49. Margaret Lonsdale, *Sister Dora: A Biography* (London: C. Kegan Paul, 1880).

50. Margaret Lonsdale, "Platform Women," *Nineteenth Century* 15 (1884): 415.

51. Samuel Carter Hall, *A Book of Memories of Great Men and Women of the Age From a Personal Acquaintance*, 2 vols. (London: Virtue, 1871), 2: 438.

52. [Elizabeth Sewell], *Principles of Education Drawn from Nature and Revelation and Applied to Female Education in the Upper Classes*, 2 vols. (London: Longman, Green, Longman, Roberts & Green, 1865), 2: 304.

53. John Bennett, *Strictures on Female Education* (Worcester: Isaiah Thomas, Jr., 1795), p. 88.

54. William Landels, *Woman: Her Position and Power* (London: Cassell, Petter, & Galpin, 1871), p. 111; see also *Woman's Sphere and Work, Considered in Light of Scripture* (London: J. Nisbet, 1859).

55. Alexandra Orr, "The Future of English Woman," *Nineteenth Century* 3 (1878): 1026.

56. Ibid., 1027.

57. Ibid., 1032.

58. *Journal of the Women's Education Union* 6 (1878): 123-124.

59. W. R. Hughes, *Constance Naden: A Memoir* (London: Bickers & Sons, 1890).

60. Henry Maudsley, "Sex in Mind and Education," *Fortnightly Review* 21 (1874): 475.

61. Ibid., 476.

62. Ibid., 481.

63. Elizabeth Garrett Anderson, "Sex in Mind and Education—A Reply," *Fortnightly Review* 21 (1874): 592.

64. Ibid., 587. For impact of the writings of Patrick Geddes and Arthur Thompson in the last generation of the century, see Jill Conway, "Stereotypes of Femininity in a Theory of Sexual Evolution," *Suffer and Be Still*, ed. Martha Vicinus (Bloomington: Indiana University Press, 1972), pp. 140-154.

65. "Educational Pressure," London *Times*, April 15, 1880; "Examination for Girls," *Times*, February 17, 1881; "Educational Pressure," *Times*, August 19, 1884.

66. George Romanes, "Mental Difference between Men and Women," *Nineteenth Century* 21 (1887): 667. For the continuing controversy, see Dr. Arabella Kenealy, "Woman as an Athlete," *Nineteenth Century* 45 (1899): 630-645, 915-929; L. Ormiston Chant, "Woman as an Athlete. A Reply," *Nineteenth Century* 45 (1899): 745-754.

67. Edith Simcox, "The Capacity of Women," *Nineteenth Century* 22 (1887): 402.

68. John Ruskin, *Sesame and Lilies* (London: Smith Elder, 1865), p. 171.

69. Ibid., 5th ed. (Sunnyside, Orpington, Kent: George Allen, 1882), xv-xvi; see Kate Millett, "The Debate Over Women: Ruskin vs. Mill," *Suffer and Be Still*, pp. 121-139.

70. John Ruskin, *Letters and Advice to Young Girls and Young Ladies* (New York: John Wiley & Sons, 1879), p. 41.

71. Hallam Tennyson, *Alfred Lord Tennyson: A Memoir*, 2 vols. (London: Macmillan & Co., 1897), 1: 249.

72. William Clark Gordon, *The Social Ideals of Alfred Lord Tennyson as Related to His Time* (Chicago: University of Chicago Press, 1906), pp. 234-35.

73. Alfred Tennyson, *The Princess: A Medley* (Boston: William D. Ticknor, 1848), p. 164.

74. Martha Hale Shackford, *E. B. Browning; R. H. Horne: Two Studies* (Wellesley: Wellesley Press, 1935), pp. 14-15.

75. Elizabeth Barrett Browning, *Aurora Leigh* (New York: C. S. Frances, 1887).

76. Annie Edwards, *A Girton Girl* (London: R. Bentley & Sons, 1885).


CHAPTER 3


1. Maria Grey and Emily Shirreff, *Thoughts on Self Culture Addressed to Women* (London: E. Moxon, 1850), p. vi.

2. Eric Hobsbawm, *The Age of Capital, 1848-1875* (New York: Charles Scribner's Sons, 1975), p. 239; see also David Roberts, "The Paterfamilias of the Victorian Governing Classes," *The Victorian Family*, ed. Anthony S. Wohl (New York: St. Martin's Press, 1978), pp. 59-81.

3. Grey and Shirreff, *Thoughts on Self Culture*, passim; Hoffman R. Hays, *The Dangerous Sex: The Myth of the Feminine Evil* (New York: G. P. Putnam's Sons, 1964).

4. Grey and Shirreff, *Thoughts on Self Culture*, p. 58.

5. Ibid., pp. 40-44.

6. Emily Shirreff, *Intellectual Education and Its Influence on the Character and Happiness of Women* (London: John W. Parker & Son, 1858), passim.

7. Huth, *The Life of Buckle*, 1: 80-81.

8. Grey and Shirreff, *Thoughts on Self Culture*, p. 22.

9. Shirreff, *Intellectual Education*, p. 122.

10. Ibid., p. 423.

11. *Journal of the Women's Education Union* 2 (1874): 132-33.

12. Maria Grey, "Men and Women," *Fortnightly Review* 32 (1879): 683.

13. Emily Faithfull, *Three Visits to America* (Edinburgh: David Douglas, 1854), p. 107.

14. Maria Grey, *Last Words to Girls on Life in School and After School* (London: Rivingtons, 1889), p. 213. Emily had taken a similar position in 1870. She said that claims "whether really tenable or not, must for generations—perhaps forever—remain incapable of proof on either side." See Emily Shirreff, "College Education for Women," *Contemporary Review* 15 (1870): 64.

15. Shirreff, *Intellectual Education*, p. 424.

16. Ibid., p. 418.

17. Grey and Shirreff, *Thoughts on Self Culture*, p. 146.

18. Ibid., p. 3.

19. Mrs. William Grey, "Idols of Society," *Fraser's Magazine* 39 (1874): 379-80.

20. Ibid., 382.

21. Ibid., 388.

22. Shirreff, *Intellectual Education*, p. 305.

23. Ibid., p. 403.

24. Ibid., pp. 411-12.

25. Grey and Shirreff, *Thoughts on Self Culture*, p. 20.

26. Ibid., p. 6.

27. Mrs. William Grey, *Old Maids: A Lecture*, p. 4.

28. Ibid., pp. 30-31.

29. Ibid., pp. 4-5. See also M. Jeanne Peterson, "The Victorian Governess: Status Incongruence in Family and Society," *Suffer and Be Still*, pp. 3-19.

30. Grey and Shirreff, *Thoughts on Self Culture*.

31. For Emily's discussion of the point, see *Intellectual Education*, pp. 414-15.

32. Shirreff, *Intellectual Education*, p. 453.

33. C. W. Cunnington, *The Perfect Lady* (London: Max Parrish, 1948), p. 39.

34. Grey and Shirreff, *Thoughts on Self Culture*, pp. 374-390.

35. Ibid., p. 384.

36. Ibid.

37. Shirreff, *Intellectual Education*, p. 409.

38. Grey and Shirreff, *Thoughts on Self Culture*, p. 314.

39. John Morley, "Social Responsibilities," *Macmillan's Magazine* 14 (1866): 380-382.

40. E. Lynn Linton, *Modern Women and What Is Said of Them*, p. 137.

41. Ibid., p. 135. See also Patricia Thomson, *The Victorian Heroine: A Changing Ideal* (London: Oxford University Press, 1956); Elaine Showalter, "Family Secrets and Domestic Subversion: Rebellion in the Novels of the 1860s," *The Victorian Family*, pp. 101-116.

42. Maria Grey and Emily Shirreff, *Passion and Principle* (London: Routledge, 1853), p. 200.

43. Ibid., pp. 200-01.

44. Maria Grey, *Love's Sacrifice*, 2:368.

45. Ibid., 178.

46. Henry Thomas Buckle, *History of Civilization in England* (London: J. W. Parker & Son, 1857), 4:105.

47. Emily Shirreff, "Our Modern Youth," *Fraser's Magazine* 68 (1863): 127.

48. Emily Shirreff, "The Work of the World and Women's Share in It," *Journal of the Women's Education Union* 9 (1881): 6.

49. Ibid., 12.

50. Grey, *Last Words to Girls*, pp. 204-05.

51. Ibid., pp. 316-17.

52. Ibid., p. 323.

53. Ibid., p. 324.

54. Ibid., p. 333.

55. Ibid., pp. 338-339.

56. Ibid., p. 339.

57. Ibid., p. 341.

58. Ibid., p. 259.

59. Anna Swanwick, *An Utopian Dream...and How It May be Realized* (London: C. Kegan Paul, 1888).

60. Amice Lee, *Laurels and Rosemary: The Life of William and Mary Howitt* (London: Oxford University Press, 1955).

61. Grey, *Last Words to Girls*, p. 238.

62. Ibid., p. 239.

63. Ibid., p. 327.

64. Ibid., p. 326.

65. Ibid., p. 342.

CHAPTER 4

1. Mill-Taylor Manuscript Collection, Vol. 18.

2. Maria Grey, *Is the Exercise of the Suffrage Unfeminine?* (London: Spottiswoode, 1870).

3. Ibid.

4. Helen Blackburn, *Women's Suffrage: A Record of the Women's Suffrage Movement in the British Isles* (London: Williams & Norgate, 1902), p. 144.

5. For analysis of the suffrage movement in late nineteenth and early twentieth centuries, see Sylvia Pankhurst, *The Suffragette Movement* (London: Longmans, Green, 1931); Roger Fulford, *Votes for Women* (London: Faber & Faber, 1958); Antonia Raeburn, *The Militant Suffragettes* (London: Joseph, 1973); Andrew Rosen, *Rise Up Women! The Militant Campaign of the Women's Social and Political Union, 1903-1914* (London: Routledge & Kegan Paul, 1974); Midge MacKenzie, ed., *Shoulder to Shoulder: A Documentary* (New York: Alfred A. Knopf, 1975).

6. Grey, *Memorials of Emily Anne Shirreff*, p. 29.

7. Ibid.

8. "The Married Women's Property Act," *Spectator* 4 (1882): 1161. For discussion of the Married Women's Property Acts of 1870, 1874, and 1882, see Thomas Barrett-Lennard, *The Position in Law of Women* (London: Waterlow & Sons, 1883).

9. Frances Power Cobbe, "Wife-Torture in England," *Contemporary Review* 32 (1878): 55-87.

10. E. Moberly Bell, *Josephine Butler: Flame of Fire* (London: Constable, 1962); Arthur S. Butler, *Portrait of Josephine Butler* (London: Faber & Faber, 1954).

11. J. Estlin Carpenter, *The Life and Work of Mary Carpenter* (London: Macmillan & Co., 1879), pp. 428-29.

12. *The Peace Society and Its Aims*, [London, 1884].

13. See British Library, *National Health Society Annual Reports*, and miscellaneous pamphlets issued by the society [1883-1890].

14. See British Library, *Ladies Sanitary Association Tracts* [1859-1872].

15. See British Library, *Metropolitan Association for Befriending Young Servants Reports* [1870-1886].

16. Louisa Twining, *Recollections of Workhouse Visiting and Management During Twenty-Five Years* (London: C. Kegan Paul, 1880); *Recollections of Life and Work Being the Autobiography of Louisa Twining* (London: Edward Arnold, 1893).

17. C. L. Mowatt, *The Charity Organisation Society* (London: Methuen, 1961); Joseph H. Wright, *Thoughts and Experiences of a Charity Organisationalist* (London: William Hunt, 1878).

18. Octavia Hill, "The Work of Volunteers in the Organization of Charity," *Macmillan's Magazine* 26 (1872); C. Edmund Maurice, ed., *Life of Octavia Hill as Told in Her Letters* (London: Macmillan & Co., 1913); Enid Bell, *Octavia Hill: A Biography* (London: Constable, 1942).

19. Janet Henderson Robb, *The Primrose League, 1883-1906* (New York: Columbia University Press, 1942), p. 135.

20. Ibid., p. 130.

21. Maria Grey, "What Are the Special Requirements for the Improvement of the Education of Girls?" *Transactions of The National Association for the Promotion of Social Science* (1871), pp. 366-68.

22. Emily Shirreff, "What Public Provision Ought to be Made for the Secondary Education of Girls?" Ibid (1872), pp. 271-72.

23. Maria Grey, "On the Organization of Lectures and Classes for Women," Ibid. (1873), pp. 361-62.

24. Emily Shirreff, "Is a Fair Proportion of the Endowments of the Country Applicable to Female Education?" Ibid. (1875), pp. 445-46.

25. Emily Shirreff, "On the Training of Teachers," Ibid. (1876), pp. 469-70.

26. Emily Shirreff, "On the Kindergarten and Froebel's System of Education," Ibid. (1878), pp. 442-44.

27. Brian Rodgers, "The Social Science Association, 1857-1886," *The Manchester School of Economics and Social Studies* 20 (1952): 283-310.

28. *The Englishwomen's Review* 19 (1888): 276. Comparison of the Census of 1861 with that of 1871 in regard to employment of women is as follows:

| OCCUPATION | NUMBER IN 1861 | NUMBER IN 1871 |
| --- | --- | --- |
| Civil Service | 1,931 | 3,314 |
| Law Stationers | 21 | 51 |
| Painters and Artists | 853 | 1,069 |
| Photographers, including Assistants | 168 | 694 |
| Commercial Clerks, Accountants, etc. | 404 | 1,755 |
| Saleswomen | 1,055 | 1,721 |

| | | |
|---|---|---|
| Drapers and Assistants | 11,993 | 19,112 |
| Shopwomen | 4,520 | 8,333 |
| Apprentices | 185 | 743 |
| Stationers | 1,752 | 3,004 |
| Booksellers and Publishers | 952 | 1,077 |
| Printers | 419 | 741 |
| Hairdressers and Wig- | | |
| makers | 501 | 1,240 |
| Gilders | 74 | 234 |

29. Jessie Boucherett, "The Industrial Movement," *The Woman Question in Europe*, ed. Theodore Stanton (New York: G. P. Putnam's Sons, 1884), p. 104. For uncollated statistics on female employment in the last three decades of the century, see *Accounts and Papers*, 1883, Vol. 80; *Accounts and Papers*, 1893, Vol. 106; *Accounts and Papers*, 1902, Vol. 118.

30. Ellis Howe and John Child, *The Society of London Bookbinders, 1780-1950* (London: Sylvan Press, 1952).

31. K. A. McKenzie, *Edith Simcox and George Eliot* (London: Oxford University Press, 1961).

32. Vivian H. H. Green, *Oxford Common Room: A Study of Lincoln College and Mark Pattison* (London: Edward Arnold, 1957); Emilia Pattison [Dilke], *The Book of the Spiritual Life...With a Memoir of the Author by the Rt. Hon Sir C. W. Dilke* (London: John Murray, 1905).

33. Stephan Gwyn, completed and edited by Gertrude Tuckwell, *The Life of the Rt. Hon. Sir Charles W. Dilke* (London: John Murray, 1917).

34. Benjamin Roberts, *The Trades Union Congress, 1868-1921* (London: Allen & Unwin, 1958).

35. Emilia Pattison Dilke, *Trade Unionism Among Women* (London: Trade Union League, 1893).

36. Jessie Boucherett and Helen Blackburn, *The Condition of Women and the Factory Acts* (London: Elliot Stock, 1896), p. 32.

37. S. Barbara Kanner, "The Women of England in a Century of Social Changes, 1848-1914," *Suffer and Be Still*, pp. 175-176; see William Lovett, *Life and Struggles*, ed. with introduction by R. H. Tawney (London: G. Bell & Sons, 1920), pp. 131, 145; "Meeting of Female Chartists," London *Times*, October 20, 1842; *The English Chartist Circular*, Vols. 1-3; P. W. Slosson, *Decline of the Chartist Movement* (New York: Columbia College, 1916); Hermann Schlueter, *Die Chartistan-Bewegung* (New York: Socialist Literature Co., 1916), Chapter 21, book III, part 3; E. P. Thompson, *The Making of the English Working Class* (New York: Pantheon Books, 1963), pp. 414-17, 717-18, 730-31.

38. Peter N. Stearns, "Working Class Women in Britain, 1890-1914," *Suffer and Be Still*, p. 120.

39. Gertrude Tuckwell, *The State and Its Children* (London: Methuen, 1894).

40. Lucy Herbert, *Mrs. Ramsay MacDonald* (London: Women Publishers, 1924), p. 96.

41. Margaret Cole, *Beatrice Webb* (London: Longmans, Green, 1945), p. 89.

42. Edward R. Pease, *The History of the Fabian Society* (New York: E. P. Dutton, 1916), pp. 189-90.

43. Virginia Woolf, Introductory Letter in Margaret Llewellyn Davies, *Life As We Have Known It* (London: Hogarth Press, 1931), pp. xxxvi-vii.

44. Louise Creighton, "The Employment of Educated Women," *Nineteenth Century* 50 (1901): 806-811.

45. E. A. Huntley, *The Study and Practice of Medicine by Women* (London: Lewes Farncombe, 1886).

46. Louisa Martindale, *The Woman Doctor* (London: Mills & Boon, 1922); K.C.H. Mead, *Women in Medicine* (London: Haddam Press, 1938).

47. Louisa Twining, "Women as Official Inspectors," *Nineteenth Century* 35 (1894): 35.

48. Eva Anstruther, "Ladies Clubs," *Nineteenth Century* 45 (1899): 598-611.

49. Maria Grey, *The School Board of London: Three Addresses of Mrs. William Grey in the Borough of Chelsea* (London: William Ridgway, 1871).

CHAPTER 5

1. Maria Grey, "The Women's Educational Movement," *The Woman Question in Europe*, p. 31.

2. *Introductory Lectures Delivered at Queen's College, London* (London: John W. Parker, 1849).

3. Emily Davies, *The Higher Education of Women* (London: Alexander Strahan Publisher, 1866).

4. *Reports from Commissioners, Report of Schools Inquiry Commission* 28 (1867-1868): 570.

5. Ibid., 548.

6. Ibid., 549-550.

7. Ibid., 570.

8. Ibid., 534.

9. Ibid., 555.

10. Ibid., 557.

11. Ibid., 570.

12. Dorothea Beale, *Reports Issued by the Schools Inquiry Commission on the Education of Girls . . . with Extracts from the Evidence and a Preface* (London: David Nutt, 1869).

13. Maria Grey, "The Women's Educational Movement," *The Woman Question in Europe*, p. 37; see also Grey, *Memorials of Emily Anne Shirreff*, p. 31.

14. *East Kent Scientific and Natural History Society: Report and Transactions* 7 (1908).

15. *Report of Manchester Field Naturalists Society, 1867* (Manchester, 1868).

16. Ann Pratt, *The Pictorial Catechism of Botany* (London: Suttaby, 1842); *Wild Flowers* (London: Society for Promoting Christian Knowledge, 1852);

*The Grasses, Sedges and Ferns of Great Britain* (London: Society for Promoting Christian Knowledge, 1866); Margaret Plues, *British Ferns* (London: L. Reeve, 1866); *British Grasses* (London: L. Reeve, 1867); Edward Wood, ed., *Geology for the Millions* (London: Routledge, 1863); Margaret Scott Gatty, *British Sea Weeds* (London: Bell & Daldy, 1867); *Parables from Nature* (London: Bell & Daldy, 1867).

17. See British Library, A collection of circulars, prospectuses, annual reports and other documents printed and in manuscript relating to the Royal Institution, 1801-1837, addressed to W. H. Pepys, 2 vols. (London, 1801-1837); *Syllabus of Lectures Commencing after Easter 1832* (London); R. Watson Frazer, *Notes on the History of the London Institution* (London: Waterlow & Sons, 1905). The London Institution between 1819 and 1854 offered 266 distinct courses comprising 1,655 separate lectures and 126 soirees.

18. Don Alvarez Espriella [Robert Southey], *Letters from England* (Boston: Munroe & Frances, 1807).

19. Louis Simond, *Journal of a Tour and Residence in Great Britain During the Year 1810 and 1811* (New York: T & W Mercein Printers, 1815), pp. 1, 182.

20. *Journal of the Women's Education Union* 6 (1878): 122.

21. Emily Faithfull, *Three Visits to America* (Edinburgh: David Douglas, 1884), p. 100; "Victoria Discussion Society: Women's Demand for the Privileges of Both Sexes," *Victoria Magazine* 15 (1870): 318-356.

22. Samuel Greg, *Speech at the Second Annual Celebration of the Three Lyceums, Ancoats, Chorlton Upon Medlock and Salford* (Manchester, 1837).

23. James Hole, *An Essay on the History and Management of Literary Scientific and Mechanics Institutes* (London: Longman, Brown, Green & Longman, 1853).

24. Robert Hunt, *On Classes for Scientific Observation in Mechanics Institutions: Lectures in Connection with the Educational Exhibition of the Society of Arts* (London, 1854).

25. Mabel Tylecote, *The Mechanics Institutes of Lancashire and Yorkshire Before 1851* (Manchester: Manchester University Press, 1957), p. 263.

26. Ibid., p. 264.

27. Ibid., p. 186.

28. *Educational Guardian* 1 (1860): 106.

29. Fanny Hertz, "Mechanics Institutes for Working Women," *Transactions of the National Association for the Promotion of Social Science, 1859* (London: John Parker, 1860), p. 349.

30. Ibid., p. 354.

31. Grey, *Memorials of Emily Anne Shirreff*, pp. 32-33.

32. Blanche A. Clough, *A Memoir of Anne Jemima Clough* (London: Edward Arnold, 1897).

33. Anne J. Clough, "Hints on the Organization of Girls' Schools," *Macmillan's Magazine* 14 (1866): 436-39.

34. A.J.C., "Suggestions on Primary Education and a Short Notice on the Method of Teaching Reading and Writing in Germany," *Macmillan's Magazine* 18 (1868): 297.

35. H.T. [Helen Taylor], "Women and Criticism," *Macmillan's Magazine* 14 (1866): 335-40.

36. *The North London Collegiate School 1850-1950: Essays in Honour of the Centenary of Frances Mary Buss* (London: Oxford University Press, 1950).

37. Anne E. Ridley, *Frances Mary Buss and Her Work for Education* (London: Longmans, 1895), pp. 202-03.

38. Ibid.

39. Scrapbook, North London Collegiate School Archives.

40. Letter, North London Collegiate School Archives.

41. Ridley, *Frances Mary Buss*, p. 282-83.

42. Dorothea Beale, *History of Cheltenham Ladies College, 1853-1904* (Cheltenham, 1904), *passim*.

43. Letter, Girls' Public Day School Archives.

44. Vera Brittain, *The Women at Oxford: A Fragment of History* (London: George G. Harrap, 1960), p. 102.

45. Dorothea Beale, "Secondary Education of Girls During the Past Fifty Years," *National Education Association Fiftieth Anniversary Volume, 1857-1906* (London, 1906).

46. Josephine Kamm, *How Different From Us: A Biography of Miss Buss and Miss Beale* (London: Bodley Head, 1958).

47. Emily Davies, *The Higher Education of Women*. Miss Clough escalated her demands for women's educational rights. In 1897 she asked from Cambridge University for women (1) unrestricted use of Cambridge University Library, (2) free competition for all university prizes and scholarships, (3) recognition in the matter of advanced study and research, (4) a general participation in academic affairs. Charles Whibley, "The Encroachment of Women," *Nineteenth Century* 41 (1897): 535.

48. Grey, *Memorials of Emily Anne Shirreff*, p. 28.

49. Barbara Stephen, *Girton College, 1869-1932* (Cambridge: University Press, 1933), pp. 233-34.

50. M. C. Bradbrook, *"That Infidel Place": A Short History of Girton College, 1869-1969* (London: Chatto & Windus, 1969), p. 50.

51. Letter, Girls' Public Day School Archives.

52. Lady Stanley of Alderley, "Personal Recollections of Women's Education," *Nineteenth Century* 6 (1879): 314.

53. Jane Ellen Harrison, *Reminiscences of a Student's Life* (London: Hogarth Press, 1925), p. 53.

54. Ridley, *Frances Mary Buss*, pp. 261, 243.

55. Maria Grey, "The Women's Education Movement," *The Woman Question in Europe*, p. 55.

56. Ibid., p. 56.

57. Ibid., p. 57.

58. Ibid., p. 55.

CHAPTER 6

1. *Journal of the Women's Education Union* 2 (1874): 132-133.
2. Emily Shirreff, *Intellectual Education and Its Influence on the Character and Happiness of Women*, p. 7.
3. Ibid., p. 378.
4. Ibid., p. 8.
5. Ibid., p. 33.
6. Ibid., p. 206.
7. Ibid., p. 351.
8. Ibid., p. 82.
9. Ibid., p. 32.
10. Ibid.
11. Ibid., p. 8.
12. Ibid., p. 47.
13. Ibid., p. 73.
14. Ibid., p. 7.
15. Ibid., p. 80.
16. Ibid., p. 81.
17. Ibid., p. 84.
18. Ibid.
19. Ibid., p. 207.
20. Ibid., p. 210.
21. Ibid., p. 211.
22. Ibid., p. 227.
23. Ibid., p. 221.
24. Ibid., p. 229.
25. Ibid., p. 262.
26. Ibid., pp. 271, 277-78.
27. Ibid., pp. 273-74.
28. Ibid., p. 276.
29. Ibid., p. 282.
30. Ibid., p. 285.
31. Ibid., pp. 286-87.
32. Ibid., p. 294.
33. Ibid., p. 295.
34. Ibid., p. 297.
35. Ibid.
36. Ibid., p. 299.
37. Ibid., p. 309.
38. Ibid., pp. 402-03.
39. Ibid., p. 322.
40. Ibid., pp. 322-23.

41. Ibid., p. 324.

42. Ibid., p. 327.

43. Ibid., p. 355.

44. Ibid., P. 349.

45. Ibid., p. 356.

46. Ibid., pp. 386-89.

47. *Athenaeum*, June 1858, p. 174.

48. *Spectator* 31 (1858): 554.

49. *Saturday Review* 6 (1858): 16.

50. Huth, *Life of Buckle* 2: 269.

51. Ibid.

52. T.H.S. Escott, *England, Her People, Polity and Pursuits* (New York: Henry Holt & Company, 1880), p. 296.

53. George Gissing, *In The Year Of Jubilee* (London: Lawrence and Bullen, 1894), 1: 14.

54. Ibid., 2: 21.

55. Mountstuart Grant Duff, "A Plea for a National Education," *Fortnightly Review* 28 (1877): 170-194; *Journal of the Women's Education Union* 5 (1877): 137.

56. Ibid., 148.

57. Ludwig Wiese, *German Letters on English Education Written During an Educational Tour in 1876*, trans. and ed. Leonhard Schmitz (New York: G.P. Putnam's Sons, 1879); see also his earlier comments, *German Letters on English Education*, trans. W.D. Arnold (London: Longman, Brown, Green & Longman, 1854).

58. *Journal of the Women's Education Union* 5 (1877): 118-21.

59. Mrs. William Grey, *On the Study of Education as a Science*, p. 11.

60. Gilbert Murray, *Jane Ellen Harrison, An Address Delivered at Newnham College, October 27th, 1928* (Cambridge: W. Heffer & Sons, 1928), pp. 6-7.

61. Ibid., p. 20.

62. Ibid.

63. Harrison, *Reminiscences of a Student's Life*, p. 88.

64. Havelock Ellis, *Women and Marriage; or, Evolution in Sex* (London: W. Reeves, 1888); *Studies in the Psychology of Sex*, 8 vols. (Philadelphia: F. A. Davis, 1905-1928); *The Erotic Rights of Women, and the Objects of Marriage* (London: British Society for the Study of Sex Psychology, 1918).

65. Havelock Ellis, Introduction, in *The Woman Movement* by Ellen Key, trans. Manah Bouton Borthwick (New York: G. P. Putnam's Sons, 1912), p. xii.

## CHAPTER 7

1. *Journal of the Women's Education Union* 1 (1873): 41.

2. Ibid.

3. Josephine Butler, *The Education and Employment of Women* (London: Macmillan & Co., 1868).

4. Arthur S. Butler, *Portrait of Josephine Butler*; Enid Moberly, *Josephine Butler*.

5. Letter, Girls' Public Day School Trust Archives.

6. Grey, *Memorials of Emily Anne Shirreff*, p. 31.

7. Letter, Girls' Public Day School Trust Archives.

8. *Journal of the Women's Education Union* (1873): No. 1.

9. Letter, North London Collegiate School Archives.

10. *Journal of the Women's Education Union* 1 (1873): No. 1.

11. Ibid.

12. *Report of Schools Inquiry Commission* 28 (1867-1868): 548.

13. Grey, *On the Study of Education as a Science*, p. 12.

14. *Journal of the Women's Education Union* 5 (1876): 186-87.

15. *Spectator* 45 (1872): 78.

16. *Journal of the Women's Education Union* 1 (1873): 119-26.

17. Grey, *Memorials of Emily Anne Shirreff*, p. 34.

18. *Journal of the Women's Education Union* 7 (1879): 125.

19. *Spectator* 56 (1883): 542.

20. Josephine Kamm, *Indicative Past: A Hundred Years of the Girls' Public Day School Trust* (London: Allen & Unwin, 1971).

21. For the work of the education committee, see Girls' Public Day School Trust Archives.

22. Notes, Girls' Public Day School Trust Archives.

23. Minutes of Education Committee, 1875-1877, Girls' Public Day School Trust Archives.

24. Notes, Girls' Public Day School Trust Archives.

25. Agnes S. Paul, *Some Memories of Mrs. Woodhouse* (London: Silas Birch, 1924), p. 31.

26. Ibid., p. 29.

27. Morley, ed., *Women Workers in Seven Professions*, p. 30.

28. Mrs. Humphrey Ward, *A Writer's Recollections*, 2 vols. (New York: Harper & Brothers, 1918), 1: 130-131.

29. Richard L. Archer, *Secondary Education in the Nineteenth Century* (Cambridge: University Press, 1921), p. 248.

30. Ibid.

31. Ibid., p. 257.

32. Joyce C. Penderson, "Schoolmistress and Headmistresses: Elites and Education in the Nineteenth Century," *Journal of British Studies* 15 (1975): 152.

33. Ibid., 159.

34. David Newsome, *Godliness and Good Learning: Four Studies on a Victorian Ideal* (London: John Murray, 1961), pp. 7-8.

35. May Charlotte Malim and Henrietta Caroline Escreet, eds., *The Book of the Blackheath High School* (London: Blackheath Press, 1927), p. 39.

36. Ibid., p. 159.

37. Harrison, *Reminiscences of a Student's Life*, p. 53.

38. M. Vivian Hughes, *A London Girl of the Eighties* (London: Oxford University Press, 1936), p. 62.

39. Ibid., p. 292.

40. Material in the last three novels of Frederic is especially relevant, *March Hares* (1896), *Gloria Mundi* (1898), and *The Market Place* (1899). Criticism of the new female education surfaced fairly regularly in late Victorian and Edwardian Britain. It was accused of being too narrow and strictly academically oriented and encouraged a pompous self-satisfaction; see Emily Constance Cook, "A Modern High-School Girl," *National Review* 17 (1891): 370-378.

41. Roland Hunter, "Sir Joshua Fitch," *Contemporary Review* 58 (1890): 245.

42. J. G. Fitch, "Women and the Universities," *Contemporary Review* 84 (1902): 807-818.

43. Penderson, "School Mistresses and Headmistresses," p. 162.


CHAPTER 8

1. *Journal of the Women's Education Union* 4 (1876): 101.

2. Ibid., 170-75.

3. *Journal of the Women's Education Union* 1 (1873): 98.

4. T. Wemyss Reid, *The Life of the Right Hon. William Edward Forster* (London: Chapman & Hall, 1888).

5. *Journal of the Women's Education Union* 6 (1879): 72-74.

6. J. G. Fitch, *Lectures on Teaching Delivered in the University of Cambridge During the Lent Term, 1880* (Cambridge: University Press, 1881).

7. *Spectator* 8 (1880): 29.

8. Maria Grey, *Paper on the Study of Education as a Science Read at the Meeting of the British Association at Belfast to which is Added the Speech Delivered by Mrs. Grey on the 25th August, 1874*, pp. 6-7.

9. Ibid., pp. 10-11.

10. Ibid.

11. Ibid., p. 16.

12. Auberon Herbert, *The Sacrifice of Education to Examination: Letters from All Sorts and Conditions of Men* (London: Williams & Morgate, 1889).

13. Max Müller, Edward Freeman, and Frederic Harrison, "The Sacrifice of Education to Examination," *Nineteenth Century* 21 (1888): 617-52.

14. Grey, *Paper on the Study of Education as a Science*, pp. 16-17.

15. Ibid.

16. Ibid., p. 19.

17. Morley, ed., *Women Workers in Seven Professions*, Section V, p. 26.

18. Ibid., p. 19.

19. Letter, Archives, Maria Grey Training College.

20. Ibid.

21. Ibid.

22. *Journal of the Women's Education Union* 4 (1876): 125-126.

23. Ibid., 5 (1876): 186-187.

24. Grey, *Memorials of Emily Anne Shirreff,* p. 45.

25. Charles Eyre Pascoe, *Schools for Girls and Colleges for Women* (London: Hardwicke & Bogue, 1879), pp. 224-25.

26. *Our Magazine: The Maria Grey Training College,* 1888, p. 67.

27. *Report of a Discussion on Training by the Head Masters Conference, December 1881* (London, 1881).

28. Alice Woods, *Educational Experiments in England* (London: Methuen, 1920).

29. Letter, North London Collegiate School Archives.

30. *Some Account of the Maria Grey Training College* (1898).

31. Letter, Girls' Public Day School Archives.

32. *Child Life,* New Series 2 (1900): 18-21.

33. Morley, ed., *Women Workers in Seven Professions,* p. 35.

34. Ibid., p. 32.

35. Alice Gordon, "The After-Careers of University-Educated Women," *Nineteenth Century* 37 (1895): 956-957.

36. *Journal of the Women's Education Union* 1 (1873): preface.

37. Ibid., 6 (1878): 17-18; 7 (1879): 33-34; 8 (1880): 81-82.

38. Ibid., 6 (1878): 61.

39. Ibid., 7 (1879): 33-34.

40. Ibid., 8 (1880): 161.

41. Grey, *Memorials of Emily Anne Shirreff,* p. 54.

42. Letter, Girls' Public Day School Archives.

43. Mary Gurney's Scrap Book, Girls' Public Day School Archives.

44. Ibid.

45. *Journal of the Women's Education Union* 1 (1873): 43-44.

46. Ibid., 41.

47. Dorothea Beale, "A Retrospect and a Forecast," *Longman's Magazine* 30 (1888): 339.

48. Quoted in Archer, *Secondary Education in the Nineteenth Century,* p. 250.

## CHAPTER 9

1. Ridley, *Frances Mary Buss,* p. 275.

2. Eleanore Heerwart, *The Kindergarten System: A Lecture* (Edinburgh: R. M. Cameron, 1883).

3. *Journal of the Women's Education Union* 4 (1876): 182.

4. Maria Kraus Boelte, "Reminiscences of Kindergarten Work," *Papers on Froebel's Kindergarten* (Hartford: Office of the *American Journal of Education,* 1894).

5. Ibid.

6. J. H. Miller, *Charles Dickens. The World of His Novels* (Cambridge: Harvard University Press, 1970), p. 239.

7. Ibid., p. 332; see also L. Mannheim, "The Dickens Hero as Child," *Studies in the Novel* 1 (1969): 189-95.

8. G. Eliot, *Silas Marner*, Ch. 4; Henry Austin, *Local Habitations. Regionalism in the Early Novels of George Eliot* (Cambridge: Harvard University Press, 1970), p. 193.

9. Amy Cruse, *The Victorians and Their Reading* (Boston: Houghton & Mifflin, 1936), p. 178.

10. Malcolm Elwin, "Christopher North," *Victorian Wallflowers* (London: Jonathan Cape, 1934), p. 43.

11. Martin Tupper, *Proverbial Philosophy* (Philadelphia: E. H. Butler & Co., 1853), pp. 177-78.

12. Robert Pattison, *The Child Figure in English Literature* (Athens: University of Georgia Press, 1978), p. x.

13. Grey and Shirreff, *Thoughts on Self Culture*, p. 424.

14. Ibid., p. 429.

15. Ibid., p. 434.

16. Ibid., p. 420.

17. Cruse, *The Victorians and Their Reading*, p. 289.

18. Ibid., p. 306.

19. Rosemary Treble, "Introduction," *Great Victorian Pictures* (London: Arts Council of Great Britain, 1978), p. 7.

20. Roy Strong, *And When Did You Last See Your Father: The Victorian Painter and History* (London: Thames & Hudson, 1978).

21. Jeremy Hass, *Victorian Painters* (London: Cresset Press, 1969), p. 14.

22. Ionides Collection, Victoria and Albert Museum.

23. Charles H. Caffin, "A Painter of Childhood and Girlhood," *Harper's Monthly Magazine*, European Edition 59 (1909-1910): 926-27.

24. *Journal of the Women's Education Union* 5 (1877): 14.

25. Ibid., 4 (1876): 183.

26. James Sully, *My Life and Friends. A Psychologist's Memoirs* (London: T. Fisher Unwin, 1918).

27. Woods, *Educational Experiments in England*, p. 43.

28. E. R. Murray, *A Story of Infant School and Kindergarten* (London: Sir Isaac Pitman & Sons, 1912), p. 53.

29. Grey, *Memorials of Emily Anne Shirreff*, p. 44.

30. Lucy Masterman, ed. *Mary Gladstone—Mrs. Drew: Her Diaries and Letters* (London: Methuen, 1930), p. 140.

31. Grey, *Memorials of Emily Anne Shirreff*, p. 57.

32. Thomas Acland, *Knowledge, Duty and Faith* (London: C Kegan Paul, 1896), p. 263.

33. Emily Shirreff, *Wasted Forces*. Froebel Society's Kindergarten Tract No. 5 (London: Sonnenschein & Allen, 1880).

34. Ibid.

35. Emily Shirreff, *Kindergarten: Principles of Froebel's System and Their Bearing on the Education of Women* (London: Chapman and Hall, 1870), p. 53.

36. Ibid., pp. 74-86.

37. Ibid., p. 79.

38. Ibid., p. 83-84.

39. Ibid., pp. 89-90.

40. Ibid.

41. Emily Shirreff, *Home Education in Relation to the Kindergarten. Two Lectures* (London: J. Hughes, 1884), *passim*.

42. Emily Shirreff, *The Kindergarten in Relation to Schools. Papers Read Before the Society of Arts, December 12th, 1877* (Reading: W. Millard, 1877), p. 10.

43. Ibid.

44. Ibid., p. 11.

45. *Child Life*, New Series 2 (1901): 57-58; 1 (1900): 163.

46. Lileen Hardy, *The Diary of a Free Kindergarten* (Boston: Houghton Mifflin, 1913), pp. 170-171.

47. Shirreff, *The Kindergarten in Relation to Schools*, p. 7.

48. Ibid., p. 11.

49. T.H.S. Escott, *Social Transformation of the Victorian Age* (London: Seeley, 1897), p. 166.

## CHAPTER 10

1. Shirreff, *Kindergarten: Principles of Froebel's System and Their Bearing on the Education of Women*, p. 30.

2. Ibid.

3. Melvin Richter, *The Politics of Conscience: T.H. Green and His Age* (Cambridge: Harvard University Press, 1964), pp. 346-50.

4. Ibid., p. 374.

5. Shirreff, *The Kindergarten in Relation to Schools*, p. 11.

6. N. Isaacs, "Froebel's Educational Philosophy in 1952," *Froebel and English Education*, ed. Evelyn Lawrence (New York: Schocken Books, 1969), p. 227.

7. Shirreff, *The Kindergarten in Relation to Schools*, p. 32.

8. Ibid., p. 34.

9. Ibid., p. 37.

10. Shirreff, *Intellectual Education*, p. 180.

11. Emily Shirreff, *Moral Training: Froebel and Herbert Spencer* (London: Phillip & Son, 1892).

12. Huth, *Life of Buckle*, 1: 313.

13. Baroness Bertha von Marenholtz-Bülow, *Reminiscences of Friedrich Froebel Translated by Mrs. Horace Mann: Sketch of the Life of Froebel by Emily Shirreff* (Boston: Lee & Shephard, 1877); pp. 350-351.

14. Mary J. Lyschinska, *The Ethical Teaching of Froebel. Two Essays* (London: Kegan, Paul & Co.), p. 45.

15. Shirreff, *Kindergarten: Principles of Froebel's System and Their Bearing on the Education of Women*, appendix, pp. 96-105.

16. *Journal of the Women's Education Union* 8 (1880): 100.

17. Ibid.

18. *Child Life* 2 (1892): 47-48.

19. H. Courthope Bowen, *Connectedness in Teaching: or the School Curriculum as One Organic Whole. A Paper Read Before the College of Preceptors....Reprinted from the Educational Times* (London: The Author, 1890).

20. Charles E. B. Reed, *Memoir of Sir Charles Reed* (London: Macmillan & Co., 1883), p. 332.

21. *The Philosophical System of Antonio Rosmini-Serbati: Translated with a Sketch of the Author's Life, Bibliography, and Notes by Thomas Davidson* (London: C. Kegan Paul, 1882).

22. William Angus Knight, *Memorials of Thomas Davidson, The Wandering Scholar* (Boston: Ginn, 1907).

23. Claude Leetham, *Rosmini, Priest, Philosopher and Patriot* (Baltimore: Helicon Press, 1958), p. xiv.

24. Antonio Rosmini-Serbati, *The Ruling Principle of Method Applied to Education... Translated by Mrs. William Grey*, preface, p. iv-v.

25. Ibid.

26. Leetham, *Rosmini*, pp. 266-67.

27. Rosmini-Serbati, *The Ruling Principle of Method*, preface.

28. *Parents Review* 8 (1897): 56.

29. *Child Life* 2 (1892): 125-26.

30. Ibid., 69.

31. Ibid., 68.

32. M. Roth, *On the Neglect of Physical Education and Hygiene by Parliament and the Education Department as the Principal Cause of the Degeneration of the Physique of the Population* (London: Groombridge, 1879).

33. *Child Life*, New Series 7 (1899): 224.

34. Essex Cholmondeley, *The Story of Charlotte Mason, 1842-1923* (London: J. M. Dent & Sons, 1960).

35. *Then and Now: The Froebel Society's Jubilee Pamphlet* (London, 1925).

36. *Child Life*, New Series 2 (1900): 57-58.

## EPILOGUE

1. Grey, *Last Words to Girls*, pp. 219-220.

2. Joseph A. and Olive Banks, *Feminism and Family Planning in Victorian England* (Liverpool: Liverpool University Press, 1964); Joseph A. Banks, *Prosperity and Parenthood: A Study of Family Planning Among the Victorian Middle Class* (London: Routledge & Kegan Paul, 1954).

3. Manton, *Elizabeth Garrett Anderson*, p. 284.

4. Joseph A. and Olive Banks, "The Bradlaugh-Besant Trial and the English Newspapers," *Population Studies* 8 (1954-1955): 33.

5. David Victor Glass, *Population Policies and Movements in Europe* (Oxford: The Clarendon Press, 1940), pp. 35-43.

6. Grey, *Last Words to Girls*, p. 303.

7. Peter T. Cominos, "Late Victorian Sexual Respectability and the Social System," *International Review of Social History* 8 (1963): 37.

8. David J. Pivar, *Purity Crusade: Sexual Morality and Social Control, 1868-1900* (Westport, Conn.: Greenwood Press, 1973), pp. 111-112, 118.

9. T. D. Traill, "The Abdication of Mrs. Grundy," *National Review* 17 (1891): 12-24; see also Peter Fryer, *Mrs. Grundy: Studies in English Prudery* (London: Dennis Dobson, 1963).

10. A somewhat similar attitude was in evidence in the United States of America. William Chafe noted that the middle-class reform movement which brought about female enfranchisement did not seek to overthrow traditional values toward women. Jane Addams in her settlement work, Florence Kelley in the labor cause and the National Consumer's League, and Carrie Chapman Catt sought improvement, not a total recast of the economic and social systems. William M. Chafe, *Women and Equality: Changing Patterns in American Culture* (New York: Oxford University Press, 1977), pp. 39-40.

11. Madame Bessie Rayner Parkes Belloc, "Voluntaries, 1851," *In Fifty Years* (London: Sands, 1904), p. 17.

# Bibliography

Pamphlets and books written by Emily Shirreff and Maria Shirreff Grey (Mrs. William Grey):

### Shirreff, Emily:

*Intellectual Education and Its Influence on the Character and Happiness of Women* (London: John W. Parker & Son, 1858).

*The Chivalry of the South.* Ladies London Emancipation Society Tract No. 1. (London: 1864).

*Kindergarten. Principles of Froebel's System and Their Bearing on the Education of Women* (London: Chapman & Hall, 1870).

*The Work of the National Union* (London: William Ridgway, 1872).

*Why Should We Learn* (London: John W. Parker & Son, 1872).

*The Enjoyment of Life. A Lecture by E.A.E. Shirreff* (London: William Ridgway, 1875).

*The Claim of Froebel's System to be Called "The New Education": A Paper Read at the Meeting of the Froebel Society, London, June 5, 1877* (New York: E. Steiger, 1877).

*The Kindergarten in Relation to Schools: Papers Read Before the Society of Arts, December 12th, 1877* (Reading: W. Millard, 1877).

von Marenholtz-Bülow, Bertha, *Reminiscences of Froebel Translated by Mrs. Horace Mann: Sketch of the Life of Froebel by Emily Shirreff* (Boston: Lee & Shephard, 1877).

*On the Connection Between the Kindergarten and the School: A Lecture on Mme. Portugall's Synoptical Table* (London: Sonnenschein & Allen, 1880).

*Wasted Forces.* Froebel Society's Kindergarten Tract No. 5 (London: Sonnenschein & Allen, 1880).

*Home Education in Relation to the Kindergarten. Two Lectures* (London: J. Hughes, 1884).

*The Kindergarten at Home* (London: J. Hughes, 1884).
*Kindergarten Teachers and Their Qualification: The Annual Address Delivered Before the Froebel Society, 1885* (London: W. Rice, 1885).
*A Short Sketch of the Life of Frederick Fröbel. . . New edition including Froebel's Letters to His Wife* (London: Chapman & Hall, 1887).
*Moral Training: Froebel and Herbert Spencer* (London: Phillip & Son, 1892).

**Grey, Maria:**

*Love's Sacrifice: A Novel,* 3 vols. (London: Hurst & Blackett, 1868).
*Is the Exercise of the Suffrage Unfeminine?* (London: Spottiswoode, 1870).
*On the Education of Women: A Paper Read by Mrs. William Grey at the Meeting of the Society of Arts, May 31st, 1871* (London: William Ridgway, 1871).
*The School Board of London: Three Addresses of Mrs. William Grey in the Borough of Chelsea, with a Speech by William Grove Esq., Q.C., F.R.S.* (London: William Ridgway, 1871).
*On the Special Requirements for Improving the Education of Girls: Paper Read at the Social Science Congress, October 1871* (London: William Ridgway, 1872).
*The National Union for Improving the Education of Women. A Letter to the Editor of the "Times," May 22, 1872* (London: William Ridgway, 1872).
*Old Maids: A Lecture* (London: William Ridgway, 1875).
*Last Words to Girls on Life in School and After School* (London: Rivingtons, 1889).
Rosmini-Serbati, Antonio. *The Ruling Principle of Method Applied to Education. . . Translated by Mrs. William Grey* (Boston: D. C. Heath, 1893).
*Memorials of Emily Anne Eliza Shirreff, with a Sketch of Her Life* (privately printed, 1897).

**Grey, M., and Shirreff, E.:**

*Thoughts on Self Culture Addressed to Women* (London: E. Moxon, 1850).
*Passion and Principle* (London: Routledge, 1853).


GENERAL BIBLIOGRAPHY

Adamson, J. W. *English Education* (London: Cambridge University Press, 1930).
Anderson, Louisa Garrett. *Elizabeth Garrett Anderson* (London: Faber & Faber, 1939).
Anthony, Sylvia. *Women's Place in Industry and Home* (London: Routledge, 1932).
Archer, Richard L. *Secondary Education in the Nineteenth Century* (Cambridge: University Press, 1921).
Armitage, Angus. *William Herschel* (Garden City, N.Y.: Doubleday, 1963).

Armytage, Walter H. G. *The Civic Universities: Aspects of a British Tradition* (London: Ernest Bonn, 1955).

Bailey, E. B. *Charles Lyell* (Garden City, N.Y.: Doubleday, 1963).

Bailey, John, ed. *The Diary of Lady Frederick Cavendish* (London: John Murray, 1927).

Banks, Joseph A., and Olive Banks. *Feminism and Family Planning in Victorian England* (Liverpool: Liverpool University Press, 1964).

Barnard, H. C. *A Short History of English Education from 1760 to 1944* (London: University of London Press, 1947).

Beale, Dorothea, et al. *Work and Play in Girls' Schools* (London: Longmans, 1898).

Bell, Enid Moberly, *Josephine Butler* (London: Constable, 1962).

Besant, Annie. *An Autobiography* (London: T. Fisher Unwin, 1893).

_____. *Principles of Education* (Adyar, India: Theosophical Publishing House, 1932).

Binns, Elliott L. *Religion in the Victorian Era* (London: Lutterworth Press, 1936).

Birchenough, Charles. *History of Elementary Education in England and Wales from 1800 to the Present Day* (London: University Tutorial Press, 1914).

Bishop, A. S. *The Rise of a Central Authority for English Education* (Cambridge: University Press, 1971).

Bosanquet (Dendy), Helen. *Rich and Poor* (London: Macmillan & Co., 1896).

_____. *Social Work in London 1869-1912: A History of the Charity Organisation Society* (London: John Murray, 1914).

_____. *The Family* (London: Macmillan & Co., 1906).

Bott, Alan, and Irene Clephane. *Our Mothers* (London: V. Gollanz, 1932).

Boucherett, Jessie, and Helen Blackburn. *The Condition of Working Women and the Factory Acts* (London: Elliot Stock, 1896).

Bremner, C. S. *Education of Girls and Women in Great Britain* (London: Swan Sonnenschein, 1897).

Brittain, Vera. *The Women at Oxford: A Fragment of History* (London: George G. Harrap, 1960).

Brownlow, Jane. *Women and Factory Legislation* (Congleton, England: Women's Emancipation Union, 1896).

_____. *Women's Work in Local Government; England and Wales* (London: David Nutt, 1911).

Buckle, Henry Thomas. *History of Civilization in England* (London: John W. Parker & Son, 1857).

Burdett-Coutts, Baroness, ed. *Women's Mission. Congress Papers on Philanthropic Work of Women* (London: Sampson Low, Marston & Co., 1893).

Burgess, H. J. *Enterprise in Education: The Story of the Work of the Established Church in Education of the People prior to 1870* (London: Society for Promoting Christian Knowledge, 1958).

Burstall, Sara. *English High Schools for Girls* (London: Longmans, 1907).

_____. *Frances Mary Buss* (London: Society for Promoting Christian Knowledge, 1938).

_____. *Retrospect and Prospect: Sixty Years of Women's Education* (London: Longmans, 1933).

_____. *The Story of Manchester High School for Girls*(Manchester: Manchester University Press, 1911).

Burstall, S. A., and M. A. Douglas. *Public Schools for Girls: A Series of Papers on their History* (London: Longmans, Green, 1911).

Burton, Hester. *Barbara Bodichon* (London: John Murray, 1949).

Butler, Arthur S. *Portrait of Josephine Butler* (London: Faber & Faber, 1954).

Butler, Josephine. *Personal Reminiscences of a Great Crusade* (London: Horace Marshall, 1898).

Byrne, Muriel, and Catherine Mansfield. *Somerville College, 1879-1921* (Oxford: University Press, 1922).

Cadbury, Edward, et al. *Women's Work and Wages, 1906* (London: T. Fisher Unwin, 1909).

Candler, W. I., et al. *King Edward VI High School for Girls*, Birmingham (London: Ernest Benn, 1971).

Carr-Saunders, Alexander M., and Paul A. Wilson. *The Professions* (Oxford: Clarendon Press, 1937).

Clayton (Needham), Eleanor. *English Female Artists* (London: Tinsley Brothers, 1876).

Cleveland, Arthur R. *Women under English Law: From the Landing of the Saxons to the Present Time* (London: Hurst & Blackett, 1896).

Clough, Blanche A. *A Memoir of Anne Jemima Clough* (London: Edward Arnold, 1897).

Cobbe, Frances Power. *Life of Frances Power Cobbe as Told by Herself: With Additions by the Author and Introduction by Blanche Atkinson* (London: Sonnenschein, 1904).

Costelloe (Strachey), Ray. *Careers and Openings for Women: A Survey of Women's Employment and a Guide for Those Seeking Work* (London: Faber & Faber, 1935).

_____. *Our Freedom and Its Results By Five Women* (London: Hogarth Press, 1938).

_____. *"The Cause": A Short History of the Women's Movement in Great Britain* (London: G. Bell & Sons, 1928).

_____. *Women's Suffrage and Women's Service. The History of the London and National Society for Women's Service* (London: Fawcett Society, 1927).

Crow, Duncan. *The Victorian Woman* (London: Allen & Unwin, 1971).

Cunnington, C. W. *Feminine Attitudes in the Nineteenth Century* (London: Heinemann, 1935).

Curtis, Stanley J. *History of Education in Great Britain*, 6th edition (London: University Tutorial Press, 1965).

Davies, Emily. *The Higher Education of Women* (London: Alexander Strahan Publisher, 1866).

Ensor, Robert C. *England, 1870-1914* (Oxford: Clarendon Press, 1936).

Faithfull, L. M. *In the House of My Pilgrimage* (London: Chatto, 1924).

Fawcett, M. G. *What I Remember* (London: T. Fisher Unwin, 1924).

Figes, Eva. *Patriarchal Attitudes: Women in Society* (London: Faber & Faber, 1974).

Fryer, Peter. *Mrs. Grundy. Studies in English Prudery* (London: Dennis Dobson, 1963).

_____. *The Birth Controllers* (New York: Stein & Day, 1966).

Gardiner, Dorothy. *English Girlhood at School* (London: Oxford University Press, 1929).

Glynne-Grylls, R. *Queen's College, 1848-1948* (London: Routledge, 1948).

Gollanz, Victor, ed. *The Making of Women: Oxford Essays on Feminism* (London: Allen & Unwin, 1917).

Goodsell, Willystine. *Education of Women: Its Social Background and Problems* (New York: Macmillan Co., 1933).

Graveson, R. H., and F. R. Crane, ed. *A Century of Family Law, 1857-1957* (London: Sweet & Maxwell, 1957).

Grossmith, George, and Weedon Grossmith. *The Diary of a Nobody* (London: Collins, 1894).

Gunn, J. *The Infant School* (London: Nelson, 1924).

Hamilton, Mary Agnes. *Newnham: An Informal Biography* (London: Faber & Faber, 1936).

Harrison, J.F.C. *Learning and Living, 1789-1960: A Study in the History of the English Adult Education Movement* (Toronto: University of Toronto Press, 1961).

Harrison, Jane Ellen. *Reminiscences of a Student's Life* (London: Hogarth Press, 1925).

Hays, Hoffman R. *The Dangerous Sex: The Myth of the Feminine Evil* (New York: G. P. Putnam's Sons, 1964).

Hecker, Eugene A. *A Short History of Women's Rights from the Days of Augustus to the Present Time* (London: G. P. Putnam's Sons, 1911).

Hewitt, Margaret. *Wives and Mothers in Victorian Industry* (London: Rackliff, 1958).

Hobsbawm, E. J. *The Age of Capital, 1845-1875* (New York: Charles Scribner's Sons, 1975).

Holcombe, Lee. *Victorian Ladies at Work: Middle-Class Working Women in England and Wales, 1850-1914* (Hamden, Conn.: Archon Books, 1973).

Houghton, Walter, *The Victorian Frame of Mind, 1830-1870* (New Haven: Yale University Press, 1963).

Hughes, Mary Vivian. *A London Child of the Eighties* (London: Oxford University Press, 1934).

_____. *A London Girl of the Eighties* (London: Oxford University Press, 1936).

_____. *A London Home in the Nineties* (London: Oxford University Press, 1937).

Johnson, G.W. *The Evolution of Women: From Subjection to Comradeship* (London: R. Holden, 1926).

Johnson, G.W. and L.A. Johnson, eds. *Josephine E. Butler. An Autobiographical Memoir*, 3rd edition (London: Arrowsmith, 1928).

Johnstone, Grace. *Leading Women of the Restoration* (London: Digby, Long, 1891).

Kamm, Josephine. *Hope Deferred: Girls' Education in English History* (London: Methuen, 1965).

_____. *Indicative Past: A Hundred Years of the Girls' Public Day School Trust* (London: Allen & Unwin, 1971).

_____. *Rapiers and Battle-axes: The Women's Movement and Its Aftermath* (London: Allen & Unwin, 1966).

Key, Ellen. *The Woman Movement* (New York: G. P. Putnam's Sons, 1912).

Killham, John. *Tennyson and "The Princess": Reflections of an Age* (London: Athlone Press, 1958).

Klein, Viola. *The Feminine Character: History of an Ideology* (London: C. Kegan Paul, 1946).

Laslett, Peter, and Richard Wall. *Household and Family in Past Times* (Cambridge: University Press, 1972).

Lee, Amice, *Laurels and Rosemary: The Life of William and Mary Howitt* (London: Oxford University Press, 1955).

Leetham, Claude. *Rosmini: Priest, Philosopher and Patriot* (Baltimore: Helicon Press, 1958).

Lennard, Thomas Barrett. *Woman: Her Power, Influence and Mission: Twenty-One Sermons . . . With a Preface by the Countess of Jersey* (London: Skeffington & Sons, 1910).

Lewis, Roy, and Angus Maude. *The English Middle Classes* (London: Phoenix House, 1949).

Lockhead, Marion. *The Victorian Household* (London: John Murray, 1964).

_____. *Their First Ten Years: Victorian Childhood* (London: John Murray, 1956).

_____. *Young Victorians* (London: John Murray, 1959).

Mack, Edward. *Public Schools, 1780-1860* (London: Methuen, 1938).

_____. *Public Schools and British Opinion Since 1860* (New York: Columbia University Press, 1941).

McKenzie, K. A. *Edith Simcox and George Eliot* (London: Oxford University Press, 1961).

MacPherson, Robert G. *Theory of Higher Education in Nineteenth-Century England* (Athens: University of Georgia Press, 1959).

Manton, Jo. *Elizabeth Garrett Anderson* (New York: E. P. Dutton, 1965).

Marcus, Steven. *The Other Victorians: A Study of Sexuality and Pornography in Mid-Nineteenth-Century England* (New York: Basic Books, 1966).

Martin, G. Currie. *The Adult School Movement, Its Origin and Development* (London: National Adult School Union, 1924).

Martyn, Edith, and Mary Breed. *The Birth Control Movement in England* (London: J. Bale, 1930).

Moulton, R. G. *The University Extension Movement* (London: Bemrose & Sons, 1887).

Neff, W. F. *Victorian Working Women* (London: Allen & Unwin, 1929).

Newsome, David. *Godliness and Good Learning: Four Studies on a Victorian Ideal* (London: John Murray, 1961).

Oakley, Ann. *Housewife* (London: Allen Lane, 1974).

Ogilvie, Vivian. *The English Public School* (London: B. T. Batsford, 1957).

O'Malley, Ida. *Women in Subjection* (London: Duckworth, 1933).

Pankhurst, Sylvia. *Save the Mothers* (London: Alfred A. Knopf, 1930).

_____. *The Suffragette Movement* (London: Longmans, 1931).

Percival, Alisia C. *The English Miss Today and Yesterday* (London: George G. Harrap, 1939).

Phillips, M., and W. S. Tomkinson. *English Women in Life and Letters* (New York: Benjamin Blom, 1971).

Pinchbeck, Ivy. *Women Workers and the Industrial Revolution, 1750-1850* (London: G. Routledge & Sons, 1930).

Raikes, Elizabeth. *Dorothea Beale of Cheltenham* (London: Constable, 1900).

Reiss, Erna. *Rights and Duties of Englishwomen: A Study in Law and Public Opinion* (Manchester: Sherratt & Hughes, 1934).

Ridley, Anne E. *Frances Mary Buss* (London: Longmans, 1895).

Roach, J.P.C. *Public Examinations in England, 1850-1900* (Cambridge: University Press, 1971).

Rogers, Annie M.A.H. *Degrees by Degrees: The Story of the Admission of Oxford Women Students to Membership of the University* (London: Oxford University Press, 1938).

Roth, Mathias. *A Plea for the Compulsory Teaching of the Elements of Physical Education in Our Elementary Schools* (London: Groombridge, 1870).

Royden, Agnes Maud. *Women and the Sovereign State* (London: New Commonwealth Books, 1917).

_____. *The Church and Women* (London: James Clarke, 1924).

Royden, Agnes Maud. *A Threefold Cord* (London: Victor Gollanz, 1947).

Ruskin, John. *Sesame and Lilies* (London: Smith Elder, 1865).

Schilling, Bernard N. *Human Dignity and the Great Victorians* (New York: Columbia University Press, 1946).

Schreiner, Olive. *Women and Labour* (London: T. Fisher Unwin, 1911).

Selleck, R.J.W. *English Primary Education and the Progressives, 1914-1939* (London: Routledge & Kegan Paul, 1972).

Sidgwick, Arthur. *School Homilies*, 2 vols. (London: Sidgwick & Jackson, 1915-1916).

Sidgwick, A. S. and E.M.S. *Henry Sidgwick: A Memoir* (London: Macmillan & Co., 1906).

Sidgwick, Eleanor M. *University Education of Women* (Cambridge: Macmillan and Bowes, 1897).

_____. *Health Statistics of Women Students of Cambridge and Oxford and of Their Sisters* (Cambridge: University Press, 1890).

Sidgwick, Ethel. *Mrs. Henry Sidgwick: A Memoir* (London: Sidgwick & Jackson, 1938).

Silver, Harold. *The Concept of Popular Education* (London: MacGibbon & Kee, 1965).

Simon, Brian. *Studies in the History of Education, 1780-1870* (London: Lawrence & Wishart, 1960).

Smelser, Neil J. *Social Change in the Industrial Revolution* (Chicago: University of Chicago Press, 1959).

Smiles, Samuel. *Character* (New York: Harper & Brothers, 1880).

_____. *Duty, with Illustrations of Courage, Patience and Endurance* (London: John Murray, 1880).

_____. *Self Help* (London: John Murray, 1859).

Smith, Frank. *A History of English Elementary Education* (London: University of London, 1931).

Stephen, Barbara. *Emily Davies and Girton College* (London: Constable, 1927).

Stewart, W.A.C., and W. P. MacCann. *The Educational Innovators* (London: Macmillan & Co., 1967).

Stuart, D. M. *The Girl through the Ages* (London: George G. Harrap, 1933).

Swanwick, Anna. *An Utopian Dream (i.e., The Improvement of the Condition of the Lower Classes in London and How It May Be Realized)* (London: C. Kegan Paul, 1888).

Swanwick, Helen M. *I Have Been Young* (London: Victor Gollanz, 1935).

Taylor, G. R. *Sex In History* (New York: Ballantine Books, 1954).

Thicknesse, Ralph. *The Rights and Wrongs of Women: A Digest* (London: Women Citizen Publishing Society, 1909).

Thompson, Donna F. *Professional Solidarity Among the Teachers of England* (New York: Columbia University Press, 1927).

Thomson, Patricia. *The Victorian Heroine: A Changing Ideal* (London: Oxford University Press, 1956).

Thorne, Isabel. *The Foundation and Development of the London School of Medicine for Women* (privately printed, 1905).

Tillyard, Alfred. *A History of University Reform from 1800 to the Present Time* (Cambridge: W. Heffer & Sons, 1913).

Tomalin, Claire. *The Life and Death of Mary Wollstonecraft* (London: Weidenfeld & Nicolson, 1974).

Tomkinson, W. S., and M. Phillips. *Englishwomen in Life and Letters* (London: Oxford University, 1927).

Tropp, Asher. *The School Teachers* (New York: Macmillan Co., 1957).

Tuke, Margaret. *A History of Bedford College for Women, 1849-1918* (London: Oxford University Press, 1939).

Tylecote, Mabel. *The Education of Women in Manchester University, 1883-1933* (Manchester: University of Manchester Press, 1941).

Vicinus, Martha, ed., *Suffer and Be Still* (Bloomington: Indiana University Press, 1972).

Wallas, Ada. *Before the Bluestockings* (London: Allen & Unwin, 1929).

Webb, Beatrice. *The Case for the Factory Acts* (London: Grant Richards, 1901).

_____. *The Co-operative Movement in Great Britain* (London: Sonnenschein, 1891).

Ward, W. "Sir M. E. Grant Duff's Diary," *Ten Personal Studies* (London: Longmans, Green, 1908).

Wardle, David. *Education and Society in Nineteenth-Century Nottingham* (Cambridge: University Press, 1971).

Wheeler, Ethel R. *Famous Blue Stockings* (London: Methuen, 1910).

White, Cynthia. *Women's Magazines, 1693-1968* (London: Joseph, 1970).

Wilson, Leonard G. *Charles Lyell: The Years to 1841: The Revolution in Geology* (New Haven: Yale University Press, 1972).

Winstanley, Denys A. *Early Victorian Cambridge* (Cambridge: University Press, 1940).

_____. *Later Victorian Cambridge* (Cambridge: University Press, 1947).

Wohl, Anthony S., ed. *The Victorian Family* (New York: St. Martin's Press, 1978).

*Women in a Changing World: The Dynamic Story of the International Council of Women Since 1888* (London: Routledge & Kegan Paul, 1966).

Woods, Alice. *Educational Experiments in England* (London: Methuen, 1920).

Young, Agnes F., and Elwyn T. Ashton. *British Social Work in the Nineteenth Century* (London: Routledge and Kegan Paul, 1956).

Young, G. M. *Victorian England: Portrait of an Age* (London: Oxford University Press, 1936).

Zahm, John A. *Women in Science* (New York: D. Appleton & Company, 1913).

Zimmern, A. *The Renaissance of Girls' Education in England* (London: Longmans, 1898).

Bibliographies for the women's movement and history of women in nineteenth-century Britain:

Kanner, S. Barbara. "The Women of England in a Century of Social Change, 1845-1914," in *Suffer and Be Still*.

McGregor, O. R. "The Social Position of Women in England, 1850-1914. A Bibliography," *The British Journal of Sociology* 6 (1955).

Altholz, Josef L. *Victorian England, 1837-1901* (Cambridge: University Press, 1970).

# Index

**About the Author**
Edward W. Ellsworth is professor of history at Wheelock College, Boston. He is the author of *Massachusetts in the Civil War: A Year of Crisis, 1862-1863* and has had articles published in the *Journal of the Royal Asiatic Society* and the *Lincoln Herald*.